Out of the Silence...

...Into the Silence

Out of the Silence...
...Into the Silence

Prayer's Daily Round

❖ ❖ ❖ ❖ ❖ ❖ ❖ ❖ ❖ ❖ ❖ ❖ ❖ ❖ ❖ ❖ ❖ ❖ ❖ ❖

*An unfolding of prayers, psalms, and canticles
for daily or occasional use*

JIM COTTER

with music composed by

PAUL PAYTON

CAIRNS PUBLICATIONS
ABERDARON 2010
Second Impression

British Library Cataloguing in Publication Data.

A record for this book is available from the British Library.

10-DIGIT ISBN 1 870652 44 4
13-DIGIT ISBN 978 1 870652 44 5

CAIRNS PUBLICATIONS

www.cottercairns.co.uk
jim@cottercairns.co.uk

Typeset in Monotype Baskerville by
Strathmore Publishing Services, London EC1

First published in 2006
Second impression 2010
(with minor amendments and corrections)

For
the sisters and brothers of the
Community of the Transfiguration
at Breakwater, Geelong,
in the State of Victoria, Australia:
with affection and in solidarity

A NOTE ON TREES

How many trees have been used in preparing this book? Well, only the pulp is used, which comes from the trimmings. The trunks are used for furniture. A commercially grown softwood tree produces, on average, about one-sixth of a ton of pulp. Since this book has used between one and two tons, it has needed between six and twelve trees to produce it – but of course not all of those trees. By weight it has needed something between three-quarters and one-and-a-half trees. So Cairns Publications will donate the wherewithal for the planting of three trees, in appreciation and gratitude.

CONTENTS

PREFACE

In the twenty-five years since 1981 Cairns has published five books which are part of the story of the compiling of this volume. For those who do not know the link, I had better say immediately that Cairns Publications is Jim Cotter by another name. In 1981 I put together a version of the late evening prayer, Compline, calling it *Prayer at Night*. 200 photocopies found their way into the hands of friends, parishioners, and colleagues in and around Watford.

That book and the ones that followed it, including this one, have the classic structure of the kind of prayer known as an 'office' – with its implications of duty, routine, and work. More on that in the Introduction. Such an order of prayer is made up of psalms and canticles, readings and prayers, and it can be short, medium, or long, depending on the time of day and the vocation of those who are praying. Each order of prayer in these earlier books is short. In this book each is a little longer. Monks and nuns go in for a mixture of short, medium, and long, the latter often being in the hours of darkness and therefore beyond most of us.

Prayer at Night has been published in a number of editions. It appeared in proper book form for the first time in 1983 and the fourth edition, still just about in print at the time of writing, in 1991. It was subtitled 'A Book for the Darkness' and included 'Cairns for a Journey' as material for meditation. In 1997 the main part, the order of prayer, became *Prayer at Night's Approaching*, produced in large print but in pocket size with generous breathing space for the words. A slightly revised version was issued in 2001, and in both hardback and paperback this is the edition which has taken the book probably as far as I am able to. ('Cairns for a Journey', much expanded, reappeared in 2001 with the title *Waymarks*. Its format is similar to that of *Prayer at Night's Approaching*.)

Prayer in the Day paralleled *Prayer at Night* for a number of years. The 1992 edition is the one in print as a paperback, in both pocket and standard size, the latter with drawings by Peter Pelz. It suits the middle of the day, time stopping at noon for a while.

The third volume, the 1989 edition, also still in print but in standard size only, is *Prayer in the Morning*. With material for a year's round, day by day, it is the most direct antecedent of this book.

However, there was not much in it specifically about the beginning of the day and it could be used, as can this book, at any time of day. So another volume appeared in parallel to *Prayer at Night's Approaching*, again similar in format, and entitled *Prayer at Day's Dawning*. It has a particular focus on the theme of creation and our care for the planet. The 2001 edition is in print.

Lastly, a week of daily prayer for people on pilgrimage appeared in 2003 in both English and Welsh, the Welsh translation being by Cynthia Davies. It is called *Pilgrim Prayer* and is in print.

Silence surrounds the words in each of these books, by spacing or by indicators, not least to deepen the praying and the sense of presence. None has so many words that the time needed for the whole sequence is more than twenty to thirty minutes, with half of that in pauses and silences distributed appropriately. Hence the title of this volume: *Out of the Silence...Into the Silence*.

The psalms are a revised version of three books that were published in 1989, 1991, and 1993 respectively: *Through Desert Places*, *By Stony Paths*, and *Towards the City*. They are not translations or paraphrases of the 150 psalms in the Bible, rather new unfoldings. The whys and wherefores are given in detail in the Introduction.

I should perhaps add that the three titles above are almost out of print in the UK, but are available in the USA as one book, published by Morehouse with the title *Psalms for a Pilgrim People*.

I am conscious of many people who have been part of a writing and praying journey, privately for some fifty years now, publicly for the last twenty-five. Most of these 'associates' are ancestors of faith, their names largely forgotten, from the first utterers of prayer in the open air to the first English translators of the Bible, the Thomas Cranmers of liturgical prose, and the Shakespeares and lesser mortals of poetry and drama. In that perspective, my contemporaries are few, though they are a crowd to me. I cannot begin to calculate the number of people who have contributed to what I hope is a living stream by means of phrases, images, criticisms, and suggestions. They range from my mother and father in my earliest years to those who have been particularly associated with this book.

To each and all, my thanks:

> Nicholas Jones, Talitha Hitchcock, Pat Saunders, and Catherine Duffy of Strathmore Publishing Services in London;
>
> Alan Dodson of Malvern, for his advice on the layout: though now frail he is still able to cast an eagle eye over a manuscript, not entirely having given up the hope that I might produce a typographically perfect book: and for all the work he did in earlier years, not least for the classic cover designs, all of which have been a direct influence on this book;
>
> Esther de Waal of Rowlestone in Herefordshire, who was one of the first people to encourage me to think of compiling *Prayer at Night*, and who has kindly written the Foreword;
>
> Brian Thorne of Norwich, for his commendation, and to the three people from whose forewords to the original psalm volumes there are quotations here: Alan Ecclestone, Sheila Cassidy, and Lavinia Byrne;
>
> Paul Payton of Lancaster, who has composed the music for the refrains to the psalms;
>
> and to Marjorie Bates and Shirley Sanders of Sheffield, Tony and Barbara Powell of Harlech, Shân Roberts of Llandecwyn, Aled Jones-Williams of Porthmadog, and Geoffrey Hooper of Llaniestyn, for help with proof-reading.

Two CDs are being issued to accompany this book, one as an introduction to it and with samples from it, with the same title, the other as a celebration of twenty-five years of Cairns Publications, a recording of *Prayer at Night's Approaching*. Again my thanks are due to Strathmore Publishing Services, to Paul Payton for his contribution to the first CD and for his singing voice on the second, and to Judith Daley for her voice on the second – and for her participation years ago in praying some of the antecedents listed in the first part of this preface.

My last thanks are again to some nameless people. The printing industry has gone through a period of bewildering change over these years, and to those who have given of their expertise with paper, ink, and machinery, my gratitude.

JIM COTTER

Harlech, September 2005

A NOTE ON COPYRIGHT

I become more relaxed about copyright as I get older, or maybe it's resignation that it's difficult to keep track of who is copying what. One thing I am clear about is that the rule that an original work is in copyright until seventy years after the author's death is ludicrous. I'd change that to 'shall expire after the author's death or the death of his or her partner, whichever be the later' – or some such legalese.

I am always touched to receive a request to reproduce something I have written, and I always say Yes. I have no problem with a copy or a few being made for small-scale personal, religious, or educational use. I rarely ask a fee in those circumstances, but I do quite firmly ask for precise and detailed acknowledgment, i.e., author, title, publisher, page number if possible, and either my mailing address, my website, or my e-mail address.

For use of material in other books or at conferences I usually ask a fee. This varies according to the amount requested, the anticipated print-run, and/or the number of participants.

One other request is that you make no alteration to the text without consultation. You may well be suggesting an improvement, and that will be gratefully received. But there may be a reason for the wording that is not obvious, but is important in context.

THIS BOOK & THE CAIRNS WEBSITE

Because *Out of the Silence...Into the Silence* is a long book and verges on being a directory, resource, or quarry, it will also be available, I hope by the summer of 2006, on the Cairns website:

www.cottercairns.co.uk

As I write Phil Gardner of Leeds is constructing a site which is currently a glorified catalogue. I am grateful to him for his hidden labour and skill. He tells me that when he has done the work under the bonnet he will be able to teach me to drive it. Hmm. I'll wait and see.

The plan has a number of parts and stages to it, and there will be free pages – publicity and samples – and different levels of subscription giving access and permission to download pages and copies.

The material in this book should be available in a form that you can read on screen or download for your own use. You will be able to have before you or in your hand simply what you need for any one day. There should also be two additional items: an extra reading for each day from the Cairns book, *Waymarks*, and the music for the psalm refrains in a harmony version. (Only the melody line appears here.)

In time I would like to add further material, for example, some intentions for the 'connecting' prayer of solidarity (commonly called 'intercession') for each day, some suggestions for a hymn for each day, and, in time, an unfolding of the Gospel readings from a perspective similar to that used in preparing the psalm versions here.

Also in preparation are arrangements, words and music, of the psalm or section of the psalm indicated for each Sunday of the three-year lectionary now widely used in most of the churches.

The way in which the relationship between books and websites will progress (or not) is unpredictable. It is currently full of fascination, but any exploration on the small scale, such as that of Cairns, feels like a roller coaster of faith. But, hey, what's new? I can always hope it will add to the pension fund – oh yes, and to our mutual spiritual nourishment...

One thing that seems to be happening is that large reference books like directories and dictionaries are fast becoming redundant, not least because websites can keep them up to date more easily and cheaply. Perhaps the majority of books will continue to be paperbacks, with short shelf lives for all but a few. And there will be a minority of hardbacks and special editions for words that are proving their worth, that need savouring and pondering, and need covers and binding that don't disintegrate on second reading. It may or may not be symptomatic of these changes that most of the recent Cairns Publications, including this one, have been published in hardback.

FOREWORDS & COMMENDATIONS

Foreword to this volume

Many people worldwide have been grateful for the work of Jim Cotter over recent years, and as time goes on what he gives us gets better, refined by honesty and reality. We have come to expect something that is new and original in thought, and different in format and presentation.

But can there be anything new to say about prayer? Yes – because, as Jim puts it so firmly and clearly at the start, if we believe that God is constantly at work creating and re-creating, then it is our responsibility to participate in the re-shaping of the language and intimations of prayer. The way in which he thus puts the art and practice of praying in a historical and theological context is refreshing and invigorating.

So what are we to expect this time? The title gives us the heart of it, and it is indicated at the beginning in words that are them- selves half way to being poetry, as he speaks of the "breathing space for the silence to surround the words." This in itself makes the book practical and flexible. It is also clearly laid out and easy to use, and it is carefully indexed, so that even if we do not wish to use the book daily, it can be a place we turn to for help for some immediate situation or need: genocide or gossip, terror or rejection.

These are not tired words. Time and again we are arrested by their strength, by lines and phrases that are vigorous and full- bodied, words that resound and resonate:

> Your words are *fierce with love*, your hands are gentle in judgment ...May we be content to travel light in this world, undistracted by *the babel of possessions*...To the beauty of your creation and grace we have responded, O God, with *desecration and greed* . (Italics mine.)

This is a book to read, to ponder, to sing, to shout aloud. Above all it is a book to carry in the heart and to allow its echoes to sound out in daily life. Who else could have made this suggestion? "...say a line out loud and then imagine you hear it back like an echo from the other side of a valley..."

ESTHER DE WAAL
Writer and lecturer, *Rowlestone*, September 2005

From the Foreword to Through Desert Places

The new turns of phrase should open to us new insights into the psalmists' rich and enduring spirituality...What is attempted in this presentation...is a supremely important and necessary task for which we have good reason to be grateful. It deserves to be used painstakingly and attentively in our own pilgrim's progress.

ALAN ECCLESTONE
Anglican priest, harrier of the powers that be, writer on prayer, d.1992

From the Foreword to By Stony Paths

(This) version is not so much a translation as a re-working, a re-fashioning. It is as if (the writer) has taken a collection of clothes, unpicked them, and then made a new garment out of each. Sometimes the result is only a mild variation, but others are radically cut, exciting, and very different...Here (is) the poet with vivid images and words that sing, the prophet reminding us that we are destroying the earth, and the priest reminding us of God in our midst.

SHEILA CASSIDY
Doctor, notably with the dying, and writer, author of *Audacity to Believe*

From the Foreword to Towards the City

...it is the language, above all, which marks this (book) as a truly inclusive collection of prayers. And that does not simply mean that women and men may use them with equal confidence. It means that God too is named in ways which invite us to draw closer to the

mystery which Christianity has consolidated by revealing to us
the deepest desire of God, namely to be with us – and not apart
from us.

LAVINIA BYRNE
Broadcaster, writer

A commendation of this volume

Jim Cotter achieves a remarkable synthesis of contemporary
psychological insight and the wisdom of the ages. Those who use
this book will be led into the sanctuary of their own hearts and will
find God waiting for them there.

BRIAN THORNE
Fellow of the British Association
for Counselling and Psychotherapy,
Honorary Lay Canon of Norwich Cathedral

INTRODUCTION

Prayer's daily round

The daily round, the common task, a worthy but hardly noticed routine. And so for prayer: nothing dramatic, a slowly changing rhythm through the weeks and seasons. Think of a revolving diamond that catches the light, now from one facet, now from another. Or think of the thesaurus, a treasury into which you take a dip day by day. Change the meaning of 'dip', and the water on any one day may be invigorating, withering, calming, holding.

The traditional name for this kind of prayer is the office. And yes, it's work. The *opus Dei*, God's work. It isn't complicated work, actually quite simple. But that doesn't mean it's easy. A duty can soon become boring. In the end it's only love that keeps you to the task. Without love it soon becomes as nothing, no more than a meaningless gabble.

There are a few, monks and nuns, who pray in this way seven times a day. Some pray four times, morning, midday, evening, bedtime. Thomas Cranmer reduced the seven to two for the Church of England, morning and evening, and hoped it would become part of the daily pattern of prayer for lay people as well as for clergy. The compiler of this book, along with others he has talked with, can manage it only once, and not always at the same time of day. What you have in your hands is the result of practising that 'once' for a number of years.

The structure of the praying is straightforward. There are always words, said or sung, a psalm, a reading from the Bible, and a canticle, topped and tailed with a prayer or two, and usually including a version of the Lord's Prayer. The Bible is in fact the main source, either of quotation or of inspiration, and sometimes by way of argument and disagreement. By means of such 'unfolding' we can absorb the best of what our ancestors of faith have given us and at the same time make it our own. We honour them in spirit if not always in exact repetition.

There is something more going on. It is hinted at by such phrases as 'all human life is here', 'solidarity with others and with creation in God', and 'here comes everybody'. At best, beyond the particularities of the Jewish-Christian tradition there are intimations of the universal. Though not without 'protests' within the praying, the aim is to be 'catholic', the whole being within the bounds of what is 'orthodox', in the sense of a tradition that is, in George Guiver's telling phrase, 'faith in momentum'. (Perhaps 'protest', 'catholic', and 'orthodox' are better as adjectives than as nouns with capital letters.)

For the monastic life, this daily round of prayer has at its heart our solidarity with all that is, a sense which, paradoxically, deepens in solitude and silence. So there is every good reason to pray in this manner if you are physically on your own: it is an excellent cure for loneliness. As to the silence, there is more on that below.

Quarries and nuggets

If you have never handled a prayer book like this, it may overwhelm you by its thickness, if not its weight. Too many pages, too many words, too heavy. It may be no consolation to know that other such books are often twice or three times the length, or split into two or three volumes, however thin and light the paper. And it's true that this book could have been somewhat shorter if the layout hadn't indicated breathing space for the silence to surround the words. If you know that silence leads you into generosity you will find the layout helpful; if not, it will seem a waste of timber.

But it's also true that the material for this kind of praying can grow and grow, and its use become complicated. Finding your way round the maze can distract from the praying. There may be too much to choose from. You find yourself in the middle of a quarry with rocks of different colour, shape, and size. Collections of such prayer books need a wheelbarrow to transport them. They become like encyclopaedias or directories, increasingly more suitable to and made available on websites. And although the compiler thinks that this book is usable as it is, with the need only for a copy of the Gospels in addition, he does recognize that it may well be used as a quarry: look at the index of themes and you may find a psalm or canticle suitable for a particular occasion of prayer or worship that is not at all framed as an 'office'. Indeed, at the same time as this book is being prepared for publication, the Cairns website is under construction, precisely to make it easy to read on screen or to download simply what is needed for one particular day of the year – and to find, via an index, material for selected themes. There is more about this on page xiii.

Rather than explore a quarry you may want to carry but a few pebbles in your pocket: a slim note book rather than Yellow Pages, nuggets rather than a builders' yard, a book you can hold if you are not well and want something light enough to pick up from a bedside table. You want fewer words at any one time, that part of the treasury that you want to learn by heart and savour. Over the years, the compiler has experimented in this direction, focusing on the time of day, for example, in *Prayer at Day's Dawning* and *Prayer at Night's Approaching*, and on a particular theme, for example, *Pilgrim Prayer*. Each of these uses the week rather than the year as the basis of the 'round'. In miniature, *Prayer in the Morning* is the antecedent to this book, and serves as a short way in to this kind of daily prayer. All these books are, at the time of writing, in print and available.

(*Prayer at Night's Approaching* has been recorded on two CDs by Jim Cotter, Judith Daley, and Paul Payton. It, too, is available through Cairns Publications.)

Words and voice, solidarity and silence

The words of the psalms range far and wide: in their content they nudge you towards a sense of solidarity. It becomes 'common prayer'. Even if I cannot personally identify with what another human being, past or present, is saying in a particular psalm, I can nevertheless imagine myself in his or her position: perhaps one of relative comfort if I am anxious about my income, or one of constriction if I am relatively free. I can put myself in another's shoes, I can inhabit for a short while that person's emotional state, in an act of co-inherence. I think of those who at any one moment need all their energy for coping with pain, or for teaching a child, or for driving a fire engine. In the movement 'Connecting' this kind of prayer can become quite specific, as we bring particular people, places, and concerns into mind's eye and heart's care, allowing them to be with us in the enfolding greater presence, breathing a blessing towards them, willing that our small energies be aligned with the divine energy, to their well-being. If God can be imaged as 'pain-bearer', we are shouldering a little of that in order that somewhere, somehow, another person may know a moment's relief. So it is that this prayer is 'work', the work of God, part of the groaning that provokes our complaint yet seems mysteriously necessary in the coming to be of wonders such as we cannot yet imagine. This is a grander vision than that of prayer for others as a plea to a distant being who may or may not be persuaded to act.

It is easy to run through a list of names in the tone of voice of a station announcer. It takes more time and effort to stay with an unfamiliar name in the way we do when it is the name of someone close to us. Refrains, especially when sung, help. But it is above all in the silences that we leave behind our isolation and the awful experience of uttering words that seem meaningless, dry, and exhausted. If we soak them in silence, not only do they reveal hidden depths, but we are drawn closer to one another, and, we may believe, to God. We become aware of the extraordinary connecting web or network that the universe seems to be. We are part of that, and in prayer may become aware too of the transcendent presence that both enfolds all that is and lures it towards greater complexity and creativity.

There is a lot of silence in monasteries. Its presence is palpable, and is sensed even in the way monks and nuns gather for their community prayer. So they do not need to punctuate the words of that prayer with as much silence as the rest of us do. Our lives are too full of noise. So take the times of pause and silence indicated in the book seriously. Start with silence, and let the words rise out of the depths of silence and fall back into silence. The words allocated to each day in this book can be said in less than fifteen minutes. Think of giving half an hour in total. Notice when you ask yourself, Do I have time for daily prayer before I have to go out? The answer is almost certainly No. You will be too conscious of the clock and will find it impossible to let yourself drop into the silences.

To 'pray' an office rather than 'say' it is to enter into a rhythm of silence and words. It needs time to settle into. Think of lobbing a pebble into a still pool, letting the ripples do their gentle work. When you hear them quietly lapping at the shore, lob another pebble. Sometimes the sound of the plop will enhance and prolong the silence – like the bark of a dog in the distance on a still evening or the sound of an occasional passing car at midnight.

Some of us remember the question from our childhood: Have you said your prayers? Again, that is not quite right. Yes, the voice is important, it is as physical and real as posture and gesture. But there needs to be something more going on. Prayer is not a 'thing', entire of itself. The words hint at modes of being and intention, at movement of mind and heart and body. And God may be more adjective and verb than noun, more flavour and activity than static enthroned being. Hence the momentum implied by the titles given to each 'movement' of daily prayer. It is the 'continuously active present'. So, in this book, each day's prayer has this sequence:

Opening	–	an invocation
Greeting	–	a psalm or other prayer
Engaging	–	the psalm for that day
Listening	–	a reading from the Bible
Delighting	–	a canticle
Connecting	–	bringing others to mind
Gathering	–	a version of the Lord's Prayer
Proceeding	–	a prayer leading into the rest of the day

The psalms at their beginning

Because the psalms are at the heart of this kind of prayer, I'd like to introduce them in more detail.

Go back in time. It is hard for us to imagine what it was like for the human beings who discovered fire. For the first time they could feel relatively safe and warm at night. Not for nothing do we still talk of hearth and home. Round a fire intimacies are shared, stories are told, ballads of our history are sung. Tell us what God is like. Tell us about our ancestors. Sing us one of the songs of our people.

In some such fertile soil we may guess the seeds of the psalms were sown, with their all too human expressions of grief, indignation, gratitude, and awe, some of them intimate and tender, others more formally telling a story suitable for acclamation and celebration at a great gathering. In the psalms we read soul-deep into the life of some of our ancestors of faith. Sometimes we read 'I', sometimes 'we'. They moved easily between the one and the

many and it is hard for us to realize that they did not have any
concept of the individual as separate from others. Each person may
indeed be distinctive, singular, unlike anybody else, but the one
could represent the many and the many could identify with the one.
There's wisdom in that. Of course certain particular people, either
anonymous or named, may well have composed a song or psalm in
a white-hot moment of inspiration, but it would not have found its
way into common prayer if it had been merely quirky or inacces-
sible to others. It is one of the amazing features of the ancient
psalms that people of other cultures and times can recognize so
much of what was eventually written down, from their self-pity and
laments, to their penitence and anger, to their quiet contentment
and exuberant joy.

But we may also find ourselves asking questions.

Why an 'unfolding'?

Over the last century in its public worship the Church has been
selective in its choice of psalms. Some of them have been put
into an ecclesiastical attic because they are long historical remem-
brances or because they relish anger and violence and slaughter,
often in the name of God, or because of a sense of complaint that
verges on paranoia. Sometimes two or three verses of a psalm have
been bracketed, indicating that the revisers have found them problematic, of intellectual interest perhaps, but not deemed suitable for
worship.

I have mixed feelings about this. But let me come clean. In much
of the Bible, including the psalms, there are at least three things
that bother me. First, God often acts violently and orders whole-
sale slaughter. Second, the people of God believe that they have
been chosen for privilege and status; some psalms reek of the self-
righteousness which pitches us – superior – against them – inferior.
Third, a range of human emotion is presented without criticism.

Now I believe in a God who discerns and purifies, and so can be
pictured as wise and healing in judgment – but not condemning
and obliterating. Yes, I believe that individuals and communities
sense the pressure of God to do something special, but this is a call
to costly service, not to wealth and position at others' expense. Yes,
I wish to acknowledge that I have angry and destructive feelings:

but in prayer I seek to be penitent about that, and to transform such undoubtedly fierce energy that it might be channelled in the service of the common good, into a power that protects, restrains, and encourages, and towards a justice which stands for reconciliation and restoration, not for revenge and rejection – and therefore for a judge who never discourages, destroys, or demeans.

I continue to be uneasy at the predominance in the psalms and elsewhere in the Bible, and in hymns and prayers, of one-sided imagery for God, far more masculine than feminine, far more connected to the realities of worldly power than those of godly vulnerability, far more about lordship than about friendship, far more about shepherds, usually men, than about weavers, usually women, far more about distance than about intimacy. And while we do well to learn from history, we should be more critical of our own than of others', not least when two sides both claim God for their cause.

Such thoughts and hesitations are dealt with in various ways in this book. When an ancestor is speaking, inverted commas are often used. What is an absolute conviction is turned into an uncertain question. Doubts are taken seriously and allowed room for pondering. Never far away is the faith that the God of Jesus does not know how not to love. Indeed, 'Love your enemies' as the goal of our 'spiritual direction' has never been far from mind in the unfolding of this inheritance of prayer. And if you remember that the Jewish traveller who had been attacked received help from a Samaritan, someone he might well have despised, perhaps we have to learn to let our enemies love us. (That's not an original thought but comes from an American scholar, Robert Funk's commentary on the parable.)

If we believe that the Spirit of God is guiding us into the truth, has yet more to reveal to us from these ancient texts, and is constantly at work creating and re-creating, then it is our responsibility to participate in the re-shaping of the language and intimations of prayer. Truths are not simply propositions to which we do or do not give our assent, but rather are they discovered in and among human beings living in relationship with one another. So we can expect new unfoldings in each generation, some of which will doubtless be further criticised and changed by the next. We may be in communion with our ancestors of faith, but surely not slavishly.

It is our burden and delight to listen for and articulate fresh thoughts for a new day, reflections charged with the poetry and passion of our experience, bringing treasure old and new from the scriptural songs of the past and writing our own as well.

This kind of critical solidarity with our ancestors can be illustrated from within the psalms themselves. Psalm 51 gives a clear example. It is a deeply personal penitential psalm: the sacrifice that God desires is a humbled spirit and a contrite heart. But the two verses at the end are so different in tone that they are now thought to have been added by a later hand. An official in the Temple in Jerusalem? Well, somebody who, whilst conceding that the right *intention* is necessary in the worshipper, is eager to affirm that animal sacrifices are still important. (A touch of ecclesiastical vested interest, I wonder?) We may not necessarily think this particular addition an improvement, but it does show that the next generation doesn't always agree with everything it inherits, nor does it need to.

We might want to ask a similar question, but with our own dilemmas in mind. Can the nonconformist (*my* way of praying) and the conformist (we've always done it this way) both give way to an approach to prayer which recognizes a variety of acceptable ways of praying within a common loyalty to one another and to God, ways which honour the past but seek to transform it?

Further, in our own day we are living with the bewilderment of not being able to claim we belong to one overarching culture, and it is an acute question how we can foster the well-being of the one globe with its increasing diversity and complexity. What was once regarded as universal is not now experienced as such: and we rightly fear disintegration. But how do we find our way?

Well, the aim in these unfoldings has been to take us in a direction where specific thoughts and images may be recognized by as many people as possible, and where the universal is, even if tentatively, affirmed. But it is very much work in progress. It is only a printing deadline that has stopped the writing and amending. Take courage if you are using it. Make alterations in the margin. Add question marks. Make it your own. We are living through a profound technological revolution, as convulsing as the invention of printing itself. It is now so easy to make changes on the screen. And the 'manuscript' (the word means 'that which is written by hand') needs to be typed only once, rather than the three or four times of living memory. There is every likelihood that in a couple of years' time the version of this book on the website will have at least minor alterations.

Before you think this is a descent into anarchy, let me take a step back. There are some psalms in these pages that have been hardly altered at all. When I was beginning this work around 1980 I asked various parish groups and students to let me have their choice of 'desert island psalms'. Which eight would you take with you? (You might like to pause, pick up a Bible, and make your own selection.) Again and again, the same psalms were chosen. Nobody included more than one psalm (and even that was usually because of one or two particular verses) that did not come from a range of only thirty-seven out of the hundred and fifty in the Bible. For the record, here is the list: 4, 8, 15, 16, 19, 22, 23, 24, 27, 31, 42, 43, 46, 51, 67, 84, 90, 91, 95, 98, 100, 102, 104, 107, 121, 122, 126, 127, 128, 130, 131, 133, 134, 137, 139, 148, 150. So nearly three-quarters of the psalms were not chosen at all. When I hear people referring to the 'treasury' of the Psalter I think they mean only a selection. But that selection is indeed a treasury to dip into, for the themes are so universal that they speak directly across two and a half thousand years and more. It is these that give us a deep sense of solidarity with our ancestors of faith and with our contemporaries across the globe. It is the rest that present the challenge of unfolding them afresh to make them prayable in our own time.

Even Psalm 23 has many versions

Our Presbyterian ancestors of the sixteenth century would have disagreed. Though they were the first to put the psalms into English metrical verse, they were careful not to introduce any other vocabulary than was there in the original.

Later hymn writers and compilers of hymn books have not felt so constrained. Take Psalm 23 for instance, one of the inevitable 'desert island' choices. Many of us know the psalm in the version from the Scottish Psalter of 1650, 'The Lord's my shepherd', sung to the tune Crimond. Almost equally well known is H. W. Baker's nineteenth-century version, 'The King of Love my shepherd is'. For a start, neither the word 'King' nor the word 'Love' occur in Psalm 23. Baker is letting his faith in Jesus Christ inform the psalm.

Hence later we have the line, 'Thy cross before to guide me.'
Similarly, the 'sweet and wondrous love' of God is central to
George Herbert's seventeenth-century version, 'The God of love
my shepherd is'.

But what of the version, 'The Lord my pasture shall prepare'?
It is by Joseph Addison, English essayist of the eighteenth century.
I wonder if he wrote it while staying for the weekend in a friend's
country house, amongst newly laid out gardens and park? After
mentioning fainting in 'the sultry glebe' he writes these lines:

> To fertile vales and dewy meads
> My weary wandering steps he leads,
> Where peaceful rivers, soft and slow,
> Amid the verdant landscape flow.

In the next verse we find ourselves among 'sudden greens and
herbage' and 'murmuring' streams, followed at the end by the 'aid'
of 'thy friendly crook', a noun easily misunderstood. And the
description is hardly one that would have been familiar to a desert
nomad, even when resting at an oasis.

Well, such a version is not untrue to the spirit of the original
psalm, but it certainly reflects a time and place now known only
in nostalgia by those who long for a vanished countryside which
in fact can have been delectable only to the privileged few.
Eighteenth-century rural life was rather different for most of the
people who lived and worked there. The lord of the manor was not
averse to moving a whole village if it interfered with the view from
his mansion.

Addison's language may verge on the sentimental and it is certainly quaint to our ears. We may wish to use different imagery and
reflect different landscapes. But the task of the writer of hymns and
psalms is, at times, to be as contemporary in our generation as our
ancestors were in theirs. The next generation will have to discern
how much we were in thrall to the spirit of our age.

A personal contribution

Having written so far it still feels faintly ludicrous, and not a little
arrogant, for me to be offering this new unfolding. The book has
been written by an ordained, English, middle class, educated man,

with the cadences of his native language echoing almost physically in his mind from the sixteenth and seventeenth centuries. Through it, however, the language of the silenced finds some expression because of his roots in some of the first peoples of these islands of north-western Europe, and because of his experience of the struggles of a sexual minority to find a way of speech that gives some shape and coherence to their experience. But I have tried to hold firm to my conviction that what is in these pages is but partial and temporary. And I am clear and sincere in my hope that those who use them find themselves making their own alterations, subtractions, and additions.

These versions of the psalms are offered as a form of prayer *for the time being*. They have been used in their original edition (those three separate books, *Through Desert Places*, *By Stony Paths*, and *Towards the City*, and in an American edition, *Psalms for a Pilgrim People*) by all manner of folk, from an elderly man quietly musing on his own, to a nurse who found some of them an adequate container for her distress at the end of a harrowing day in a hospital, and by congregations who found the Sunday handout containing something unexpected. An author has no way of telling from such scraps of response what else is going on. But doubtless these versions will fade sooner or later: few contemporary prayers last beyond the generation in which they were written. It is good that we can prune the past and that we do not need to carry a heavy load.

Address and response

A debate continues among people for whom the word 'God' has become problematic. Is God best pictured as a supra-human being or as the ground of all being? Is God real or only the sum of our best ideals and aspirations? Can we imagine God as someone we can relate to and converse with in a way that is at least analogous to our human relationships? Or are we being lured into a mysticism for the many which will savour words like absence, presence, mystery, no-thing, nothing and everything, emptiness and all things?

If you are in the midst of this kind of question, the way in which the prayers and psalms are cast may not be particularly helpful, for they are an address seeking a response. Now it seems to me that it is hard to do without this mode of prayer, though we may well grow beyond it. After all, we have no higher language than the personal, and while we may believe God to be more than personal, we rarely believe that presence to be less than personal. We may be being drawn to greater fulfilment of our humanity, but surely not to be less than human. That is our conviction either in conventional religious language like that of transfiguration or resurrection, or in the evolutionary and holistic language of the 'whole greater than the sum of the parts' and 'increasing levels of complexity'. In either case, 'we ain't seen nothin' yet.'

Personal language that respects the otherness of the other may also help us to avoid the kind of spirituality that merely inflates the ego. The inner conversation that we have may be nothing more than an obvious ego talking with a more subtle but still self-centred ego. At the very least the form of address and response can be translated into the surface self addressing the deeper self, or, in Thomas Merton's words, our smoke self addressing our flame self.

Or try this as a spiritual practice, in the silences when the words of prayer have done as much as they can. Suppose you are reflecting awhile on justice, human and divine. Ask what the face of a wise and compassionate judge looks like. Perhaps add to it memories of the faces of wise healing women – though don't forget that there are a few wise healing men and more than a few good women judges. And you may want to add the faces of good mothers and good fathers. Let the faces meld. If you have difficulty in doing this, look out for portraits and photographs of such faces, and use these in your prayer. Then imagine such a face opposite you, and contemplate it – dare to look steadily at it. That may renew a conversation. After a while, when the words cease again, imagine that face becoming your own as you move from the activity of prayer to that of family, social, and political life. Through the prayer you have been seeking to embody the God of justice, and, incognito, become something of the divine for others. When prayer and life become seamlessly connected, there is no distinction between them. Prayer can then be led into deeper silence and union, images left far behind. And you can give this book away.

(The compiler hastens to add that he hasn't yet reached that point, whether through personal failings or commercial ambition it's hard to say...)

Praying faithfully today

Let me give some examples of how some of the psalms have been unfolded in this book in an attempt to link what is contemporary with what we have inherited. For we human beings are being pressed protestingly into the reality of a citizenship of one world. Each religious tradition is being challenged to look carefully at its tendencies towards being exclusive and hostile to others. If we relish this crisis as opportunity, we may find ourselves willing to use the language and imagery of a global culture in our praying – from the huge issues of nuclear power and ecology on a vulnerable planet to the particular experiences of cars and bicycles, T-shirts and jeans, traffic lights and television, propaganda and sporadic violence, viruses and bacteria in food and bloodstreams – in each and every city of the world.

So, in these unfoldings:

...invisible rain falls on the mountains,
even the caves fill with rubble. (Psalm 11)

Save us from the corruption of language,
from manipulators of words, greedy for power. (Psalm 12)

In country lanes we have hidden and pounced,
in city streets we have stalked and murdered. (Psalm 10)

The young prowl the streets and the malls,
alienated, rootless, pain turning to violence. (Psalm 7)

In the Hebrew Psalm 22, which Jesus may have prayed as he was dying, there is the picture of the huntsmen and their dogs encircling their victim. In the version in this book similar experiences are added from our own recent past: the prisoner in the concentration camp, the patient in hospital gasping for air, the person quarantined and left alone by those who withdraw in terror.

Again, with our new understanding of the vastness of the universe,

The beginning was all flame,
and the flame unfurled into time;
all that has come into being
began at the heart of the flame. (Psalm 104)

The laws of God

> ...dance as the stars of the universe,
> perfect as the parabolas of comets,
> like satellites and planets in their orbits,
> reliable and constant in their courses. (Psalm 19)

And we human beings are called to be guardians of the planet
which is our home:

> How awesome a task you entrust to our hands,
> how fragile and beautiful is the good earth. (Psalm 8)

Praying for our 'enemies'

I have touched already on the theme of 'us' and 'them', 'superior'
and 'inferior'. Let me go into it a little more.

When that good earth was more forested than it is now, only spo-
radically settled, it is not surprising that those over the mountains
or across the river, unknown and possibly more powerful, were
feared as enemies. Nor is it surprising that wars broke out over
disputed territory as the population grew and the land was cleared.
Only in our generation have we reached the point where co-
operation for the sake of the survival of the planet is rendering war
a wasteful, outmoded, and increasingly suicidal means of resolving
conflict.

As our consciousness changes, the use of many of the psalms
becomes more and more problematic. They often assume an 'over-
againstness', of enemies beyond the gate – with that wearisomely
repeated claim that God is always on our side. 'We' are innocent in
our integrity while 'they' are spurned as hypocrites and deceivers.
I suspect that this should sound more shrill and defensive to our
ears than it often does, especially when politicians manipulate our
patriotism into jingoism. We have suffered and still do suffer from
so-called 'holy' wars.

By contrast, and very slowly over the centuries, we have had
glimpses of a different kind of God, one who indeed strives with
those who rebel against the ways and laws of love, but little by little
impinges on human beings exactly as a persuasive rather than a
coercive power, one who seeks always to redeem tragedy and to

travel the second mile in pursuit of the bewildered, the lost, and the maimed. Our problem is our continuing projection on to God of our suspicion of the stranger, so that we can self-righteously slaughter our enemies on God's behalf.

You can see these two viewpoints struggling with each other in different people's attitudes to the words of Jesus, as reported in chapter 8 of the Gospel according to John, to the woman who had been caught in the act of adultery. Having challenged her accusers to throw the first stone only if they were themselves without sin, he says to the woman, "Neither do I condemn you; go, and do not sin again." (verse 11). I have noticed over the years that some people emphasize the first part of that sentence, others the second. But I wonder what Jesus would have said to the person who asked him, "What if she commits adultery again?" If you focus on, "Go, and do not sin again," you might well say, "She has had a second chance, but now the law must take effect and she must be stoned." If you focus on, "Neither do I condemn you," you might say, "I cannot condemn you even now – even though you are brought to me seventy times seven." But the sorrow in the voice and the hurt in the eyes might make the questioner pause. Here is a man who bears the pain of her and my wrongdoing, one who feels it right through his very being. And in turn that thought might enable the response, "Let me share the pain too. Let me stop acting in ways that hurt you. You are so utterly loving, so totally attractive, that I cannot but love you in return." In such fragmentary moments of reconciliation I think we do from time to time *know* that this is the gospel way.

The process of the prayer of recognition and reconciliation

So, if we seek to transform our praying for our enemies in this light, then we must find our way, with clarity and courage, through this process of recognition and reconciliation. At least seven stages can be discerned, and they have been incorporated into these unfoldings:

1 Honestly admitting our hostile feelings:

> Slay them with your iron fist,
> may they choke on the grapes of your wrath. (Psalm 17)

Denial of anger never does any good, and it is mealy-mouthed to pretend that our feelings are any more civilized than those of our ancestors. But of course such anger rarely helps if it is not transformed into a passion for justice and reconciliation. We are challenged not to keep ourselves totally separate from those with whom we are so angry.

2 Becoming aware of our own hatreds and potential for evil:

> Purge me of hatred and smugness,
> of self-righteous satisfied smile. (Psalm 17)

This is a discipline of deliberately willing to be less condemning of others and more sternly truthful with ourselves:

> Forgive the boast of your people, O God,
> self-righteous and blind in our mouthings. (Psalm 26)

3 Becoming aware also of the forces that threaten us from within as well as from others:

> I am afraid of the powers that prowl within me,
> howling in the dark of the moonless nights. (Psalm 3)

4 Recognizing the love that is expressed through both judgment and mercy:

> You thunder so fiercely in love for us,
> you whisper so gently in judgment. (Psalm 50)

5 Focusing this awareness in contemplation of Christ, recognizing that the extremes of some of our prayer need to be tempered:

> We resist the wrath of your love,
> the searing of judgment and truth.
> Bring us in awe and trembling
> to wake up to ourselves in your presence.

> But who is this, your presence clear among us,
> your human face on earth, true human being at the last?
> You take our rage upon yourself,
> mocked and despised, yet meeting all with love. (Psalm 2)

6 Being brought to true repentance, through a clear recognition of
   ourselves in relation to God:

> You are the fire that shrivels up our hates,
> and brings us to our knees in awe.
> You are the light that pierces all our fury,
> laying bare our greed and pride.
> You are the truth that shines light in our darkness:
> forgive us, for we know not what we do. (Psalm 2)

God's love may be stern but it is not vindictive. In the imagery of fire,
it refines but does not utterly destroy. God brings good out of seem-
ing total evil, a good that is beyond our imagining, yet the hope of
which can become more securely embedded in our prayer than
many of the words we have inherited would lead us to suppose.

7 Offering ourselves, willing a new direction:

> Dear God, we offer you our lives this day,
> the gift of love in our hearts and our loins,
> the incense of prayer, the myrrh of our suffering,
> the gold of all that we hold most dear... (Psalm 45)

Such kindness towards others needs to be extended to our own
enemy within:

> Blessed are those who care for the poor and the helpless,
> who are kind to the outcast within them. (Psalm 41)

In some such way I believe it is possible for us to draw closer to the
true and living God, overcoming the unnecessary distancing that
we often experience when we try to pray many of the psalms in
their original form.

Claiming the story of our ancestors as our own

Some psalms recall in detail the stories of the past. No doubt the
beliefs stated or implied were held sincerely, but inevitably they do
not bring God alive for us in quite such a vivid and immediate
way as they did for those who had direct memories of the events.
Only if we can imaginatively leap the centuries can we make
them part of our own story. Moreover, the history is written in the

third person, which makes the psalm more of a description than a prayer.

Two changes can help. One is to alter the grammar so that the words become a more direct prayer to God in I/We–You language. Immediately the psalm engages and involves us more.

The second is to refer to the present and the future as well as to the past, petition and hope becoming part of the prayer as well as thanksgiving and penitence. We need to take seriously the Hebrew sense of the *continuing* activity of God: creation is not so much a past event as a ceaseless active process. For example, in this book Psalm 33 gives a perspective on both history and creation, Psalm 104 reminds us of the continuing processes of creation, and Psalm 105 brings the notion of the covenants of God with the people into the present day.

A call to adventurous faith

So, again, this task of re-shaping, unfolding, renewing needs to be attempted in a spirit of humility. But it may be more than mere fancy to hope that our ancestors will one day be eager to learn what new things God has revealed to us through our questing spirit in our own generation. And maybe some truths will dawn on us in the midst of the very process of arguing with those half-forgotten and shadowy people of faith.

Years ago my mind stored the sixth verse of Psalm 84 in the Book of Common Prayer of 1662:

> Who going through the vale of misery use it for a well,
> And the pools are filled with water.

Those words haunt me with the hope of their content and the beauty of their expression. But their truth is tough as well as glistening. They challenge us to dig deep into faith's uncompromising terrain, and although there is hope of refreshment, it is in the midst of the desert. Sustained we may be, but to bore a hole for the well is not easy. The drill biting into the rock frequently breaks, and the heat of the day echoes the harsh landscape. It was in such unpromising circumstances, like many of our own, that the psalms were created, in an anguished trust in a seemingly absent God. It is because of this that they have resonated soul-deep in human beings ever since.

If there is a God, only a pain-bearing God can help. That is the
hope – embodied, so we may believe, in God-in-Christ. And that
hope keeps alive the possibility of praise.

> Many are the afflictions of those who seek good,
> but the pain-bearing God is with them.
> You penetrate to the heart of their suffering,
> that they come to no lasting harm. (Psalm 34)

And in the words of the prayer that follows that psalm:

> Pain-bearer God, in our affliction we sense your presence, moving
> with our sufferings to redeem them, bringing joy out of tragedy,
> creating such music as the world has not yet heard. We praise you
> with great praise.

If such faith holds, it does so only just. And it does so in the very
act of falling into an abyss. We do not know whether we shall crash
on the rocks, or how fearful it may be to fall into the hands of the
living God. We are promised that underneath us are the everlasting
arms, but we are not meant to be infants for long. Will the great
white bird of the southern ocean that is the Spirit of God seize us
and teach us how to fly?

Jesus

If you look at the index to this book you will find that there are
more entries for 'Jesus' in the psalms than for any other word. This
is because he is the key figure for this writer and for any praying
Christian, the lens through which the past of the psalms has to go
if they are to be prayed in the present. For convenience, these are
the references: 2, 16, 22, 27, 45, 62, 68, 69, 74, 78, 89, 93, 99, 105,
108, 114, 116, 132, 135, 136, 149.

Sometimes the word 'anointed' is used, not least because it is the
best English translation for 'Christos' or 'Messiah'. In our prayer it
often seems that 'Christ' is functioning merely as a surname.

Also, 'Yeshua' sometimes replaces 'Jesus' to remind us that he is
so often strange to us as we peer back over two millennia. We need
to remember his disturbing wildness if we are to resist the temptation to domesticate him to our comfort and prejudices.

You will also find these phrases used: 'in the Spirit of Jesus', 'in the name of Jesus', 'after the pattern of Jesus', and in the running foot at the bottom of each double page, 'the kaleidoscope of Jesus'. That one-liner, repeated throughout the book, serves as a reminder that the ideas and images that are its content, between the silence out of which they come and the silence into which they drop, are focused on the person of Jesus.

It may seem odd to end with a note about Psalm 119

The longest psalm can seem the most repetitive and boring. But that is only from the outside. From within it is more like the statements lovers make to each other. This psalm is a love song to the God of wisdom. It celebrates the Law, the Torah, the Living Way, the whole counsel of the living God in covenant with the people. It reminds me again of the image of the diamond. As with the annual round of daily prayer, so with Psalm 119. Each section is a facet, illuminating one or other aspect of the wisdom of God.

If we find it difficult to have 'law' so central to a psalm we do well to remember that the meaning here is not that of rules and regulations which must be mechanically obeyed in every single detail, imposed on us externally. Rather do the 'laws' unfold for us certain characteristics of our lives which become typical once we have responded to the gracious invitation of the living loving God. A nineteenth century rabbi, Yerachmiel ben Yisrael, wrote that it is in the practice of prayer that we come to "what is right in so powerful a way that we feel commanded to do it. There is no real choice. The knowing is too strong." So law and love are not in the end opposed to each other.

And if you have once said or sung Psalm 119 as a delighted lover, then the rest of prayer's daily round may take on this character too.

THE MUSIC

by Paul Payton

If one were to put a psalm text into a pan of boiling water and reduce it down to its essence what would be left might be little more than a single verse refrain: a pithy, flavoursome distillation of the text's main theme or themes; a psalmic sound-bite, representing the emotional and spiritual base camp to which the reciter keeps returning; a wake-up call, bringing the reciter back from monotony or over-familiarity or forgetfulness or mind-meandering. And through its regular repetition within the psalm the refrain is a text the reciter might come to memorize, and at another time, on the bus, doing the dishes, lying awake in the middle of the night, meditate upon and pray through.

If little else of the psalm sticks in the memory the refrain might, especially if it's sung. Through singing a text we unwittingly engage the two hemispheres of the brain. Singing makes the brain work holistically and by so doing gives extra force to the power and potential of memory. When St Augustine said that singing is praying twice I don't imagine that he was aware of the scientific basis of his observation. Singing was, for him, a means of connecting with a deeper spiritual reality within and beyond the singer's own breath and voice box. The music on which the words were floated allowed them to travel to places beyond the surface level of communication, connecting the human realm of speech with the divine music of the spheres.

It was with some of this in mind that I approached the composition of 150 psalm refrains. I had to engage with a number of problems: How to articulate musically the textual nuances, the emotional tenor, the rhythmic subtleties of the individual refrains? How to capture and contain the essence of the whole psalm in a few bars of music? How to balance the need for accessibility – to compose melodies that are both singable and memorable and which celebrate a range of musical and liturgical traditions – without being trite or patronizing.

Here are two examples which illustrate something of how these considerations were carried through into the compositional process.

The refrain for Psalm 39 is a good example of musical word painting.

My-ste-rious is___ the_ God who throws us to the ground
and con-tin-ual-ly,_ con-tin-ual-ly, rai-ses us up.

First, to capture something of the mystery implied by the text, the refrain is in the dark key of C minor. Notice that at the midpoint of the refrain the words 'throws us to the ground' are mirrored by an element of musical instability. The pace is suddenly quicker, the rhythm noticably more awkward, and melodically the shape is angular. The musical setting of the refrain's final words, 'raises us up', literally picks us up off the ground, rising in pitch to the highest point of the whole refrain.

Those of you who are familiar with contemporary worship songs and choruses will recognize something of their influence on the refrain for Psalm 97.

God reigns:_ the gen-tle peo-ple_ in-he-rit the earth,
the lit-tle is-lands re-joice_____ to see the day.
God reigns! God_ reigns!_

The melodic line is lyrical and largely stepwise in its movement from note to note. The repetition of the final words 'God reigns' helps bring the more active and angular middle section to a close, echoing the gentleness of the refrain's opening. The refrain has a satisfying musical shape, describing an arc moving from a point of stillness through greater activity and then back to stillness.

Rather than try to overcompose the refrains for the longest psalm, 119, I took my cue from the masterly internal repetitions of the text and decided to follow an integrated sequence of melodic refrains. Each section of the text has its own refrain or refrains, but each is a musical variation on the one which precedes it and the one which follows it. Thus the psalm has both textual and musical continuity, and internal logic.

How might the refrains be used? Some people might choose not to sing the refrains at all. Some might choose a cantor to sing the refrains solo on behalf of others. Some might have the cantor sing through the refrain once and then support the rest as it is repeated. Some might have the refrain played first on an instrument and then repeated as all sing. Some might accompany the refrains on a keyboard instrument, adding their own harmony or the harmonization soon to be available on the website. Whatever is decided, above all the refrains are designed to suit and serve those who use them as flexibly as possible. Poetic license is encouraged.

PAUL PAYTON
Lancaster, October 2005

HOW TO USE THIS BOOK

* Some suggestions about bodies. Take posture seriously. Gently keep your back as straight as you can, and with no strain or stiffness, specially when bored and tempted to slouch. Keep your feet on the ground. Otherwise your head may well be in the clouds. So don't cross your legs. And if your hands are in your pockets you are probably not taking the prayer seriously – unless of course you're trying to keep warm.

* Take the silence seriously and the words steadily. Remember the book's title and the words at the bottom of each double page.

* Allow ten to fifteen minutes for the words, and a similar amount of time for the silence. Let the silences and pauses punctuate the words at suitable places. Some of these are indicated in the text. Other places may be after the reading, and as part of the prayer of solidarity, also before any words are said, and after the last one has been said.

* Suggestion: experiment with counting seconds to get the feel of the length of a pause – perhaps five to eight seconds – and of a silence – perhaps twenty to thirty seconds. And allow a moment's pause at the end of each line, and after a comma or full stop. Then you will be praying with a background rhythm and not be tempted to read continuously as if you were giving out information. Let there be breathing spaces.

* You may like to make this experiment. After saying a line out loud, imagine you hear it back, like an echo from the other side of a valley.

* Psalms and canticles can be sung in various ways, even simply holding one note as you move through a line, or with a higher or lower note or two at the end of the line. Simple plainsong is

not difficult. Don't be put off by the glories of Gregorian chant on a CD. A straightforward chant can help 'carry' the prayer.

* But find your own rhythm if you are on your own, or experiment in a group until you can all settle. Then the mechanics won't get in the way of the praying. Above all, keep the words rooted in the silence.

* Use the Calendar if you wish. It suggests a particular psalm, reading, and canticle for each day of the year. The days are dated except for the period before and after Easter. After the pancakes of Shrove Tuesday in February or March turn to Ash Wednesday (see pages 15–18), and after Pentecost in May or June turn back to the dated day.

* The suggested reading from the Calendar is usually short and invariably from the Gospels. There are of course lectionaries galore, and courses of biblical readings with commentary, such as *Words for Today*.

* Words in italics are titles, indicators, and prompts, none of which need to be spoken aloud.

* Words in ordinary, roman, type are for solo voices, perhaps in turn if a small group of people are praying together.

* Words in bold type are for everybody to say or sing.

* You may find candles, pictures, and music give focus to and enhance the prayer.

* Let the sense of praying to God relax into the sense of praying in God. Let the prayer be more of re-membering and solidarity rather than petition and intercession. And don't forget it's work. At the end you may feel nothing – you may even feel worse.

SUGGESTED CALENDAR

OF PSALMS,
GOSPEL READINGS,
AND CANTICLES
FOR EACH DAY
OF THE YEAR

		Psalm	Gospel Reading	Canticle
January				
1		103	Luke 2.33–35	32
2		8	Luke 2.36–38	34
3		19	Luke 2.39–40	35
4		23	Luke 2.41–52	32
5		33	John 1.14–18	34
6	Epiphany	113	Matthew 2.1–12	37
7		5	Matthew 2.13–18	37
8		17	Matthew 2.19–23	37
9		18.i	Mark 1.16–20	37
10		18.ii	Mark 1.21–28	36
11		40	Mark 1.29–39	36
12		45	Mark 1.40–45	36
13		91	Mark 2.1–12	36
14		57	Mark 2.13–17	38
15		99	Mark 2.18–28	38
16		63	Mark 3.1–6	38
17		138	Mark 3.7–19a	38
18		125	Mark 3.19b–35	32
19		72	Mark 4.1–9	32
20		119.xix	Mark 4.10–20	32
21		127	Mark 4.21–34	32
22		89.i	Mark 4.35–41	12
23		89.ii	Mark 5.1–20	12
24		122	Mark 5.21–43	12
25	St Paul	67	Mark 6.1–6a	58/59/60
26		119.xx	Mark 6.6b–13	15
27		119.xxi	Mark 6.14–29	15
28		119.xxii	Mark 6.30–44	15
29		131	Mark 6.45–56	28
30		146	Mark 7.1–23	28
31		147	Mark 7.24–30	28

		Psalm	Gospel Reading	Canticle
February				
1		148	Mark 7.31–37	22
2	*Presentation*	48	Luke 2.22–40	5
3		15	Mark 8.1–10	5
4		16	Mark 8.11–21	5
5		2	Mark 8.22–26	5
6		3	Mark 8.27—9.1	1
7		4	Mark 9.2–8	2
8		14	Mark 9.9–13	3
9		90	Mark 9.14–29	4
10		44	Mark 9.30–37	8
11		49	Mark 9.38–50	6
12		50	Mark 10.1–12	12
13		52	Mark 10.13–16	1
14		53	Mark 10.17–31	2
15		119.i	Mark 10.32–34	3
16		119.ii	Mark 10.35–45	4
17		119.iii	Mark 10.46–52	9
18		119.iv	Mark 11.1–11	7
19		119.v	Mark 11.12–26	13
20		58	Mark 11.27–33	1
21		59	Mark 12.1–12	2
22		93	Mark 12.13–17	3
23		76	Mark 12.18–27	4
24		80	Mark 12.28–34	10
25		83	Mark 12.35–44	16
26		95	Mark 13.1–13	14
27		126	Mark 13.14–27	1
28		39	Mark 13.28–37	2
29		65	Matthew 4.1–11	3

On Ash Wednesday turn to page 15.
For dates of Ash Wednesday turn to page 18.

		Psalm	Gospel Reading	Canticle
March				
1	St David	1	Matthew 4.1–11/4.12–17	4
2		7	Matthew 4.12–25/4.18–25	11
3		46	Matthew 5.1–12	17
4		47	Matthew 5.13–16	15
5		9a	Matthew 5.17–26	1
6		9b	Matthew 5.27–37	2
7		10a	Matthew 5.38–48	3
8		10b	Matthew 6.1–8	4
9		62	Matthew 6.9–18	1

*Because the following dates always occur during the Lent and Easter seasons
they have been left blank, but you may find them useful for your own additions.*

10

11
12
13
14
15

16
17   *St Patrick*
18
19   *St Joseph*
20

21
22
23
24
25   *Annunciation*

26
27
28
29
30
31

	Psalm	Gospel Reading	Canticle

April

1
2
3
4
5

6
7
8
9
10

11
12
13
14
15

16
17
18
19
20

21
22
23   *St George*
24
25   *St Mark*

26
27
28
29
30

		Psalm	*Gospel Reading*	*Canticle*

May

1	*SS Philip & James*			
2				
3				
4				
5				
6				
7				
8				
9				
10				
11		2	Mark 8.22-26	54
12		3	Mark 8.27—9.1	54
13		5	Mark 9.2-8	54
14	*St Matthias*	14	Mark 9.9-13	54
15		90	Mark 9.14-29	54
16		44	Mark 9.30-37	54

The canticle chosen for each day over the next few weeks depends on whether it is the week after Pentecost, the week following Trinity Sunday, or ordinary time.

17		49	Mark 9.38-56	54 or 55
18		50	Mark 10.1-12	54 or 55
19		52	Mark 10.13-16	54 or 55
20		53	Mark 10.17-31	54 or 55
21		119.i	Mark 10.32-34	54 or 55
22		119.ii	Mark 10.35-45	54 or 55
23		119.iii	Mark 10.46-52	54 or 55
24		119.iv	Mark 11.1-11	54 or 55 or 10
25		119.v	Mark 11.12-26	54 or 55 or 16
26		58	Mark 11.27-33	54 or 55 or 14
27		59	Mark 12.1-12	54 or 55 or 1
28		93	Mark 12.13-17	54 or 55 or 2
29		76	Mark 12.18-27	54 or 55 or 3
30		80	Mark 12.28-34	54 or 55 or 4/5
31	*Visitation*	83	Mark 12.35-44	54 or 55 or 11

		Psalm	Gospel Reading	Canticle
June				
1		95	Mark 13.1–13	54 or 55 or 17
2		126	Mark 13.14–27	54 or 55 or 15
3		39	Mark 13.28–36	54 or 55 or 1
4		1	Matthew 4.1–11	54 or 55 or 2
5		75	Matthew 4.12–17	54 or 55 or 3
6		94	Matthew 4.18–25	54 or 55 or 4/5
7		98	Matthew 5.1–12	54 or 55 or 22
8		9a	Matthew 5.13–16	54 or 55 or 18
9		9b	Matthew 5.17–26	54 or 55 or 21
10		106.i	Matthew 5.27–37	54 or 55 or 1
11	St Barnabas	106.ii	Matthew 5.38–48	54 or 55 or 2
12		129	Matthew 6.1–8	54 or 55 or 3
13		130	Matthew 6.9–18	54 or 55 or 4/5
14		141	Matthew 6.19–24	54 or 55 or 24
15		144	Matthew 6.25–34	54 or 55 or 19
16		132	Matthew 7.1–12	54 or 55 or 20
17		114	Matthew 7.13–29	54 or 55 or 22
18		119.xvii	Matthew 8.1–13	54 or 55 or 1
19		87	Matthew 8.14–27	54 or 55 or 2
20		21	Matthew 8.28—9.1	54 or 55 or 3
21		85	Matthew 9.2–8	55 or 4/5
22		111	Matthew 9.9–17	55 or 6
23		13	Matthew 9.18–34	55 or 12
24	St John the Bap.	12	Matthew 9.35—10.4	55 or 1
25		36	Matthew 10.5–15	55 or 2
26		11	Matthew 10.16–31	55 or 3
27		84	Matthew 10.32–42	4/5
28		119.xviii	Matthew 11.1–15	7
29	St Peter	103	Matthew 11.16–19	9
30		8	Matthew 11.20–30	26

		Psalm	Gospel Reading	Canticle
July				
1		19	Matthew 12.1−14	26
2		137	Matthew 12.15−30	26
3	*St Thomas*	33	Matthew 12.31−37	57
4		113	Matthew 12.38−45 (−50)	26
5		64	Matthew 13.1−9	26
6		17	Matthew 13.10−17	1
7		18.i	Matthew 13.18−23	2
8		18.ii	Matthew 13.24−30	3
9		40	Matthew 13.31−35	4/5
10		45	Matthew 13.36−43	16
11		91	Matthew 13.44−52	14
12		57	Matthew 13.53−58	1
13		99	Matthew 14.1−12	2
14		63	Matthew 14.13−21	3
15		138	Matthew 14.22−36	4/5
16		125	Matthew 15.1−20	17
17		102	Matthew 15.21−28	15
18		119.xix	Matthew 15.29−39	1
19		127	Matthew 16.1−12	2
20		89.i	Matthew 16.13−28	3
21		89.ii	Matthew 17.(1−)14−21	4/5
22	*St Mary Magdalene*	122	Matthew 17.22−27	57
23		67	Matthew 18.1−11	18
24		119.xx	Matthew 18.12−14	21
25	*St James*	119.xxi	Matthew 18.15−20	58
26		119.xxii	Matthew 18.21−35	1
27		131	Matthew 19.1−12	2
28		146	Matthew 19.13−15	3
29		147	Matthew 19.16−30	4/5
30		148	Matthew 20.1−16	19
31		48	Matthew 20.17−28	20

		Psalm	Gospel Reading	Canticle
August				
1		65	Matthew 20.29–34	22
2		51	Matthew 21.1–17	1
3		38	Matthew 21.18–22	2
4		22.i	Matthew 21.23–32	3
5		22.ii	Matthew 21.33–46	4/5
6	Transfiguration	80	Matthew 17.1–13	56
7		22.iii	Matthew 22.1–14	56
8		37.i	Matthew 22.15–22	56
9		37.ii	Matthew 22.23–46	56
10		56	Matthew 23.1–15	56
11		6	Matthew 23.16–26	56
12		32	Matthew 23.27–39	56
13		26	Matthew 24.1–14	8
14		28	Matthew 24.15–31	6
15	St Mary	34	Matthew 12.46–50	57
16		73	Matthew 24.32–41	12
17		54	Matthew 24.42–51	1
18		121	Matthew 25.1–13	2
19		128	Matthew 25.14–30	3
20		101	Matthew 25.31–46	4/5
21		77	Luke 4.1–13	9
22		86	Luke 4.14–30	7
23		120	Luke 4.31–37	13
24	St Bartholomew	140	Luke 4.38–44	58
25		112	Luke 5.1–11	1
26		136	Luke 5.12–16	2
27		60	Luke 5.17–26	3
28		139	Luke 5.27–39	4/5
29		143	Luke 6.1–11	10
30		71	Luke 6.12–19 (–30)	16
31		35	Luke 6.31–38	14

	Psalm	Gospel Reading	Canticle
September			
1	31	Luke 6.39–49	1
2	41	Luke 7.1–10	2
3	79	Luke 7.11–17	3
4	61	Luke 7.18–28	4/5
5	25	Luke 7.29–35	11
6	55	Luke 7.36–50	17
7	142	Luke 8.1–8	15
8	42–43	Luke 8.9–15	1
9	69	Luke 8.16–21	2
10	88	Luke 8.22–25	3
11	117	Luke 8.26–39	4/5
12	30	Luke 8.40–56	23
13	29	Luke 9.1–11	18
14	66	Luke 9.12–17	21
15	81	Luke 9.18–27	1
16	135	Luke 9.28–36	2
17	118	Luke 9.37–50	3
18	92	Luke 9.51–62	4/5
19	96	Luke 10.1–16	21
20	97	Luke 10.17–24	19
21	*St Matthew*	105.i	Luke 10.25–37	58
22		105.ii	Luke 10.38–42	20
23		108	Luke 11.1–13	22
24		115	Luke 11.14–20	1
25		116	Luke 11.21–26	2
26		124	Luke 11.27–36	3
27		82	Luke 11.37–54	4/5
28		110	Luke 12.1–12	6
29	*Michaelmas*	150	John 1.35–51	58
30		123	Luke 12.13–21	12

		Psalm	Gospel Reading	Canticle
October				
1		20	Luke 12.22–34	1
2		133	Luke 12.35–48	2
3		134	Luke 12.49–59	3
4		129	Luke 13.1–9	4/5
5		22.iv	Luke 13.10–21	7
6		74	Luke 13.22–30	13
7		109	Luke 13.31–35	1
8		24	Luke 14.1–11	2
9		100	Luke 14.12–24	3
10		104.i	Luke 14.25–35	4/5
11		104.ii	Luke 15.1–10	16
12		107	Luke 15.11–32	14
13		27	Luke 16.1–9	27
14		149	Luke 16.10–18	27
15		145	Luke 16.19–31	27
16		70	Luke 17.1–19	27
17		71	Luke 17.20–37	27
18	*St Luke*	119.i	Luke 18.1–14	57
19		119.ii	Luke 18.15–30	1
20		119.iii	Luke 18.31–43	2
21		119.iv	Luke 19.1–10	3
22		119.v	Luke 19.11–27	17
23		119.vi	Luke 19.28–48	15
24		119.vii	Luke 20.1–19	1
25		119.viii	Luke 20.20–26	2
26		119.ix	Luke 20.27–47	3
27		119.x	Luke 21.1–19	4/5
28	*SS Simon & Jude*	119.xi	Luke 21.20–38	18
29		139	John 1.19–34 (–51)	21
30		23	John 2.1–11	19
31		121	John 2.12–25	20

		Psalm	Gospel Reading	Canticle
November				
1	*All Saints' Day*	15	Luke 6.20–31	59
2	*All Souls' Day*	16	John 6.22–40	60
3		2	John 3.1–21	57
4		3	John 3.22–36	57
5		5	John 4.1–30	57
6		14	John 4.31–42	57
7		90	John 4.43–54	57
8		44	John 5.1–18	59
9		49	John 5.19–47	58
10		50	John 6.1–21 (–40)	58
11	*Remembrance*	52	John 6.41–48	58
12		53	John 6.49–71	58
13		119.xii	John 7.1–13	58
14		119.xiii	John 7.14–36	59
15		119.xiv	John 7.37–52	57
16		119.xv	John 8.1–11	59
17		119.xvi	John 8.12–30	60
18		58	John 8.31–47	60
19		59	John 8.48–59	60
20		93	John 9.1–17	60
21		76	John 9.18–41	61
22		80	John 10.1–21	61
23		83	John 10.22–42	61
24		95.ii	John 11.1–16	61
25		126	John 11.17–44	61
26		39	John 11.45–54	62
27		1	John 11.55—12.11	62/29
28		7	John 12.12–19	62/30
29		46	John 12.20–36	62/31
30	*St Andrew*	47	John 12.37–50	57/29

		Psalm	Gospel Reading	Canticle
December				
1		9a	Mark 1.1–8	30
2		9b	Mark 1.9–15	31
3		10a	John 1.1–5	29
4		10b	John 1.6–9	30
5		62	Matthew 3.1–6	31
6		64	Matthew 3.7–10	29
7		70	Matthew 3.11–12	30
8		75	Matthew 3.13–17	31
9		94	Luke 3.1–6	29
10		98	Luke 3.7–9	30
11		102	Luke 3.10–14	31
12		106.i	Luke 3.14–17	29
13		106.ii	Luke 3.18–20	30
14		137	Luke 3.21–22	31
15		129	Luke 3.23–38	29
16		130	Matthew 1.1–17	30
17		141	Matthew 1.18–25	31
18		144	Luke 1.1–4	29
19		132	Luke 1.5–25	30
20		114	Luke 1.26–38	31
21		119.xvii	Luke 1.39–45	33
22		87	Luke 1.46–56	33
23		21	Luke 1.57–66	33
24		85	Luke 1.67–80	33
25	*Christmas Day*	111	Luke 2.1–7	35
26	*St Stephen*	13	Luke 2.8–14	32
27	*St John Evangelist*	12	John 1.10–14	34
28	*The Innocents*	36	Luke 2.15–20	35
29		11	Luke 2.21	32
30		84	Luke 2.22–24	34
31		119.xviii	Luke 2.25–32	35

	Psalm	Gospel Reading	Canticle
Ash Wednesday	51	Mark 14.1–11	42
Thursday	38	Mark 14.12–25	42
Friday	22.i	Mark 14.26–31	42
Saturday	22.ii	Mark 14.32–42	42
1st Sunday in Lent	22.iii	Mark 14.43–52	46
Monday	37.i	Mark 14.53–65	40
Tuesday	37.ii	Mark 14.66–72	40
Wednesday	56	Mark 15.1–15	40
Thursday	6	Mark 15.16–28	40
Friday	78.i	Mark 15.29–32	40
Saturday	78.ii	Mark 15.33–39	40
2nd Sunday in Lent	32	Mark 15.40–41	46
Monday	26	Mark 15.42–47	39
Tuesday	28	Matthew 26.1–13	39
Wednesday	34	Matthew 26.14–16	39
Thursday	73	Matthew 26.17–29	39
Friday	54	Matthew 26.30–35	39
Saturday	121	Matthew 26.36–46	39
3rd Sunday in Lent	128	Matthew 26.47–56	46
Monday	101	Matthew 26.57–68	41
Tuesday	77	Matthew 26.69–75	41
Wednesday	86	Matthew 27.1–10	41
Thursday	120	Matthew 27.11–26	41
Friday	140	Matthew 27.27–37	41
Saturday	112	Matthew 27.38–44	41
4th Sunday in Lent	136	Matthew 27.45–54	46
Monday	60	Matthew 27.55–61	46
Tuesday	139	Matthew 27.62–66	46
Wednesday	143	Luke 22.1–6	46
Thursday	71	Luke 22.7–13	46
Friday	35	Luke 22.14–23	46
Saturday	31	Luke 22.24–27	46

	Psalm	*Gospel Reading*	*Canticle*
5th Sunday in Lent	41	Luke 22.28–34	43
Monday	79	Luke 22.35–38	43
Tuesday	119.vi	Luke 22.39–46	43
Wednesday	119.vii	Luke 22.47–53	43
Thursday	119.viii	Luke 22.54–62	44
Friday	119.ix	Luke 22.63—23.5	44
Saturday	119.x	Luke 23.6–12	44
Palm Sunday	61	Luke 23.13–25	45
Monday in Holy Week	25	Luke 23.26–31	45
Tuesday	55	Luke 23.32–34a	45
Wednesday	142	Luke 23.34b–38	45
Maundy Thursday	42–43	Luke 23.39–43	45
Good Friday	69	Luke 23.44–49	45
Holy Saturday	88	Luke 23.50–56	62
Easter Day	117	Luke 24.1–12	47
Monday	30	Luke 24.13–27	47
Tuesday	29	Luke 24.28–35	47
Wednesday	66	Luke 24.36–43	47
Thursday	81	Mark 16.1–8	47
Friday	135	Mark 16.9–13	47
Saturday	118	Mark 16.14–20	25
2nd Sunday of Easter	30	Matthew 28.1–7	48
Monday	92	Matthew 28.8–10	48
Tuesday	96	Matthew 28.11–15	48
Wednesday	97	Matthew 28.16–20	48
Thursday	105.i	John 13.1–11	48
Friday	105.ii	John 13.12–17	48
Saturday	108	John 13.18–20	25

	Psalm	*Gospel Reading*	*Canticle*
3rd Sunday of Easter	29	John 13.21–30	49
Monday	115	John 13.31–38	49
Tuesday	116	John 14.1–7	49
Wednesday	124	John 14.7–14	49
Thursday	67	John 14.15–21	49
Friday	82	John 14.22–26	49
Saturday	110	John 14.27–31	25
4th Sunday of Easter	150	John 15.1–10	50
Monday	123	John 15.11–17	50
Tuesday	127	John 15.18–25	50
Wednesday	20	John 15.26—16.11	50
Thursday	133	John 16.12–15	50
Friday	46	John 16.16–24	50
Saturday	68	John 16.25–33	25
5th Sunday of Easter	134	John 17.1–10	51
Monday	119.xi	John 17.11–19	51
Tuesday	119.xii	John 17.20–26	51
Wednesday	119.xiii	John 18.1–11	51
Thursday	119.xiv	John 18.12–27	51
Friday	119.xv	John 18.28–40	51
Saturday	119.xvi	John 19.1–7	51
6th Sunday of Easter	22.iv	John 19.8–16a	1
Monday	33	John 19.16b–24	1
Tuesday	74	John 19.25–27	1
Wednesday	109	John 19.28–30	1
Ascension Day	24	Luke 24.44–53	52
Friday	100	John 19.31–37	52
Saturday	72	John 19.38–42	52

	Psalm	*Gospel Reading*	*Canticle*
7th Sunday of Easter	84	John 20.1–10	52
Monday	104.i	John 20.11–18	52
Tuesday	104.ii	John 20.24–31	53
Wednesday	107	John 21.1–8	53
Thursday	27	John 21.9–14	53
Friday	149	John 21.15–19	53
Saturday	145	John 21.20–25	53
Pentecost	147	John 20.19–23	54

On the Monday after Pentecost turn back to the dated calendar.

Dates of Ash Wednesday

2010	17 February	2021	17 February
2011	9 March	2022	2 March
2012	22 February	2023	22 February
2013	13 February	2024	14 February
2014	5 March	2025	5 March
2015	18 February	2026	18 February
2016	10 February	2027	10 February
2017	1 March	2028	1 March
2018	14 February	2029	14 February
2019	6 March	2030	6 March
2020	26 February		

The cloth is unravelling.

Some of the threads crumble to dust.

Some need dipping in dye to give them colour again.

New threads need to be spun.

New patterns need to be designed.

The compiler of this book

has let some old threads disintegrate
and they will not be found here,

has dipped some old threads into dye
and tried to give them back their colour,

has found himself a spinner of new threads,

and as a tentative weaver
has tried out a design or two in a corner of the loom.

The skilled weavers we need
are probably being born about now.

After Gilbert Shaw
&
Mary Clare of the Sisters of the Love of God

SEQUENCE

Opening

Greeting

Engaging

Listening

Delighting

Connecting

Gathering

Proceeding

We breathe these words out of the Silence within us, into the Silence beyond us…
. . .in the Spirit that stirs amongst us the kaleidoscope of Jesus.

OPENING

Sunday

Eternal Spirit of the living God,
be for us the fountain of water
creating and sustaining us each day,
be for us the enlivening wind
searching us out and scouring us clean,
be for us the refining warming flame
steadying and transforming our desires,
that, lovingly and truthfully,
we may pray and we may live.

Monday

Living One,
open our lips
and we shall sing of your wonders;
open our eyes
and we shall see your glory;
open our hearts
and we shall embrace your love;
open our minds
and we shall discover your wisdom;
open our hands
and we shall show your generosity;
open our flesh
and we shall embody your presence.

Tuesday

We stand in the presence of the One who is making us.
We stand in the presence of the One who is healing us.
We stand in the presence of the One who is guiding us.
We stand in love and adoration.

...in the Spirit that stirs amongst us the kaleidoscope of Jesus.

Wednesday

Giver of life,
Giver of the nights and days,
Giver of this moment now,
open our lips
that we may speak truthfully,
open our hearts
that we may love wholeheartedly,
open our minds
that we may think clearly,
open our loins
that we may create passionately,
open our whole being
that we may act courageously,
this moment now,
through this and all our days,
and at the last.

Thursday

We live and die, die and live,
in flow and ebb, in ebb and flow.
We live and die in the Three-in-One,
we die and live in the One-in-Three.

Friday

Let us be silent…
let us be still…
empty…
in the presence…
saying nothing…
asking nothing…
being silent…
being still.

We breathe these words out of the Silence within us, into the Silence beyond us…

Saturday

Companion, Lover, open my heart,
and I shall embrace you, my beloved.
Grandfather, Grandmother, open my mind,
and I shall discern you, my wise one.
The One That Shall Be, open my imagination,
and I shall dream you, my future.
Yeshua, born of Miriam, open my flesh,
and I shall embody you, my brother.
Great Spirit, open my whole being,
and I shall dance your life this day.

...in the Spirit that stirs amongst us the kaleidoscope of Jesus.

GREETING

ORDINARY TIME

3 February
to Shrove Tuesday

First Sunday after Trinity
to Saturday before Advent Sunday

Sunday morning

We praise you, O God, holy and beloved.
We praise you for your glory and wisdom.
We praise you for your creative power.
We praise you for your deeds of deliverance.

We praise you in a glorious symphony.
We praise you on the flute and harp.
We praise you with the caress of the trumpet.
We praise you with the solace of the cello.

We praise you on the quickening horn.
We praise you on the strumming guitar.
We praise you with the pipes of the clans.
We praise you on the deep resounding drums.

We praise you in the unnoticed pauses
that make music of disordered sounds.
We praise you in the depths of the silence,
in the music that dances between eyes that love.

We praise you for all your gifts.
We praise you for your mysterious being.
We praise you for weaving us together.
We praise you that we belong to the universe.

Let everything that breathes under the sun,
let the voices of our ancestors of old,
let worlds unknown, within and beyond,
all on this glad day give you praise.

...in the Spirit that stirs amongst us the kaleidoscope of Jesus.

Sunday evening

Hail, gladdening Light, of God's pure glory poured,
who is the great Creator, heavenly, blest,
holiest of holies, Jesus Christ who reigns.

Now we are come to the sun's hour of rest,
the lights of evening round us shine;
we hymn the God of love, eternal Spirit divine.

You are worthy, O God, at all times to be sung,
with clear and truthful voice,
light of light, giver of life, alone!
Therefore in all the world your glories, Christ, we own.

Monday, Wednesday, and Friday

Let us sing to the One who is creating us,
let us renew our covenant with God.

Dear God, we celebrate your presence with thanksgiving,
and with our whole heart sing psalms of praise.
We greet you with love, Creator of the universe,
Spirit who strives with the chaos of the world.
With your finger you shape the mountains of the earth,
and the depths of the valleys are scoured by your power.
The wings of your Spirit brood over the seas,
and your hands mould the dry land.

O come let us worship and lift our hearts high
and adore our God, our Creator.

For you indeed are God,
and we are your people,
crafted by the skill of your hands.

We breathe these words out of the Silence within us, into the Silence beyond us...

Tuesday, Thursday, and Saturday

Let the whole earth be joyful in you, O God,
greet you with gladness,
and celebrate your presence with a song.
For we know that you are creating us,
you are alive in us and we belong to you.
You are weaving us into a marvellous tapestry,
a people of diverse threads and colours.
We enter your gates, a motley procession,
with heartfelt thanksgiving and joy.
We dance with delight and bless one another,
in the Spirit of your love, intimate and just.
For you are gracious and courteous,
compassionate in embrace,
faithful through all generations.

SPECIAL TIME

Advent: 1–24 December *(from Advent Sunday if in November)*

Maranatha!
Come, universal Christ, come soon!

The glory of God shall be revealed:
all humankind shall see it together.

Maranatha!
Come, universal Christ, come soon!

Sing aloud,
waste places of Jerusalem,
cities devastated by war.
Sing with hope,
torn landscapes of the earth,
eroded by human greed.
Sing to the God who gives courage and strength.

Maranatha!
Come, universal Christ, come soon!

Those who are losing their faith, listen,
and those burdened with oppression and failure:
soon God's restoration will come,
God's justice will be revealed.

Maranatha!
Come, universal Christ, come soon!

For a woman will conceive and bear a son,
and will call his name Emmanuel,
God for ever with us,
always at home in human flesh,
never to be separated from the earth.

Hosanna! Blessed is the One who comes in the name of our God.
Hosanna in the highest!

Maranatha!
Come, universal Christ, come soon!

We breathe these words out of the Silence within us, into the Silence beyond us…

Christmas: 25 December to 2 February

Blessed be the God of wonder and mystery!
Blessed for ever be God's glorious name!

Through the tender mercy of our God
the day has dawned upon us from on high,
to give light to those who sit in darkness
and in the shadow of death,
and to guide our feet into ways of peace.
Living Word of light and love,
taking form as flesh and blood among us,
living the fulness of our humanity,
full of grace and truth, we greet you.

A child is born to us, alleluia!
A son is given to us, alleluia!
The dream of the beginning takes shape among us. Alleluia!
The human face of God is ours for ever. Alleluia!
The heart hopes and yearns!
The downtrodden can hardly believe!
The very stones of the earth cry out!
The day of freedom dawns!
Alleluia! Alleluia! Alleluia!

Lent

Let us listen to your voice this day
and harden not our hearts.
Let us not be like our ancestors
who saw the great deeds you had done,
yet put you to the test in the desert,
at the place called 'Bitterness' and 'Quarrel'.
They were wayward in their hearts,
they were ignorant of your ways.
So they could sense your love only as wrath,
and were trapped in their restless wandering.   >

If we listen to your voice deep within us,
we shall know the mercy and grace of your love.
We shall see you as Judge of the earth,
doing right in the sight of all peoples,
enfolding us in your faithfulness,
quelling our rebellious strife.

Spirit of Yeshua, take shape among us,
Spirit of the One who fulfilled God's promise.
Humble us in awe at your presence:
let us adore you in the silence of love.
Deepen our gratitude in obedience and trust,
in your covenant made sure for ever.

Passiontide

Come, let us turn again to the living God,
the God whose love sears and refines us.
For you have torn us and you will heal us,
you have stricken us and you will bind us up.
After two days you will revive us:
on the third day you will raise us up.

Let us know you, let us press on to know you:
your going forth is as sure as the dawn.
You will come to us as the showers,
as the spring rains that water the earth.

What will you do with us, your fickle people?
What will you do with us, who have turned away?
Our love is like the morning mist,
like the dew that vanishes in the sun.

You have hewn us by your prophets,
you have laid us low by the words of your mouth.
For you do not desire rituals of anxious pleading,
nor the bargainings of desperate petition.
It is steadfast love that is your heart's desire,
intimate knowledge of your compassion and justice.

We breathe these words out of the Silence within us, into the Silence beyond us...

Easter: the first four weeks

Christ is risen! **Alleluia!**

Let the gospel trumpets speak,
and the news, as of holy fire,
burning and flaming and inextinguishable,
run to the ends of the earth.

Christ is risen! **Alleluia!**

Let all creation greet the good news with jubilant shout,
for the end of its travail has come,
death's ancient grip has been released.

Christ is risen! **Alleluia!**

Death and life have engaged each other in a wondrous struggle,
and death is swallowed up by life.

Christ is risen! **Alleluia!**

Death yields strange gifts to life,
its colours rich and deep and radiant,
life more solid and more real.

Christ is risen! **Alleluia!**

Glory shines through everything that is:
unconquerable is the power of love.

Christ is risen! **Alleluia!**

Sleeping cells, awake, rise from the dead,
the light will shine out from within you.

Christ is risen! **Alleluia!**

Embrace the living hope. Death has no final word.
In the resurrection of Jesus is life in God for ever.

Christ is risen! **Alleluia!**

...in the Spirit that stirs amongst us the kaleidoscope of Jesus.

Easter: the last three weeks

Let us give thanks for your goodness, dear God,
let the people of old shout their joy.
**Let the children yet unborn hear its sound,
the harmony of a people of praise.**

No one shall die and be forgotten,
not one of the little ones is lost.
**If the hairs of our heads are numbered,
who can doubt your care and compassion?**

We shall not die but we shall live,
even in the dazzling at the heart of your darkness.
**Even though you test us to the limit,
you do not abandon us to final death.**

The stone which the builder rejected
has become the head of the corner.
**The very ones we despised
are known as your specially beloved.**

This is the festival day,
the day you have made for our joy.
**We shall be glad and rejoice,
feasting with laughter and song.**

Pentecost – and the following six days

Spirit of God, renewing the face of the earth!
**Spirit of God, filling the hearts of your people!
Spirit of God, raising the dead to new life!**

Living God, we give you thanks and praise:
your Spirit breathes life into every creature,
your Spirit in Yeshua leaps into our lives:
**our eyes are opened as we recognize you at last,
we cry out with every fibre of our being,
our Father, our Mother, our Friend, our God.**

We breathe these words out of the Silence within us, into the Silence beyond us...

Spirit of God, renewing the face of the earth!
Spirit of God, filling the hearts of your people!
Spirit of God, raising the dead to new life!

Trinity Sunday – and the following six days

Great praise and everlasting glory be to God,
Father, Son, and Holy Spirit,
Creator, Redeemer, Sanctifier,
Lover, Beloved, and Mutual Friend,
Giver of life, Bearer of pain, Maker of love,
Alpha and Omega, the Beginning and the End.

Great praise and everlasting glory be to God,
at all times, in all places,
through the centuries, throughout the universe.
Holy, holy, holy, great God of power and love,
who was and who is and who is to come.

Saints' days

You have triumphed over the power of death,
and draw us to your presence with songs of joy.
We hear the echo of your angels praising you,
and the whole communion of your saints,
those who have walked in your narrow ways,
and heard the voice of your yearning,
whose food is to do your will,
and in whom you take great delight.
From the widest bounds of the universe
to the depths of my very being,
the whispers and cries of joy
vibrate to a shining glory.

...in the Spirit that stirs amongst us the kaleidoscope of Jesus.

Kontakion for the departed

Give rest O Christ to your servant with your saints,
where sorrow and pain are no more,
neither sighing, but life everlasting.
Creator and maker of humankind,
you only are immortal,
and we are mortal, formed of the earth,
and to the earth we shall return.
For so you did ordain when you created us, saying,
Dust thou art and unto dust thou shalt return.

**All we go down to the dust,
and, weeping o'er the grave, we make our song:
Alleluia, alleluia, alleluia.
Give rest O Christ to your servant with your saints,
where sorrow and pain are no more,
neither sighing, but life everlasting.**

We breathe these words out of the Silence within us, into the Silence beyond us…

ENGAGING

I   The two ways – a wisdom song

In solidarity with those who are called to tell the truth, as teachers of the young, as researchers, as witnesses, as prophets.

Woe to us when we walk in the way of wickedness,
when we bend our ear to the counsel of deceit,
and scoff at what is holy from the seat of pride.

Keep   us   true   to   your   way.

Pause

Blessings upon us when we delight in the truth of God,
and ponder God's law by day and by night,
when we stand up for truth in face of the lie,
when we mouth no slogans and betray no friends.

Keep us true to your way.

Pause

Then we shall grow like trees planted by streams of water,
that yield their fruit in due season,
whose leaves do not wither.

Keep us true to your way.

Pause

We struggle with evil in our hearts,
tossed to and fro like chaff in the wind,
a rootless people whose lives have no meaning,
unable to stand when judgment comes,
desolate, outside the house of our God.

Keep us true to your way.

Pause

…in the Spirit that stirs amongst us the kaleidoscope of Jesus.

May ways of wickedness perish among us:
forgive us, O God, and renew us,
lead us in paths of justice and truth,
obedient to your wisdom and will,
trusting in the hope of your promise.

Silence

Giver of life, **save us from the desert of faithlessness, and
nourish us with the living water of your word, that we may
bring forth fruit that will last.**

2   God's Anointed One

*In solidarity with the powerful; that they may serve the common good; and in solidarity
with one another that we may be purged and refined in the murky places of our lives.*

Why do the nations rage at one another?
O God, why do we plot and conspire?
The powerful of the earth set themselves high,
and the rest of the people collude with their pride.

Pause

We even whisper against those whom you call,
those whom you challenge to embody your will.
We despise them for their weaknesses,
and glibly forget our own.

Pause

We resist the wrath of your love,
the searing of judgment and truth.
Bring us in awe and trembling
to wake up to ourselves in your presence.

Come, re - fin - ing fire of love.

Pause

We breathe these words out of the Silence within us, into the Silence beyond us...

But who is this, your presence clear among us,
your human face on earth, true human being at the last?
You take our rage upon yourself,
mocked and despised, yet meeting all with love.

Come, refining fire of love.

Pause

You are the fire that shrivels up our hates,
and brings us to our knees in awe.
You are the light that pierces all our fury,
laying bare our greed and pride.
You are the truth that shines light in our darkness:
forgive us, for we know not what we do.

Come, refining fire of love.

Silence

Living God, **raising us from our death-dealing, giving us life
in abundance, work in us the power and wisdom of your
love and make it visible among us as your justice.**

3   The struggle between fear and trust

*In solidarity with those who are afraid of being attacked; and that they may find
courage.*

God of gentle strength and steadfast courage,
be present to us now,
in the midst of those who oppose us.

Pause

For our foes rise up against us,
surrounding us in the night,
adversaries and friends alike,
whispering that you cannot help us,
that you have faded from human sight,
lost in silence for ever.

...in the Spirit that stirs amongst us the kaleidoscope of Jesus.

Does the reach of your love fall___ short?

Pause

Are you a shield about us, defending us from harm?
Are you our glory, do you lift our heads high?
We cry to you as we sleep and when we wake,
listening for the voice of your presence to sustain us.

Does the reach of your love fall short?

Pause

We are afraid of the powers that prowl among us,
howling in the darkness of a moonless night.
We tremble at the thousands upon thousands
of weapons and armies swarming around us.
The stockpiles, the landmines, the sudden explosions,
all paralyze us with terror.

Pause

Is your power failing, O God?
What of our cry that you smite them to the ground,
breaking their teeth, grinding them to dust?

Does the reach of your love fall short?

Pause

But no, do not destroy: call out to us all:
Rebellious powers, lay down your arms,
return to the ways of your buried conscience,
to the path of wisdom and justice.
Cease your oppression and calm your fury,
and return to the mercies of God.

Your stead-fast love ne-ver fails._____

We breathe these words out of the Silence within us, into the Silence beyond us...

Pause

Liberator, setting free your burdened people,
in the deepest places of our being renewing our trust,
refining us, judging us, reconciling us,
may your blessing be upon us for ever.

Your steadfast love never fails.

Silence

Protector and deliverer of humankind, **hear our desperate
cries, set us free from violence, relieve the pressure of
persecution, melt the ice of our fears. Even from the place
of your silence, give us the words and the deeds to embody
your way.**

4   The peace of God

In solidarity with one another; and that our doubt may move gently into deeper trust.

Answer me when I call, O God,
for you are the God of justice.
You set me free when I was hard-pressed:
be gracious to me now, for you hear my prayer.

Pause

How long will I shun your glory and shame you?
How long will I love what is worthless and run after lies?

Our hearts are a - wry: can we be - lieve__
that all will come right   in the end?

Pause

...in the Spirit that stirs amongst us the kaleidoscope of Jesus.

You have shown me such wonderful kindness.
When I call out in prayer you hear me.

Pause

Let me tremble, admit defeat, and sin no more.
Let me look deep into my heart before I sleep, and be still.
I bring my gifts, just as I am,
and put my trust in you, my God.

**Our hearts are awry: can we believe
that all will come right in the end?**

Pause

Many are asking: "Who can make us content?
The light of your countenance has gone from us, O God."
Yet you have given my heart more gladness
than those whose corn and wine and oil increase.
I lie down in peace and sleep comes at once,
for in you alone, O God, do I dwell unafraid.

**Our hearts are awry: can we believe
that all will come right in the end?**

Silence

Faithful defender, **do not let our hearts be troubled, but fill us
with such confidence and joy that we may sleep in peace
and wake in your presence.**

5   A prayer for repentance

*In penitence for the times when we have been twisted by lies and deceit; in solidarity
with those who wield the weapons of words; and that we may all serve the truth and
the common good.*

At the turning of the day
I make ready for my prayer,
emptying my mind, opening my heart,
my whole self watching and waiting.

Pause

We breathe these words out of the Silence within us, into the Silence beyond us...

Out of the silence comes my cry,
the groaning of my spirit,
profound, beyond words:
O God my deliverer, listen, and answer.

Gent - ly turn_ my face to the sun.

Pause

You take no delight in wickedness:
evil may not sojourn with you.
The boastful may not stand before your eyes,
the proud wither at your glance.
You silence those who speak lies,
you withstand the thrust of the vengeful.

Pause

Only through the gift of your steadfast love
do I dare to enter your presence.
I have courage only to whisper,
my whole being trembles in awe.

Pause

So easy it is to fall in false ways:
lead me, O God, in your justice,
make my path straight before me.

Gently turn my face to the sun.

Pause

For there is no truth in our mouths,
our hearts are set on destruction,
our throats are an open sepulchre,
we flatter with our tongue.

Pause

Our speeches are honeyed with peace,
smooth words slide from our lips.
The wavelengths dance with lies,
siren songs deceptive in the dark.

Pause

Make us feel together the weight of our guilt,
let us fall by the burden of our deceits,
crumbling by reason of our trespass,
lost because of our rebellion.

Pause

Pluck us from the despair that follows the lie,
no longer weighed down with the burden of falsehood.
Strengthen our steps in obedience to truth,
turn our lamentation to dancing and joy.
Set us on fire with unquenchable love:
we shall honour your name, exulting with praise.

Gently turn my face to the sun.

Pause

Blessed be God,
showering blessings on the just and the unjust.
Blessed be God,
enduring with us the showers of black rain.
Blessed be God,
shuddering with pain when sirens wail.
Blessed be God,
our blasts but a feather in the wind of the Spirit.
Blessed be God,
our evil but a drop in the ocean of love.
Blessed be God,
redeeming our wastes and our sorrows.
Blessed be God.

Silence

God of all justice and goodness, **hating deception and evil,
lead us in the paths of truth and godliness, and keep us
from all lasting harm.**

We breathe these words out of the Silence within us, into the Silence beyond us...

6   A desperate cry in time of illness

In solidarity with those with HIV and AIDS; and with those enduring long drawn-out affliction, cancer, Alzheimer's, and the like.

Hideous afflictions of a turbulent age –
virus, cancer, thrombosis, ulcer –
warheads in the fluids of my being:

Pause

I am caught in a world that is twisted,
trapped in its web of corruption,
tempted to blame my ills on to 'them',
tempted to avoid the hatred within.

I cry out to the void:

How long, O God, how long?

Pause

Hard pressed by anxiety and discord,
by carriers of disease, by injectors of poison,
overwhelmed by malice and fear,
paralyzed, depressed, we cannot move,
spun in the vortex of death.

Pause

Distressed in the very depths of our being,
bones shaking, cells mutating,
we are thrown to the depths of despair.

I cry out to the void:
How long, O God, how long?

Pause

...in the Spirit that stirs amongst us the kaleidoscope of Jesus.

In your mercy and grace set us free.
Refine us in the fire of your love.
Our cry is of hope, yet struggling with doubt,
a stammer gasping for breath in the night.

Pause

Turn your face to me, save my life;
deliver me in the endurance of love,
ease the burden of guilt and of pain.
Let me know the grace of your presence,
now in this life and through the shades of the grave.

I cry out to the void:
How long, O God, how long?

Pause

I am weary with my suffering,
every night I flood my bed with tears.
I drench my couch with weeping,
my eyes so full of grief I can no longer see.
I grow weak through the weight of oppression,
my very life seeping into the ground.

I cry out to the void:
How long, O God, how long?

Pause

You that work evil and seek to destroy,
loosen your grip, away from my presence.
For God has heard the sound of my weeping,
forgives me with delight and lightens my gloom.

Pause

The destroyers will be ashamed and sore troubled:
trembling, they will be stripped of their power,
no longer able to harm.

Pause

We breathe these words out of the Silence within us, into the Silence beyond us...

And no, rebellious powers, I will not gloat or hate,
in the love of God I will hold on to you yet.
In the anger and hope of the wrath of our God,
come to the place of repentance and mercy.

Pause

And you, silent virus, invisible, malignant,
bound up with my bodily being,
are you an enemy I can befriend,
or at least contain in a place of your own –
your power to harm taken away,
brought with us to the glory of God?

Silence

God of merciful tenderness, **giver of life and swallower of death, gently embrace our weakness and pain, and bring us to health and to wholeness, that we may sing a new song of joy and delight. We pray this in the Spirit of Yeshua, redeeming the powers, giving hope to humankind, calling us to follow this perplexing path to glory.**

7   A society in fragments

In penitence that our hearts are often cruel and greedy; that they may be softened; and that together we may renew our communities and cherish the vulnerable.

O God, we are shaken by terror,
our hearts grow cold through fear.
The lions roar, their teeth are bared,
they pounce at our throats and tear us apart.

Pause

The powers that be stand over us,
whispering treason to workers for peace,
declaring redundant the awkward and angular,
destroying by rumour the worth of a name.

...in the Spirit that stirs amongst us the kaleidoscope of Jesus.

Judge of the world, come and save us.___

Pause

Old loyalties no longer bind us,
family, neighbourhood, union, factory.
The young prowl the streets and the precincts,
alienated, rootless, pain turning to violence.
And the old, the weak, and the poor all cringe,
their welfare, their lives, threatened and vulnerable.

Pause

Your will for us, dear God, is sure and steady,
that we do justly, love mercy,
and walk humbly on your path.
You would not have us return evil for evil,
plundering our enemies and requiting our friends.

Judge of the world, come and save us.

Pause

Who can stand in your presence
with righteousness and integrity of heart?
Our hearts and our minds conceive evil:
they are pregnant with mischief and bring forth lies.

Pause

We dig the pit of others' doom,
and fall into the hole we have made.
Our wickedness returns on our head,
we are crushed by the violence we have spawned.
Our lives are trampled to the ground,
our very being spent in the dust.

Judge of the world, come and save us.

Pause

We breathe these words out of the Silence within us, into the Silence beyond us...

We cannot but sense your love as your wrath,
judge of the world come with dread to save us.
Who can stand against the blast of your fury,
fiery shafts sprung from your bow?
Who can bear the anguish and pain in your eyes
as you scour and cleanse us with lasers?

Judge of the world, come and save us.

Pause

And yet we give you thanks and praise,
for you will not let us go into the void.
You bear the cost of our redeeming,
the Judge of all the world does right,
bringing us through tears to love for our neighbour,
leading us in pathways to justice and peace.

Silence

Judge and Saviour, **pierce the secrets of our hearts and bring
to light our hidden sins. Purify and strengthen us in faith,
and give us courage to strive with evil and bear witness to
your just and loving rule.**

8   Stewards of creation

*In solidarity with those who work patiently and carefully to repair damage to people,
to buildings, to works of art, to the planet.*

Creator God, source of all life,

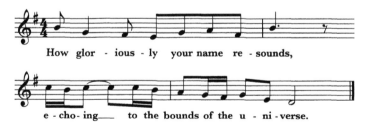

How glor - ious - ly your name re - sounds,

e - cho- ing___ to the bounds of the u - ni - verse.

...in the Spirit that stirs amongst us the kaleidoscope of Jesus.

Pause

The morning stars sing for joy,
and the youngest child cries your name.
The weak in the world shame the strong,
and silence the proud and rebellious.

Pause

When I look at creation, even the work of your fingers,
the moon and the stars majestic in their courses,
the eagle riding the air, the dolphin ploughing the sea,
the gazelle leaping the wind, the sheep grazing the fells,
who are we human beings that you keep us in mind,
children, women, and men that you care so much for us?

Pause

Yet still you bring us to life,
creating us after your image,
stewards of the planet you give as our home.
How awesome a task you entrust to our hands.
How fragile and beautiful is the good earth.

Pause

Creator God, source of all life,

**how gloriously your name resounds,
echoing to the bounds of the universe.**

Silence

Creator God, **amid the immensities of the universe you seek
us out and call us to be partners in your work of creating.
May we not fail you.**

❖

We breathe these words out of the Silence within us, into the Silence beyond us...

9a   A prayer for conciliators

*In solidarity with mediators in conflicts, with lawmakers and lawkeepers, with bomb
disposers, with clearers of landmines.*

Nuclear within and without – we are breaking apart:
cells disintegrating – virus and cancer;
the splitting of atoms – a new black death;
terrorists' dens burrowing the suburbs.

Pause

The tired game goes on – the reeds of the world trembling:
pre-emptive strikes – the tactics of bullies;
inaccurate bombings – one cell is blasted.
Hydra-like the desperate multiply:
the smallest of bombs lost in suitcase or backpack:
revenge in mind – no matter who suffers.

Pause

Tares and wheat – can you tell them apart?
Neighbour subversive – our own heart corrupt.

O___ God___ stead - y our nerve___
___ that we may see clear - ly:___
streng-then our will___ in work - ing for peace.

Pause

International law – not my country whatever,
muscle frightened of wasting sickness.
Rational policing – not the sheriff's bully.

...in the Spirit that stirs amongst us the kaleidoscope of Jesus.

Pause

Restraining force kept to a minimum –
not the unleashing of eagle or bear.
Sanctions hurting us – no wonder we're reluctant.
Complexity recognized – simple solutions are final.

O God, steady our nerve that we may see clearly:
strengthen our will in working for peace.

Pause

Can the powerful admit they have limits?
Give up their arrogance?
Know their own weakness?
Understand those they never meet?

O God, steady our nerve that we may see clearly:
strengthen our will in working for peace.

Pause

Work on in hidden ways, brave conciliators in conflicts:
patriots of earth – allied to no state – not even their own –
loyal to a future not one of us sees;
immaculately suited aliens in the strangest of lands.
Those locked in conflict – do they not see?
They all want their grandchildren to breathe the good air.

O God, steady our nerve that we may see clearly:
strengthen our will in working for peace.

Pause

Courage, bomb disposers who delve hearts and minds:
ease the finger from the trigger and button;
defuse the boiling fury, open the eyes blinded with rage.
You will come away wounded, paying a price for us all.
But judgment and mercy: these alone are left now.
We must love one another – or die.

Silence

We breathe these words out of the Silence within us, into the Silence beyond us…

O God of wisdom, **in solidarity with the b urden bearers,
patiently negotiating among the peoples of the world,
steady our nerves and strengthen our wills, that we
may pursue the way of reconciliation among our families
and communities, in the spirit of Yeshua, who pioneered
the way.**

9b   Despair and hope in a dark time

In solidarity with those whose cities are being torn apart.

What are they now but a name,
the empires of old that have vanished?
What are they now but ruins,
cities that gleamed with pride?
Where will our idolatry end?
How many more succumb to the engines of war?

Pause

Warsaw and Dresden, Geurnica and Hamburg,
Hiroshima and Beirut, Hanoi and Baghdad –
what fury to come from our darkened hearts?
We hanker after the abyss,
as we and our cities go into the night.

How long, O God, how long?

Pause

You that wept for Jerusalem,
that knew not what made for its peace,
see now your prophecy extend
as we enter the eclipse of our God.

How long, O God, how long?

...in the Spirit that stirs amongst us the kaleidoscope of Jesus.

Pause

We stare dumbly at the death camps of hell:
lo! dark evil is crowned
in the midst of the tortured and dying.

Pause

The needy are forgotten,
the oppressed know not the stronghold of God.
The hope of the weary grows dim;
the heavens are empty;
no ear hears the groan of those stricken down
beneath a pitiless sky.

How long, O God, how long?

Pause

O God, do you not hear the hard pressed cries?
Have you forgotten? When will you listen?
How long must we endure, how long?

How long, O God, how long?

Pause

I can no longer praise you for shattering my enemies,
proud of the justice of my cause.
Nor can I claim you for our side,
and urge you to slay them and blot out their name.
We are snared in the work of our own hands:
our own feet are caught in the net that we hid.

Pause

But I will not give in to despair,
for you came to your people of old,
in desert and exile, betrayal and death,
giving joy and great hope,
the light of your presence
in the least expected of places.

Pause

We breathe these words out of the Silence within us, into the Silence beyond us...

Even from the depths of our doom
comes the cry of the victory of God.
Alleluia! Alleluia!

Silence

God of hope, **be with us through the depths of our despair,
and work in us the costly ways of peace, that in justice and
with gentleness your will may be done on earth.**

10a   The pleading of the poor

*In solidarity with the destitute, the inarticulate, the landless, the stateless; and that we
may help them find their own voice.*

Why do you stand far off, O God, so mute,
hiding yourself from your people in time of our need?
We are pursued by the arrogant rich:
let them be trapped in the schemes of their devising.

Re-move___ the___   sting of the power-ful.___

Pause

They boast of the desires of their hearts:
greedy for gain, they curse and denounce you.
In the pride of their countenance they no longer seek you,
cold-eyed in denial that there is such a God.

Remove the sting of the powerful.

Pause

And yet their ways prosper:
loftily making their judgments, they scoff at us.
They think in their hearts they will not be disturbed,
through all generations never meeting adversity.

Remove the sting of the powerful.

…in the Spirit that stirs amongst us the kaleidoscope of Jesus.

Pause

But their mouths are full of deceit and cursing,
under their tongues are oppression and mischief.
They sit in ambush by the forest road:
in city streets they stalk and murder.
Their eyes watch steadily for the helpless,
they lurk like lions to seize the poor.

Remove the sting of the powerful.

Pause

The afflicted are crushed, we sink down and fall
under the weight of their scheming devices.
Denied a name, defrauded of land,
we are reduced to a number, no voice in our destiny.

Remove the sting of the powerful.

Pause

The powerful think in their hearts, God has forgotten.
God has turned away and will never see.
O God, cry aloud till they hear you:
disturb their conscience, call them to account.

Remove the sting of the powerful.

Pause

Do not forget the afflicted,
do justice to the oppressed and the orphans.
May the powerful strike terror no more.
Break the strength of their arms,
scour out all wickedness from them.

Remove the sting of the powerful.

Pause

Hear the desire of the poor,
strengthen our hearts.
May the rich denounce their pride and their greed,
the wickedness that brims with excess.

We breathe these words out of the Silence within us, into the Silence beyond us...

Remove the sting of the powerful.

Pause

May they see themselves without their fine clothes,
naked and defenceless before you.
We know that we are their judges, O God,
to purge them with truth and refine them with love,
and together be received in your mercy.

Silence

O God, **listening and suffering, your silence making us
think you are deaf to our cries, test our faith and patience
no more than we can bear, and be revealed as the Judge of
the earth who does right.**

10b   The repentance of the rich

*In solidarity with the rich; that we may all be generous and use our power wisely; and
that we may work together for a more equal and therefore more healthy society.*

In arrogance we rich have pursued the poor:
let us be trapped in the schemes we have devised.
We have boasted of the desires of our hearts:
greedy for gain we have renounced you, O God.

Melt the ice of our hearts.

Re - lease the spring of our trap.

Pause

In the pride of our countenance we have not sought you,
cold-eyed in denial we have turned away wilful.   >

Our ways prospered, our profits increased:
loftily making our judgment, we scoffed at our foes.
We thought in our hearts, We shall not be disturbed,
through all generations not meeting adversity.

Melt the ice of our hearts.
Release the spring of our trap.

Pause

Our mouths were full of cursing and scoffing.
Under our tongues were oppression and mischief.
We have sat in ambush in country lanes,
in city streets we have stalked and murdered.
Our eyes have watched stealthily for the helpless,
we lurked like lions to seize the poor.

Melt the ice of our hearts.
Release the spring of our trap.

Pause

We crushed the afflicted, they sank down and fell
under the weight of our frozen hearts.
We denied them a name, defrauded them of land.
We reduced them to a number, no voice in their destiny.
We thought in our hearts, God has forgotten.
God has turned away and will never see.

Melt the ice of our hearts.
Release the spring of our trap.

Pause

At last their cry reaches our ears,
we hear the whisper of a conscience revived.
Call us, O God, to account.
Do not forget the ones we afflicted.
Do justice through us to the orphans.

Melt the ice of our hearts.
Release the spring of our trap.

Pause

We breathe these words out of the Silence within us, into the Silence beyond us...

May we strike terror no more.
Break the strength of our arms,
return us to the ways of justice and law.
Hear the desire of the poor: strengthen our hearts.

Melt the ice of our hearts.
Release the spring of our trap.

Pause

We renounce our pride and our greed,
the wickedness that brims with excess.
Defenceless and naked before you,
may we be judged by those we oppressed.
Refine us with fire, purge us with truth,
bring us at last to your mercy.

Silence

God of light and truth, **bring us face to face with our weak-**
ness and fear, that we may be freed to greet the outcast
with love, no longer trampling them under our feet or
freezing them out of our hearts.

11   The prayer of a trembling heart

That zealots may sing songs and have a sense of humour; and that those afraid of
them may take courage and tell their stories.

I fear the fanatics who toy with the trigger,
oiling their rifles with consummate care,
ready to pounce in the dimly lit alley,
raping the makers of peace and of justice.

Pause

But to flee like a bird to the mountains –
no safety in the caves of the earth in our day:
the very foundations are splitting apart,
there is nowhere to go but the place where we are.

…in the Spirit that stirs amongst us the kaleidoscope of Jesus.

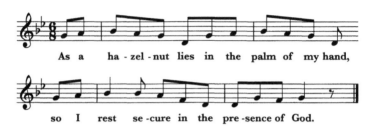

As a ha - zel - nut lies in the palm of my hand,

so I rest se -cure in the pre -sence of God.

Pause

I turn again in your presence, dear God,
seeking to renew my trust in your care.
For we tremble and shake, gripped by that fear:
the world we have known is crumbling around us,
invisible rain falls on the mountains,
even the caves of the earth fill with rubble.

**As a hazelnut lies in the palm of my hand,
so I rest secure in the presence of God.**

Pause

Within the future that is coming to meet us,
you are present with us, O God.
Though you seem so remote in our days,
turning your back, dead to the world,
yet we believe that you hold us in mind,
purging us of violence and hardness of heart,
raining coals of fire on our wickedness,
burning up our fury in your scorching wind.

**As a hazelnut lies in the palm of my hand,
so I rest secure in the presence of God.**

Pause

Give us new integrity of heart,
renew in us the deeds that you love,
of justice and mercy, compassion and courage.
Then face to face we shall see you,
knowing and known, loving and loved.

Silence

We breathe these words out of the Silence within us, into the Silence beyond us...

O God of roaring fire and kindly flame, **seeking to harness the wild winds of our winter, bu rning the decayed and warming new seeds, steady our hearts and deepen our trust, lead us through to the birth of a new age.**

12   Words and the Word

In penitence for the occasions when we have lied; that we may recognize that the truth is not always simple; and in solidarity with those compelled to learn a language not their own.

Who speaks any longer the truth of the heart,
words that are clear of corruption and lies?
Neighbour speaks falsely to neighbour,
flattery on our lips, deceit in our hearts.
The proud, silver tongued with smooth words,
control the silenced and the awkward of speech.

O   God,   ful - fil your pro - mise:___
let your word   take flesh a - mong us.___

Pause

God of truth, cut out the forked tongue,
silence the lying lips.
Save us from the corruption of language,
from manipulators of words, greedy for power.
For we drown in menacing lies:
the spring of original falsehood
now swells to torrent and spate.

O God, fulfil your promise:
let your word take flesh among us.

...in the Spirit that stirs amongst us the kaleidoscope of Jesus.

Pause

May the exiles and migrants, denied their own language,
find living words to shape their own truth,
words that give meaning to lives without purpose,
that heal and inspire and reach deep in the heart.

**O God, fulfil your promise:
let your word take flesh among us.**

Pause

Speak to us out of your silence, O God,
our minds purged of gossip and chatter.
For you are the fountain of all that is true,
a wellspring deep that never fails.

Pause

It is there that we drink long of your Word,
as sure as a friend who is tested and tried.
For your promise is true and worthy of trust,
like silver refined in the furnace.

**O God, fulfil your promise:
let your word take flesh among us.**

Silence

Spirit of truth, **lead us into all truth, and give us the words
to speak it, words that take shape deep in the heart and do
not distort or betray. We pray this in the name of the One
who lived the truth, and is the way and the life.**

13   The pain of the heart

In solidarity with those enduring the distress of emptiness and dread.

How long, O God, how long?
You hide your face from me,
you utterly forget me.

Pause

We breathe these words out of the Silence within us, into the Silence beyond us...

How long, O God, how long?
My being is in anguish and torment,
my heart is grieved day and night.

Pause

How long, O God, how long?
Icy death, dread and despair,
insidious foes, they strengthen their grip.

Pause

Dull are my eyes and lifeless,
as I stare at the desolate places.
Give light to my eyes,
stir up my will and my passion,
my trust in your life-giving Spirit.

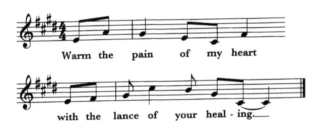

Warm the pain of my heart
with the lance of your heal - ing.

Pause

Fill my heart with compassion and strength,
that I may rejoice in your generous love,
able to strive with my foes,
no longer dead in the depths of my being.

**Warm the pain of my heart
with the lance of your healing.**

Pause

Yes, at the moment of emptiness and dread
you surprise me with joy and deliverance.
I will sing and shout with delight,
for you have overwhelmed me with grace.

...in the Spirit that stirs amongst us the kaleidoscope of Jesus.

**Warm the pain of my heart
with the lance of your healing.**

Silence

Living loving God, **taking to yourself the pains of the world,
cherish our wounded hearts in a tender embrace, and
cradle our scars, that we may witness to your glory. In
solidarity with the pain-bearer Christ we pray.**

14   The folly of the rich

*That when we are greedy and corrupt we may turn to those we have wronged and seek
forgiveness, and pay the price of justice.*

Like fools we say in our hearts, "There is no God."
We have become so vile in our deeds
that no one among us does good.

Pause

God searches long among the children of earth
to see if any act wisely,
any who seek to follow the Way.
But we have turned aside from our God,
we are caught in the web of corruption.

Pause

There is none that does good, no, not one.
The mists of evil cloud our understanding:
we devour one another like bread,
delighting in the slaughter of peoples:
no longer do we pray with penitence.
Far from the ways of justice and friendship,
we frustrate the hopes of the poor.

Pause

Our hearts will be struck with compunction and grief
when we see God embracing the destitute,
bringing their faces alive with gladness and joy.

We breathe these words out of the Silence within us, into the Silence beyond us...

Pause

Humble us, O God, our wealth turned to ash;
empty us, that we may be filled with your grace.
Turn our feet into the ways of your justice,
that we may ask forgiveness of those we have wronged.

Fill   our   hearts   with com - pas - sion,—
our—   wills—   with—   jus - tice.———

Pause

Then our ancestors of faith will rejoice,
and the whole earth will sing and be glad,
all the peoples content on that day.
Those hard of heart, shrivelled within,
will be warmed to life by those they have wronged,
even the wealthy led at last to the dance.

**Fill our hearts with compassion,
our wills with justice.**

Silence

God of the destitute, **prune our lives of all that we cling to.
God of true wealth, draw us through the narrow gate of
loss. God of Yeshua, living in those we neglect, through
their generosity turn us to repentance, that we may be
forgiven.**

…in the Spirit that stirs amongst us the kaleidoscope of Jesus.

15   Friends of God

That friendship may flourish.

Dear God, who are the honoured guests in your tent?
Who may dwell in your presence upon your holy mountain?
Who may commune with those who are your heart's desire,
lovingly embraced in the union of friends?

Pause

Those who lead uncorrupt lives,
and do the thing that is right,
who speak the truth from their hearts,
and have not slandered with their tongue.

Pause

Those who have not betrayed their friends,
or rained down abuse on their neighbours,
in whose eyes the shifty have no honour,
but hold in high esteem those who fear God.

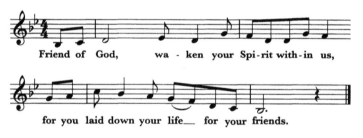

Friend of God,   wa - ken your Spi-rit with-in us,

for you laid down your life__ for your friends.

Pause

Those who give their word to their neighbour,
and do not go back on their promise,
who have not grown wealthy at the expense of the poor,
or grown sleek with flattery and bribes.

Pause

Those who recognize the outcast as the one whom they need,
who forgive to seventy times seven,

We breathe these words out of the Silence within us, into the Silence beyond us...

who depend on the mercy of God,
and live the highest law that is love.

**Friend of God, waken your Spirit within us,
for you laid down your life for your friends.**

Pause

Those who are steadfast and kind,
who are resilient and patient and humble,
who know the cost of a morsel of justice,
a glimpse of compassion in times that are savage.

Pause

Their roots are deep in the being of God,
their arms are spread wide in welcome embrace.
They are faithful, joyful, and blessed,
God's sisters and brothers and friends.

**Friend of God, waken your Spirit within us,
for you laid down your life for your friends.**

Silence

Loving God, **whose name is friendship, so guide us in
your Spirit that we may embrace the way that finds joy
in giving all for others, so that even our enemies may
become our friends, after the pattern of Jesus of Nazareth
who loved his own even to the end.**

16   Prayer in communion with those who have died

*In solidarity with those who have died before us; and that we may deepen our trust in
a faithful Creator.*

O God our refuge and strength,
preserve us from lasting harm.
Again and again we affirm,
in times both of doubt and of trust,
You are our faithful Creator,
in you alone is our bliss.

…in the Spirit that stirs amongst us the kaleidoscope of Jesus.

Pause

We thank you for all your holy people,
all whose lives give you glory.
We praise you for your martyrs and saints,
in whom you take great delight.

Greet us all____ in the joy of your pre-sence.__

Pause

As for those held in high esteem,
those idols adored by the crowd,
those gods they fête and run after,
we shall not take their name on our lips.
They are bloated with pride and success,
punctured by thorns in the late autumn wind.

Pause

Your name alone do we praise,
our resting place now and for ever.
You feed us with the bread of life,
you nourish us with the cup of salvation.

Greet us all in the joy of your presence.

Pause

We have been so fortunate in our days,
and in the places where we have lived.
To no one else belongs the praise,
but to you, the great giver of gifts.

Greet us all in the joy of your presence.

Pause

We give you thanks for the wisdom of your counsel,
even at night you have instructed our hearts.
In the silence of the darkest of hours
we open our ears to the whisper of your voice.

We breathe these words out of the Silence within us, into the Silence beyond us...

Pause

We have set your face always before us,
in every cell of our being you are there.
As we tremble on the narrowest of paths,
the steadying of your hand gives us courage.
Fleet of foot, with our eyes on the goal,
headlong in the chasm we shall not fall.

Pause

Therefore our hearts rejoice and our spirits are glad,
our whole being will rest secure.
For you will not give us over to the power of death,
nor let your faithful ones see the pit.

Greet us all in the joy of your presence.

Pause

You will show us the path of life:
in your countenance is the fulness of joy.
From the spring of your heart flow rivers of delight,
a fountain of water that shall never run dry.

Greet us all in the joy of your presence.

Silence

O God of the living, **keep our eyes fixed on the goal of our
journey, that we may be fleet of heart, and in all our
dyings leap to the embrace of the One who lures us with
love, the pioneer of our salvation, Jesus, our elder brother
and our faithful friend.**

17   An angry cry for justice

In solidarity with those struggling to be free from oppression; and that the power of our anger may be channelled in striving for justice.

Do you hear my cause, O God? I believe it to be just.
Do my lips speak the truth, or do they lie?
Let judgment come forth from your presence:
let your eyes discern what is right.

Pause

You test me by fire, searching my heart in the dark of night,
probing whatever wickedness there is in me.
I do not think I deceive,
but have I been true to your word?
Have my steps held firm to your paths?
I cannot claim my feet have not stumbled.

Pause

Take the sword, O God, from our hands,
wield it with truth and with healing.

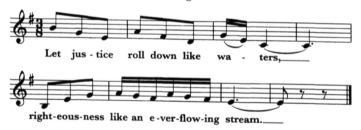

Let jus-tice roll down like wa-ters,
right-eous-ness like an e-ver-flow-ing stream.

Pause

I call upon you, O God, for you will answer:
incline your ear to me, and hear my words.
Show me the wonders of your steadfast love,
protector of those who come to you for refuge.

Pause

By your firm and gentle hand you keep them
from the deadly grip of those who surround them.

We breathe these words out of the Silence within us, into the Silence beyond us...

Keep me as the apple of an eye,
hide me under the shadow of your wings
from the onslaught of those who oppose me,
from those who threaten to put me in chains.

Pause

They have closed their hearts to pity:
their mouths speak pride and arrogance.
They track me down and surround me on every side,
watching how to bring me to the ground.
They are like lions greedy for their prey,
like young lions lurking in ambush.

Pause

By the power of your law restrain them,
by the power of your love soften their hearts.
And help me examine my own thoughts and deeds,
to take back the hatred I project on to others.

Pause

Take the sword, O God, from our hands,
wield it with truth and with healing.

**Let justice roll down like waters,
righteousness like an everflowing stream.**

Pause

Though I trust I am safe in your presence,
yet I am afraid, there is terror in my heart.
My feelings run high, my anger brims over,
I raise my own sword to wreak havoc on my foes.

Pause

"Arise, stand in their way and cast them down:
deliver me from the wicked by your sword.
Slay them with your iron fist,
slay them that they perish from the earth,
destroy them from among the living."

Pause

...in the Spirit that stirs amongst us the kaleidoscope of Jesus.

"May they choke on the grapes of your wrath,
let their bellies be filled with maggots.
May their children never come of age,
their heritage dying with them.
As for me, I shall see your face because my cause is just:
when I awake and see you as you are, I shall be satisfied."

Pause

Take the sword, O God, from our hands,
wield it with truth and with healing.

**Let justice roll down like waters,
righteousness like an everflowing stream.**

Pause

O God, like the psalmist of old I am angry
at the ways of the brutal on earth.
Afraid of their cruelty and greed,
I tremble on the point of their sword.

Pause

Yet the hammer of my words and my cries
is held in my hands, poised in the air.
For I know the evil in my own heart,
the lying, the pride, and the arrogance.

Pause

I cannot cut myself off even from those I distance:
we belong or we perish together.
Purge me of self-righteousness and hatred,
of smugness and satisfied smile.
Help me to love my enemies with truth,
for we are all children of your love.

Pause

Even as I pray for your justice,
for the vindication of your promise,
that oppressors may triumph no more,
that their victims may run free in the wind,
so I pray for my deliverance too.

We breathe these words out of the Silence within us, into the Silence beyond us...

Save us through judgment and mercy,
dependent as we are on your faithfulness.

Pause

Take the sword, O God, from our hands,
wield it with truth and with healing.

**Let justice roll down like waters,
righteousness like an everflowing stream.**

Silence

O God, compassionate and just, **wielder of the one sword that
pierces with truth and healing, penetrate the murk and
fury of our hearts, that our anger may be shaped by the
power of your Spirit, that we may create with you that
commonwealth of justice and peace that is yours alone.**

18   Rescue

*In solidarity with those who are trapped; that we may be rescued and forgive our
enemies; and for a new vision of God.*

Part i

I love you, O God: my strength,
my crag, my fortress, and my deliverer,
the rock to which I cling for refuge,
my shield, my saviour, and my stronghold.
I called to you with loud lamentation,
and you released the trap which held me fast.

...in the Spirit that stirs amongst us the kaleidoscope of Jesus.

Pause

The waves of death swept over my head,
the floods of chaos surged around me.
The cord of the grave tightened about my neck,
the snares of death sprang shut in my path.
In my anguish I called to you, O God:
I cried in desperation for your help.

Pause

Your ear was closer to me than I thought:
you heard me from the depths of my heart.
Then it seemed that the earth was quaking:
the foundations of the hills were shaken:
they trembled because of the power of your anger.

Pause

Down you came like a dragon,
swooping on the wings of the wind.
Smoke went forth from your nostrils,
and a consuming fire from your mouth.
You parted the heavens and came down,
riding upon the cherubim,
thick darkness under your feet.

Pause

Your voice roared through the heavens,
sharp arrows of lightning,
roll upon roll of thunder,
laying bare the foundations of the world.

Pause

Like an eagle you swooped down and took me,
lifting me from the jaws of the sea.
You delivered me from all that imprisoned me,
from those I thought stronger than I.

Pause

They fell upon me in the day of calamity,
yet you rescued me and led me to safety.
You brought me into a broad place,
you gave me freedom because you delight in me.

**Praise to the God of compassion and love,
the power that rescues and saves.**

Pause

I deserve no reward for anything I have done,
no recompense for the cleanness of my hands.
Have I kept to your ways, O God,
and not turned aside to do evil?

Pause

Was my eye always on your command,
did I take your wisdom to my heart?
I dare claim no innocence in your presence,
corrupt have been the deeds of my hands.

Pause

Yet still you delight in me – I am astonished –
loving and pursuing the one you are creating,
yearning for me to live in your image.
You are faithful even when I betray you,
when I feel the wrath of your love.
You carefully smooth out my crookedness,
forgiving my sin and wrongdoing.

**Praise to the God of compassion and love,
the power that rescues and saves.**

Pause

Such are the faces of your love,
each reflected in the pool of my being.
For you will save a humble people,
and bring down the high looks of the proud.

Pause

…in the Spirit that stirs amongst us the kaleidoscope of Jesus.

You light a lamp for my path,
you make my darkness to be bright.
With your help I can meet all that comes,
neutering the power of evil.

**Praise to the God of compassion and love,
the power that rescues and saves.**

Part ii

O God, your way is perfect,
your word has been tried in the fire.
You are a shield to all who trust in you.
You are my rock and I hold to you.

Pause

You gird me with strength
and make my way safe before me.
You make my feet like those of the deer,
you set me surefooted on the mountain path.

Pause

You teach my hands to fight,
and my arm to aim true with an arrow.
You have given me the shield of salvation;
your right hand guides and supports me.

Pause

Your swift response has made me great:
you lengthen my stride beneath me,
and my feet do not slip.

Pause

I pursue my enemies and overtake them,
striving till they cease their rebellion.
I fight them till they surrender their arms,
stumbling and falling before me.

Pause

We breathe these words out of the Silence within us, into the Silence beyond us…

Wild in their panic they stagger,
and cry out for mercy and help.
Tempted as I am to be cruel,
to beat them fine as dust in the wind,
to cast them out like the mire of the streets,
yet in your mercy I spare them.

Pause

In my struggle with them you deliver me,
and people I have not known become your servants.
Their strength of resistance withers away,
they come trembling from the last of their strongholds.

Praise___ to the God___ of com-pas-sion and love,
the___ power that res-cues and___ saves.___

Pause

I cannot ignore the evil in my ways,
however loyal I have been to your covenant.
I cannot deny the good in my enemies,
however hidden and obscured from my sight.

Pause

Though I must strive to put an end to their power,
humbly believing that their evil is monstrous –
for no longer do they see their victims as human,
they see only the power of missile and jet –
yet I resist evil means to disarm them,
refusing to treat them as numbers.

Pause

...in the Spirit that stirs amongst us the kaleidoscope of Jesus.

O God, renew in us your covenant of peace,
a promise that you gave to all peoples:
desperate is the need of our day.

Pause

God lives! God reigns!
Blessed be the rock of my salvation!
Those who set themselves against you have been subdued,
you have set me free from their grip,
delivering me from days of violence and bloodshed.
For this I give you thanks among the people,
and sing praises to your name.

Pause

Great love do you show to those whom you care for,
great triumph in fulfilling your purpose of glory,
keeping faith with David your servant,
with his descendants in flesh and in faith.

**Praise to the God of compassion and love,
the power that rescues and saves.**

Silence

God of freedom, **lead us through the taut place of our
despair, that we may emerge into a land broad and free, in
the Spirit of Jesus, who pioneered the way for us to follow.**

19   The love that moves the stars

That we may trust and embody the rhythms of reliable love.

The web of the world trembles,
the whisper of a great wind breathing.
The caressing of strings makes music,
its sighs reach the ends of the world.

Praise   to   the love that moves the stars,

We breathe these words out of the Silence within us, into the Silence beyond us...

and stirs in the depths   of___   our___   hearts.

Pause

The stars in the heavens chant the glory of God,
pulsing their praise across aeons of space.
From the soft radiance of a summer dawn
to the stormy sunset of a winter's evening,
from the darkest and wildest of mountain nights
to the stillness of moonlit seas,
the voice of praise is never silent,
yet all without speech or language
or sound of any voice.

**Praise to the love that moves the stars,
and stirs in the depths of our hearts.**

Pause

So too with the mighty sun,
come forth as a bridegroom from his tent,
rejoicing at his wedding day,
exulting in youthful splendour and beauty.
He climbs the sky from the eastern horizon,
he declines to the west at the end of the day,
and nothing can escape the fire of his presence.

**Praise to the love that moves the stars,
and stirs in the depths of our hearts.**

Pause

Galaxies beyond take up the cry,
suns ever more brilliant and huge:

Arcturus twenty times the size of Earth's sun,
Sigma in Dorado hundreds of thousands,
Aldebaran millions of miles in diameter,
Alpha in Lyre three hundred thousand light years away:
all, all proclaim the glory of God.

...in the Spirit that stirs amongst us the kaleidoscope of Jesus.

Praise to the love that moves the stars,
and stirs in the depths of our hearts.

Pause

The law of God is perfect,
refreshing the soul;
the words of God are sure,
and give wisdom to the simple;
the justice of God is righteous,
and rejoices the heart;
the commandment of God is pure,
and gives light to the eyes;
the fear of God is clean,
and endures for ever;
the judgments of God are true,
and just in every way.

Pause

So they dance as the stars of the universe,
perfect as the parabolas of comets,
like satellites and planets in their orbits,
reliable and constant in their courses.
Just in every way, enduring for ever.

Pause

The wisdom of God – more to be desired than gold,
sweeter than syrup and honey from the comb.
And by her is your servant taught,
in the very keeping of her there is great reward.
Rejoicing the heart, giving light to the eyes.

Pause

Who can tell how often I offend?
Cleanse me from my secret faults.
Keep your servant from pride and conceit,
lest they get the dominion over me.
So may I stand in your presence,
innocent of great offence.

We breathe these words out of the Silence within us, into the Silence beyond us...

Let the meditations of my heart
be always acceptable in your sight,
O God, my strength and my redeemer.
Refreshing the soul, giving wisdom to the simple.

Silence

Creator God, **yearning and striving to bring harmony out of chaos, so fill with your wisdom the inscape of our being, and so move with the wind of your presence among the landscapes of our world, that the earth may reflect the wonder of the universe, in the glory of the transfigured Jesus, at one with you in the cost of creating.**

20   A prayer for those who govern

In solidarity with those who wield much power; that they may be wise.

God of Abraham and Sarah, God of our ancestors,
creating among us your realm and your glory,
bless those who rule on the people's behalf,
give them strength in time of our troubles.

Pause

Send them the help of your light and your wisdom,
give them support through the prayers of our hearts.
Remember their promise to serve all the people,
take from them their lust for power and for wealth.

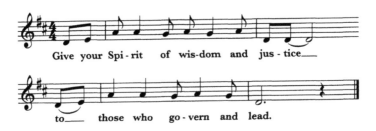

Give your Spi-rit of wis-dom and jus-tice___
to___ those who go-vern and lead.

Pause

...in the Spirit that stirs amongst us the kaleidoscope of Jesus.

Remember our promise to serve others' good,
remember the lives that are broken because of love's cost.
Give to your people the desire of their hearts,
fulfilling within them all that they cherish.
We shout for joy for your blessings towards us,
we lift our hearts high in the name of our God.
For you saved us with the power of unbroken love,
and indeed you fulfil what we deeply desire.

**Give your Spirit of wisdom and justice
to those who govern and lead.**

Pause

May the rulers of the people acknowledge your name,
serve the common good in the light of your justice.
Some put their trust in weapons of war,
but we shall trust in the power of your name.
They will decay, rust, and collapse,
but those strong in God will endure through the days.

**Give your Spirit of wisdom and justice
to those who govern and lead.**

Pause

May those who govern us trust you, O God.
Give them wisdom to lead through laws that are just.
For you will answer our prayer in the day of our cry,
fulfilling your nature and your own lasting name.

Silence

Wise and compassionate One, **guide those who bear office in
public life, that they may use their power for the common
good, in village, town and city, in this and every land, that
your commonwealth of peace and justice may indeed
come on earth.**

We breathe these words out of the Silence within us, into the Silence beyond us...

21   Royal priesthood

In solidarity with those who exercise leadership; and that they and we may find in service our true glory.

It is your royal road, O God,
it is your sovereign way –
to lead in the spirit of service,
to be stewards in your household,
to be guardians one for another,
to guide others in your paths.

To God   be the glo-ry: al-le - lu - ia!_____

Pause

As monarchs of old rejoiced in your strength,
so may we exult in your help.
As a sovereign today may trust in your faithfulness,
so do we rely on your steadfastness.

Pause

You have given us our heart's desire,
even the gift of your justice and wisdom.
You came to meet us with goodly blessings,
and placed crowns of gold on our heads.
We asked you for life and you offer your gift,
long days of contentment in your presence.

To God be the glory: alleluia!

Pause

You have destined even us for glory,
clothing us with splendour and honour.
You have promised us everlasting felicity,
and made us glad with the joy of your presence.

To God be the glory: alleluia!

...in the Spirit that stirs amongst us the kaleidoscope of Jesus.

Pause

By your light we shall penetrate the dark,
striving till they yield with our enemies.
All that is evil will wither at your coming,
as the chaff is consumed in the fire.
Those who stir malice will be overwhelmed,
their plots of mischief will come to nothing.

Pause

No longer will their infection spread through the years,
to the third and fourth generations.
You will put all their scheming to flight,
stunning them with a glance from your eye.

To God be the glory: alleluia!

Pause

Be exalted, O God, in your strength,
the power of your love and your truth,
your wisdom and your justice for ever:
we shall sing for joy and praise your name.

To God be the glory: alleluia!

Silence

Sovereign of the universe, **who has destined even us for glory,
with crowns upon our heads, enable us in your spirit to
serve one another with justice, that none may be the
victim of exploitation and violence. We pray this in the
name of the One who was crowned with thorns.**

22   Why? Why? Why?

Part i

*In solidarity with those who have been abandoned, forgotten, hounded, deserted,
quarantined.*

My God, my God, why have you forsaken me?
Why are you so far from helping me?

We breathe these words out of the Silence within us, into the Silence beyond us...

O my God, I howl in the daytime but you do not hear me.
I groan in the watches of the night, but I find no rest.

Why,   si-lent God,   why?

Pause

Yet still you are the holy God whom Israel long has worshipped.
Our ancestors hoped in you, and you rescued them.
They trusted in you, and you delivered them.
They called upon you: you were faithful to your covenant.
They put their trust in you and did not lose hope.

Pause

But as for me, I crawl the earth like a worm,
despised by others, an outcast of the people.
All those who see me laugh me to scorn:
they make mouths at me, shaking their heads and saying,
"He threw himself on God for deliverance:
let God rescue him then, if God so delights in him."

Why, silent God, why?

Pause

You were my midwife, O God, drawing me out of the womb.
I was weak and unknowing, yet you were my hope –
even as I lay close to the breast,
cast upon you from the days of my birth.
From the womb of my mother to the dread of these days,
you have been my God, never letting me go.

Pause

Do not desert me, for trouble is hard at hand,
and there is no one to help me.
Wild beasts close in on me,
narrow-eyed, greedy, and sleek.
They open their mouths and snarl at me,
like ravening and roaring lions.

...in the Spirit that stirs amongst us the kaleidoscope of Jesus.

Why, silent God, why?

Pause

My strength drains away like water,
my bones are out of joint.
My heart also in the midst of my body
is even like melting wax.
My mouth is dried up like a potsherd,
my tongue cleaves to my gums.
My hands and my feet are withered,
you lay me down in the dust of death.

Why, silent God, why?

Pause

The hunters are all about me:
a circle of the wicked hem me in on every side,
their dogs unleashed to tear me apart.
They have pierced my hands and my feet –
I can count all my bones –
they stand glaring and gloating over me.
They divide my garments among them,
they cast lots for my clothes.

Why, silent God, why?

Pause

The tanks of the mighty encircle me,
barbed wire and machine guns surround me.
They have marked my arm with a number,
and never call me by name.
They have stripped me of clothes and of shoes,
and showered me with gas in the chamber of death.

Why, silent God, why?

Pause

I cry out for morphine but no one hears me.
Pinned down by straitjacket I scream the night through.
I suffocate through panic in the oxygen tent.
Sweating with fear, I await news of my doom.

We breathe these words out of the Silence within us, into the Silence beyond us...

Why, silent God, why?

Pause

No one comes near with an unmasked face,
no skin touches mine in a gesture of love.
They draw back in terror, speaking only
in whispers behind doors that are sealed.

Why, silent God, why?

Pause

Be not far from me, O God:
you are my helper, hasten to my aid.
Deliver my very self from the sword,
my life from the falling of the axe.
Save me from the mouth of the lion,
poor body that I am, from the horns of the bull.

Silence

Silent God, **we bring the cries of our battered hearts, the
cries of those burdened by illness, the cries of those
bowed down by oppression. We bring them so that we
may not be silent...Hear us in the name of Jesus, forsaken
on a cross.**

22

Part ii

That we may be aware of God's presence whatever...

I will declare your name to my friends:
in the midst of the congregation I will praise you.
In wonder and awe I stand in your presence:
I will remember, and glorify your name.

Pause

For you have not shrunk in loathing
from the suffering in their affliction.

>

...in the Spirit that stirs amongst us the kaleidoscope of Jesus.

You have not hid your face from them,
but when they called to you, you heard them.

I re - call your mer - cies of old:___

Why have you hid-den your-self___ now?

Doubts and trem - blings o - ver-whelm_ me:

ne-ver-the-less I shall dee-pen my trust.

Pause

My praise is of you in the great congregation,
my vows I shall perform in their sight.
We shall praise you with thanksgiving and wonder.

Pause

We shall share what we have with the poor:
they will eat and be satisfied,
a new people, yet to be born.
Those who seek you will be found by you:
they will be in good heart for ever.

I recall your mercies of old:
Why have you hidden yourself now?
Doubts and tremblings overwhelm me:
nevertheless I shall deepen my trust.

Pause

We breathe these words out of the Silence within us, into the Silence beyond us...

So my life will be preserved in your sight,
and my children will worship you:
they will tell of you to generations yet to come:
to a people yet to be born
they will declare your righteousness,
that you have brought these things to fulfilment.

Pause

Let even the ends of the world remember
and turn again to their God.
Let the families of the nations worship their Creator.
In your domain all will come right in the end.

I recall your mercies of old:
Why have you hidden yourself now?
Doubts and tremblings overwhelm me:
nevertheless I shall deepen my trust.

Silence

O God of enduring love, **whom the clouds obscure, may our**
eye of faith turn steadily towards you, patiently waiting in
hope for the fulness of your salvation, bearing the pain of
evil days, in Yeshua crucified, who loved his own even to
the end, and kept on trusting even when there was no
answer to his cry.

22

Part iii

In solidarity with those who are wrestling with doubt; and for a new vision of God in
these days when the old ways do not sustain and nourish us.

Can we now hold on to such faith?
Has the name of God become an offence to our ears?
Is God deaf to the cry of the child,
offering no relief to the burning of pain,
letting the horror of life run wild,
sitting lofty and high, refusing to act?

...in the Spirit that stirs amongst us the kaleidoscope of Jesus.

Pause

So do we argue and wrestle in faith,
fiercely refusing to loosen our hold.
We demand that you listen to whisper and howl,
that your deeds may fulfil your nature and name.

Pause

This is our story from Jeremiah and Job,
from all who find you obscure and perplexing.
Who are you? Who do you say that you are?
Why must we be buffeted by malice and chance?

Pause

Is our cry no more than our pride?
Is our mind too small? Is our eye too dim?
Do not quiet our pain with dazzling display.
The open wound of the child accuses you still.

Pause

Is there a cry in the depths of your being,
in the heart and soul of your chosen Christ-Self?
Stretched between heaven and earth,
we see a striving so awesome,
a strange and harrowing love,
a bearing of pain between father and son,
a loving right through to the end,
through the worst of devil and death.

We trust___ in the fol - ly___ of a cross.

Pause

Truly you are an offence, O God,
and scandalous too are the outcries of faith.
They bite deep into the lines of our faces,
as we strive to be faithful and true.

We breathe these words out of the Silence within us, into the Silence beyond us...

Pause

Keep us from the scandal of hypocrisy,
selfish and faithless, prayers merely mouthed,
so far from the 'place of the skull',
too indifferent to be in conflict with you,
too icily cold for your friendship.

We trust in the folly of a cross.

Pause

Today if you hear the voice of *this* God,
your heart need no longer be hardened.

Silence

O God of the cross, **keep us passionate through our
wrestling with your ways, and keep us humble before the
mystery of your great love, known to us in the face of
Jesus wounded and transfigured.**

22

Part iv

That these words may be in the hearts of all who dwell now in deep darkness.

And can those who are buried give you worship,
those ground to the dust give you praise?
Will nothing be left but the wind and the silence,
a dead earth, abandoned, forgotten?

Pause

But you are a God who creates out of nothing,
you are a God who raises the dead,
you are a God who redeems what is lost,
you are a God who fashions new beauty,
striving with the weight of your glory,
bearing the infinite pain.

...in the Spirit that stirs amongst us the kaleidoscope of Jesus.

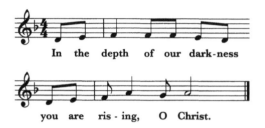

In the depth of our dark-ness

you are ris-ing, O Christ.

Pause

The footfalls of faith may drag through our days,
God's gift of a costly and infinite enduring.
We remember your deliverance of your people of old,
we remember the abundance of the earth you have given us,
we remember the millions who care day by day,
we remember your victory of long-suffering love.

**In the depth of our darkness
you are rising, O Christ.**

Pause

The power of the powers is but a feather in the wind!
Death is transfigured to glory for ever!

Silence

God of resurrection, **breaking our bonds of death, shine on
us with eyes of compassion and glory. Let light flood the
dungeons of our rejected and downtrodden selves. So may
the oppressed go free, the weak rise up in strength, and
the hungry be fed, now in these our days.**

✛

We breathe these words out of the Silence within us, into the Silence beyond us...

23   The shepherd and the host

That we and all human beings may draw close in friendship and in God.

Dear God, you sustain me and feed me:
like a shepherd you guide me.
You lead me to an oasis of green,
to lie down by restful waters.
Quenching my thirst, you restore my life:
renewed and refreshed, I follow you,
a journey on the narrowest of paths.

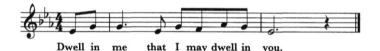

Dwell in me that I may dwell in you.

Pause

Even when cliffs loom out of the mist,
my step is steady because of my trust.
Even when I go through the deepest valley,
with the shadow of darkness and death,
I shall fear no evil or harm.
For you are with me to give me strength,
your crook, your staff, at my side.

Dwell in me that I may dwell in you.

Pause

Even in the midst of my troubles,
with the murmurs of those who disturb me,
I know I can feast in your presence.
You spread a banquet before me,
you anoint my head with oil,
you stoop to wash my feet,
you fill my cup to the brim.

Dwell in me that I may dwell in you.

Pause

...in the Spirit that stirs amongst us the kaleidoscope of Jesus.

Your loving kindness and mercy
will meet me every day of my life.
By your Spirit you dwell within me,
and in the whole world around me,
and I shall abide in your house,
content in your presence for ever.

Dwell in me that I may dwell in you.

Silence

Wise and loving Shepherd, **guiding your people in the ways of
your truth, leading us through the waters of baptism, and
nourishing us with the food of eternal life, keep us in your
mercy, and so guide us through the perils of evil and
death, that we may know your joy at the heart of all things,
both now and for ever.**

24   The glory of God

That we may see glory even in the foothills of faith.

Dear God, you are creating the earth
and all that is in it,
the whole round world
and all who dwell on land or sea.
You have founded life upon the waters,
and drawn it forth from the mysterious deeps.

Pause

Who will climb the mountain of God?
Who will stand in the holy place?
Those who have clean hands and pure hearts,
who have not set their minds on falsehood,
nor sworn to deceive their neighbours:
they will receive a blessing from God,
and justice from the God of their salvation.
Such is the fortune of those who draw near their Creator,
who seek the face of the God of Jacob.

Pause

We breathe these words out of the Silence within us, into the Silence beyond us...

Let the gates be opened, let the doors be lifted high,
that the great procession may come in.
Who is the One clothed with glory?
It is our God, the God who has triumphed,
who has striven with evil and prevailed.

Praise to the glory of God,
shining through Jesus Christ.

Pause

Let the gates be opened, let the doors be lifted high,
that the great procession may come in.
Who is the One clothed with glory?
It is the great God of all the universe,
glorious in a love that never fails.

**Praise to the glory of God,
shining through Jesus Christ.**

Silence

May the light and love of God shine in our hearts **and reach the
furthest bounds of the universe, that the whole creation
may be transfigured to glory, in and through Yeshua,
radiant in the splendour of the wounds of love.**

25   A prayer of the lonely

In solidarity with the lonely.

O God, the foundation of my trust,
you are the ground of my hope.
May I not be disappointed in my days,
may the powers of oppression fade away.

…in the Spirit that stirs amongst us the kaleidoscope of Jesus.

Pause

Let none who wait for your coming
turn away with empty hands.
But let those who break faith
be confounded and turn in repentance.

You are the source of my faith,

you are the goal of my hope.

Pause

Show me your ways, O God,
and teach me your paths.
Lead me in your truth and guide me,
for you are the God of my salvation.

Pause

I have hoped in you all the day long,
because of your goodness and faithfulness,
your steadfast love to your people,
streaming towards us from days of old.

**You are the source of my faith,
you are the goal of my hope.**

Pause

Remember not the sins of my youth,
nor my trespass and trampling on others.
According to your mercy think on me,
call to mind your agelong compassion.

Pause

You are full of justice and grace:
you guide sinners in the way.

We breathe these words out of the Silence within us, into the Silence beyond us...

You lead the humble to do what is right,
filled with the gentle strength of the meek.
All your paths are faithful and true,
for those who are loyal to your covenant.

**You are the source of my faith,
you are the goal of my hope.**

Pause

For your name's sake, O God,
be merciful to me, for my sin is great.
I come to you in trembling and awe:
guide me in the way I should choose.

Pause

I shall be at home with what is right,
I shall dwell at ease in the land.
My children will be stewards after me,
your creation cared for in days yet to come.
Your friendship is your gift to me,
revealed in the keeping of your covenant.

**You are the source of my faith,
you are the goal of my hope.**

Pause

My eyes look towards you, O God,
and you free me from the snares of the net.
Turn your face to me –
it is full of your grace and your love.

Pause

For I am lonely and in misery,
my heart is in pain and constricted:
the arteries of affection are hardened.
Open me wide and lift my heart high,
the breath of your Spirit filling my lungs.

Pause

...in the Spirit that stirs amongst us the kaleidoscope of Jesus.

Take to yourself my wretched affliction,
bring me out of my distress,
and forgive me all my sins.

**You are the source of my faith,
you are the goal of my hope.**

Pause

See how strong are the powers of oppression,
eyes full of hatred and violence.
Guard my life and deliver me,
clothe me with integrity and love.

Pause

Bring me to the innocence that no longer harms,
for you are my strength and salvation.
I wait for you: you are my hope;
may I never shrink away in shame.

**You are the source of my faith,
you are the goal of my hope.**

Silence

Compassionate and loving God, **take from me the burden
of self-hatred, the whisper of loathing that says I am
worthless. Fill me with the spirit of forgiveness and grace,
that I may deeply accept that I am accepted just as I am,
in the companionship of Yeshua, beloved of your heart.**

26   Innocent or guilty?

*In solidarity with those on trial, with those justly accused, and with those unjustly
accused.*

Examine me closely, O God,
whether I have walked in my integrity.
Have I trusted you without wavering?
Put me to the test and try me,
judge my mind and my heart.

We breathe these words out of the Silence within us, into the Silence beyond us...

For though your steadfast love is before my eyes,
I dare not claim always to have walked in your truth.

Pause

Have I never kept company with deceivers,
or consorted with hypocrites?
Have I never shunned the company of evildoers,
or sat with those who plot wickedness?

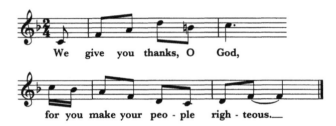

We give you thanks, O God,
for you make your peo - ple righ - teous.___

Pause

I cannot claim my own hands are innocent:
without your forgiveness I cannot stand.
But yours is the power to change and transform,
lifting my voice from trembling to gratitude.

Pause

Dear God, I love the silent presence in the places of prayer,
where glimpses of your glory shine,
and your light in the faces of those who trust you,
and the lives of the quietly faithful.
With you I shall indeed walk with integrity,
with your grace and compassion my foot will stand firm.

**We give you thanks, O God,
for you make your people righteous.**

Pause

But is this to be too easy with evil,
with my own and with those near and far?
What of those who murder with knife and gun,
those who trade in landmines and bombs?

>

...in the Spirit that stirs amongst us the kaleidoscope of Jesus.

What of those who limp through their lives,
and the bereaved who weep for those they have lost?

Pause

What is my prayer in this world of ours now?
What is the prayer of the silenced and maimed?
What of those imprisoned for conscience,
persecuted and tortured for faith?

Pause

Tempted to renounce our beliefs,
looking for courage to hold firm to your promise,
we cannot boast in your presence, O God,
we can but join with our forebears in prayer:

Kyrie eleison. Christe eleison. Kyrie eleison.

Pause

Forgive the boast of your people, O God,
self-righteous and blind in our mouthings.
We have not done a tenth of the things we should,
nor dare we plead any innocence.

Kyrie eleison. Christe eleison. Kyrie eleison.

Pause

We project the evil of our hearts on to others,
and destroy our enemies in your cause.
The drumbeat in the midst of the scriptures themselves
has sounded through inquisitions and wars.

Kyrie eleison. Christe eleison. Kyrie eleison.

Silence

We pray for the enemy, **in others and in ourselves, the one
who whispers the lie and imprisons the tellers of truth.
O God, forgive our laziness, our fears, our stupidity, and
shed on us the painful healing beams of the light of Jesus
the living truth.**

We breathe these words out of the Silence within us, into the Silence beyond us…

27   Courageous faith in turbulent times

For courage in turbulent times; and in solidarity with those caught up in war or civil strife.

God is my light and my salvation:
whom then shall I fear?
God is the strength of my life:
of whom then shall I be afraid?
In God alone do I put my trust:
how then can others harm me?

Pause

When the wicked, even my enemies,
come upon me to devour me,
they stumble and fall back.
When a mighty army is laid against me,
my heart will not be afraid.
When war rises up against me,
I shall put my trust in God.

Pause

One thing have I desired of God
that I shall seek after,
even that I may dwell in the house of my God
all the days of my life,
to feast my eyes on the beauty of my Creator,
to ponder deeply the gracious will of my God.

Pause

...in the Spirit that stirs amongst us the kaleidoscope of Jesus.

In the time of my trouble
you will hide me in your shelter;
in the shadow of your tent
you will conceal me from those who pursue me;
high on a pinnacle of rock
you will place me safe from those who surge around me.

**In time of disquiet and trouble,
with courage I will trust you.**

Pause

Therefore I shall offer in your dwelling place
gifts with great gladness:
I shall sing and praise your name.

Silence

Listen to me, O God, when I cry to you:
have mercy upon me and be gracious to me.
Do not hide your face from me,
nor cast your servant away in your anger.
The voice of my heart has impelled me:
Seek the face of the living God.

Pause

Out of the darkness I discern your presence
in the face of the risen One,
revealing your pain and your joy
in new and abundant life.

Pause

We breathe these words out of the Silence within us, into the Silence beyond us…

Indeed you have been my helper,
you have not forsaken me, O God of my salvation.
Though my family and friends may desert me,
you will sustain me in the power of the risen One.
Guide me in your way and lead me on your path.
So in the joy of your presence I can meet my adversaries,
even when false witnesses rise up against me,
or those who do me violence and wrong.

**Even through the worst of times,
I will not let go of my trust.**

Pause

I should have utterly fainted but that I truly believe
I shall see your goodness in the land of the living.
I shall patiently wait for your good time:
I put my trust in you, my faithful Creator:
I shall be strong and let my heart take courage.

**Even through the worst of times,
I will not let go of my trust.**

Pause

In all these things we are more than conquerors
through Christ who loves us.
For I am sure that neither death nor life,
nor angels nor principalities nor powers,
nor things present nor things to come,
nor height nor depth, nor anything else in all creation,
will be able to separate us from the presence of God
in Christ Jesus our Liberator in the power of great love.

Silence

Creator God, **faithful to your covenant with the earth,
steady our hearts and wills in times of great turbulence,
that we may in deed fulfil your purpose for us as heralds
of your just and lasting peace.**

…in the Spirit that stirs amongst us the kaleidoscope of Jesus.

28   The silence and the voice

That we may see God in those whose eyes we refuse to meet; and that they may see God in us.

Dear God, are you the friend I can trust?
You seem so deaf to my prayer,
to the urgent sound of my voice.
Do you turn away silent, do you not hear,
when I cry out for help?
I lift up my hands in the holy place,
but still I hear no answer.

Pause

Let me pause and remember the holy ground of your presence –
the bush burning with light at the moment of despair.

Pause

You are here in the ones I ignore:
the shuffling old man in the street,
the hollow-eyed woman unkempt,
the neighbour I pass hurriedly by.

Come, wind of the Spi - rit,____
with the voice of our God.____

Pause

I see neither their need nor mine,
it is I who turn silent away.
I collude with the ways of wickedness,
speaking peace with my lips,
unaware of the mischief of my heart.
No wonder I do not hear your voice.

We breathe these words out of the Silence within us, into the Silence beyond us...

I turn away from your presence,
pulled down by my selfish desires.

**Come, wind of the Spirit,
with the voice of our God.**

Pause

Open our eyes that we may see,
unblock our ears that we may hear.
Send us the fury of the desert wind,
or the gentle breeze through the trees.
Whether by shout or by whisper,
face us with dark truths of our ways.

**Come, wind of the Spirit,
with the voice of our God.**

Pause

No reward dare we claim,
no generosity from your heart.
No wonder we fall in the midst of our devices,
to be built up in strength no more.

Pause

Then once again your will stirs within us:
we are in touch once more with our passion,
with our anger at the traps of the poor,
of those without power or numbers.

Pause

The voice of the voiceless is heard in our land,
and the sound of your rejoicing, O God.
You are the strength of our hands
as we strive with the powers for your truth.
Our hearts trust you and we thank you,
we dance for joy and with songs give you praise.

**Come, wind of the Spirit,
with the voice of our God.**

Pause

...in the Spirit that stirs amongst us the kaleidoscope of Jesus.

Save your people, bless your heritage,
be our shepherd and guard us.
Protect us and bear with us,
both now and forever.

Silence

Remove from our hearts, O God, our apathy and fear, **and give us
the Spirit of love and freedom, that we may give passionately of ourselves in companionship with the poor and
oppressed, and so serve your just and holy rule, revealed
to us in Yeshua the Liberator.**

29   Awe in the presence of power

*That we may ponder the powers of nature, and recognize within ourselves awe, fear,
and glory, and our trembling response.*

Let all the powers of the universe praise the Creator,
ascribing to God glory and strength.
In the beauty of holiness we worship you, O God,
giving you the honour due to your name.

Pause

Your voice rolls over the waters,
your glory thunders over the oceans.
Your voice resounds through the mountains,
echoing glory and splendour.

Giv-ing   voice____   to the cry of cre - a - tion,____
we shout Glo - ry to God in the high - est.____

Pause

We breathe these words out of the Silence within us, into the Silence beyond us...

Your voice splits even the cedar trees,
breaking in pieces the cedars of Lebanon.
The trees of the mountainside howl in your wind,
uprooted like matchsticks in the roar of your passing.

Giving voice to the cry of creation,
we shout Glory to God in the highest.

Pause

Your voice divides the lightning flash,
flames of fire come from your tongue.
Your voice whirls the sands of the desert,
the whistling sands of the desert storm.

Giving voice to the cry of creation,
we shout Glory to God in the highest.

Pause

Your voice makes the oaks shake and shudder,
and strips the forest bare,
and all in your presence cry, Glory!

Giving voice to the cry of creation,
we shout Glory to God in the highest.

Pause

O God, more powerful than tempest and flood,
present throughout your creation,
stillness in the eye of the storm,
give strength to your people in awe of you,
give your people the blessing of peace.

Silence

Awesome God, **your love embraces all the powers of**
creation, and in the presence of love we need never be
afraid. Give us steadiness and courage and skill to strive
with the energies you have placed in our hands, that
the wise use of heat and light, of atom and laser, may
enable the earth and its peoples to flourish and prosper,
according to your will shown to us in Yeshua, true image
of you, our Creator.

...in the Spirit that stirs amongst us the kaleidoscope of Jesus.

30   The two conversions

That we may be thankful for rescue and humbled by our frequent stumbling.

From the depths of despair I cried out,
seared with pain and with grief.
Where are you, O God?
How long must I suffer?

Pause

You drew me up from the depths,
like a prisoner out of a dungeon,
a flesh-body touched by your hand,
flickering and trembling with life.

With gen-tle hand you raise___ me,
from___ death you call me to life.___

Pause

You brought me out of a land full of gloom,
a place of hollow silence and cold.
You melted my paralyzed fear:
your warmth like the sun's coursed through my veins.

**With gentle hand you raise me,
from death you call me to life.**

Pause

The wrath of your love lasts but a moment,
for a lifetime your mercy and healing.
Heaviness and weeping last through the night,
yet day breaks into singing and joy.

**With gentle hand you raise me,
from death you call me to life.**

We breathe these words out of the Silence within us, into the Silence beyond us...

Pause

I shall praise you, O God, for you have made me whole.
I shall give you thanks in the midst of your people.

Silence

In the strength you gave me I felt secure,
built upon rock, firm as the hills.
Basking in the warmth of your favour,
the prosperity of my days increased.

Pause

I slipped into the worship of money,
the goods of this world ensnaring me.
They gathered like a turbulent cloud,
blotting out the sight of your face.

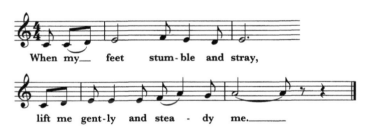

When my— feet stum-ble and stray,
lift me gent-ly and stea - dy me.——

Pause

Then I was greatly dismayed,
feeling foolish in toppling pride,
unable to praise you from the wasteland of hell,
to proclaim your name from the graveyards of death.

**When my feet stumble and stray,
lift me gently and steady me.**

Pause

O God, pour mercy upon me,
forgive my self-satisfied pride,
disentangle the web I have woven,
patiently probe me with the scalpel of truth.

...in the Spirit that stirs amongst us the kaleidoscope of Jesus.

When my feet stumble and stray,
lift me gently and steady me.

Pause

You turn my lamentation into dancing,
lifting me to my feet, clothing me with joy.
In the depths of my being I explode into laughter,
and sing with gratitude the triumph of love.

Silence

Living God, **look on us with eyes of compassion; call us**
with the word of forgiveness, again and again, to seventy
times seven, that we may at last hear and see, and turn our
stricken and wounded faces, and know ourselves accepted
and embraced, loved beyond measure and without
reserve.

31   A prayer for deliverance

In solidarity with those who are grieving, those who are overburdened, those who are
burnt out, those who are worn down.

I am bowed down by the heat of battle;
exhausted I limp back to my tent.
Here is my shelter, my refuge,
the place where I know God is with me.

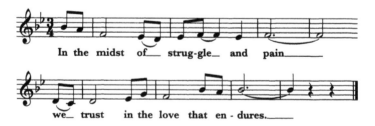

In the midst of__ strug-gle__ and pain_____

we__ trust   in the love that en - dures.____

Pause

We breathe these words out of the Silence within us, into the Silence beyond us...

Deliver me, rescue me, redeem me,
for you are just, and swift to save.
You are a stream of refreshment, an oasis of shade;
you give me manna in the wilderness, ever drawing me on.

**In the midst of struggle and pain
we trust in the love that endures.**

Pause

Lead me and guide me for the sake of your name:
deliver me out of the nets that entangle me,
for you alone are my strength.

Pause

Into your hands I cast my whole being,
knowing that you will redeem me,
O God of salvation and truth.

**In the midst of struggle and pain
we trust in the love that endures.**

Pause

I hate those who cling to vain idols,
for my trust is in you, living God.
I will be glad and rejoice in your love,
for you have seen my affliction,
and soothed my distress.

Pause

You have not abandoned me to the power of my enemy:
you have set my feet in a broad place,
where I may walk at liberty.

**In the midst of struggle and pain
we trust in the love that endures.**

Pause

Have mercy on me, O God,
for I am distressed and in pain:
no one hears the cry of my loneliness.   >

...in the Spirit that stirs amongst us the kaleidoscope of Jesus.

My eyes have become dimmed with grief,
the whole of me, body and soul.

Pause

My life is worn away with sorrow,
and my years with mourning.
My strength fails me because of my affliction,
and my bones are wasting away.

**In the midst of struggle and pain
we trust in the love that endures.**

Pause

I am the scorn of my enemies,
and a burden to my neighbours.
My acquaintances, they are afraid of me,
shrinking away from my sight.

Pause

I am clean forgotten,
like a dead man out of mind.
I have become like a broken vessel.
For I hear the conspiring of many,
the whispering of threats on every side,
as they plot to take away my life.

**In the midst of struggle and pain
we trust in the love that endures.**

Pause

The hope of my days is in your hands:
I trust you, my God, Thou that art Thou.
Deliver me from the power of my enemies,
from the grip of those who persecute me.
Show your servant the light of your countenance,
and save me in your steadfast love.

**In the midst of struggle and pain
we trust in the love that endures.**

Pause

We breathe these words out of the Silence within us, into the Silence beyond us...

Let me not be confounded, O God,
for I have called upon your name.
Let ungodliness be put to confusion,
and brought to silence in the grave.

Pause

Let lying lips be made dumb,
the voices of cruelty and pride
that speak with spite against the just.

**In the midst of struggle and pain
we trust in the love that endures.**

Pause

How great is your goodness towards us,
poured out on the just and the unjust,
saving us from whisperings within,
from the betrayals of hearts that are frightened,
sheltering us in your refuge
from the strife of tongues.

**In the midst of struggle and pain
we trust in the love that endures.**

Pause

O God, I give you thanks
for you have shown me marvellous great kindness.
When I was alarmed, like a city besieged,
I felt cut off from your sight.
Nevertheless, you heard the voice of my prayer,
when I cried to you for help.

Pause

All your servants love you, O God,
for you enfold us in your faithfulness,
and retrieve us sternly when we are proud.
With firmness of will and courage of heart,
we shall follow your way,
trusting that you are our God,
our faithful Creator and Friend.

...in the Spirit that stirs amongst us the kaleidoscope of Jesus.

Silence

Living God, **faithful to your covenants, loyal to your people, deepen our trust in your loving purposes for all human-kind, that not one of us may come to lasting harm.**

32   Release from burdens

In solidarity with those whose lives fester because of unrecognized and undeclared wrongdoing; and that we may all welcome the steady and never-ending forgiveness of God.

Blessed are those whose sin is forgiven,
the trace of whose trespass is erased.
Blessed are those whom God does not blame,
in whose heart is no guile.

Pause

I kept my secret sins to myself,
I refused to bring them to the light.
My energy wasted away,
my days were full of complaint,
a grumble murmuring in my ears.

Pause

Day and night your hand was heavy upon me:
the flow of my being became sluggish and dry,
like parched land in the drought of summer.

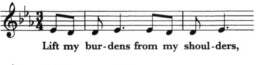

Lift my bur-dens from my shoul-ders,

for the yoke of your love___ is   light._____

Pause

We breathe these words out of the Silence within us, into the Silence beyond us...

Then I acknowledged my sin in your presence:
I hid no longer from myself or from you.
I said, "I will confess my evil to God."
So you released me from the guilt of my sin.

Pause

For this cause all those who are faithful
pray in their hearts in the day of their troubles.
Even in times of overwhelming distress,
with the thunder and force of waters in flood,
your grace is for me like a temple of rock,
standing firm in the face of the powers,
ordering the discord and chaos within,
preserving my life from utter destruction.

Pause

In the eye of the storm I hear the whisper of mercy,
the peace of those who are completely forgiven.

**Lift my burdens from my shoulders,
for the yoke of your love is light.**

Pause

I know you will instruct me and guide me,
you will teach me the way I should go.
You will counsel me with your ear to the truth,
a keen and kindly eye fixed upon me.
Let me not be like horse or mule, with no understanding,
whose course must be curbed with bridle and bit.

**Lift my burdens from my shoulders,
for the yoke of your love is light.**

Pause

Many are the pangs of the wicked:
steadfast love surrounds those who trust God.
People of integrity, rejoice in God and be glad:
shout for joy all you that are true of heart.

Silence

...in the Spirit that stirs amongst us the kaleidoscope of Jesus.

Compassionate Friend, **warm the frozen places of our fears, irrigate the deserts of our apathy, dismantle the wall around our pain and love, lift the burdens of our past, that we may be free to live in the joy of your presence.**

33   The God of creation and history

That we may discern God in things great and small, in creation and in history.

Let those who serve you praise you, O God,
let the true of heart give you thanks.
Let the melodies of the strings be played,
accompanying our words in your praise.

Pause

For your word, O God, is true,
your deeds fulfil your covenant.
You love the justice of relationships made right,
the world is full of your steadfast love.

Pause

O God, you are the God of creation:
by your word the universe begins, again and again,
the numberless stars by the breath of your mouth.
You held the waters of the seas in the hollow of your hand,
you gathered to yourself all the treasures of the deep.

**Praise to the love that moves the stars
and stirs the hearts of the people.**

We breathe these words out of the Silence within us, into the Silence beyond us...

Pause

Let the whole earth be in awe of you,
all the inhabitants of the world greet you with joy.
For you spoke, and the wonderful deed was done;
you commanded, and it all came to pass.

Pause

O God you are the God of history:
all the ways of the nations are but nothing in your sight.
You frustrate the devices of the peoples,
and your counsel and truth stand for ever,
the purpose of your heart to all generations.
Blessed are the people who put their trust in you,
whom you have chosen to serve a high destiny.

**Praise to the love that moves the stars
and stirs the hearts of the people.**

Pause

Not one of the children of earth can escape you;
all the inhabitants of the world are in your sight.
You fashion all our hearts
and comprehend all our ways.

Pause

A ruler is not saved by a mighty army,
a warrior is not delivered by much strength.
A war horse is a vain hope for victory,
and by its great might it cannot save.

Pause

But your eye, O God, is on those who are in awe of you,
who trust in your unfailing love.
You deliver them from the pangs of death,
and feed them in the time of famine.

**Praise to the love that moves the stars
and stirs the hearts of the people.**

Pause

...in the Spirit that stirs amongst us the kaleidoscope of Jesus.

We wait for you eagerly, O God,
for you are our hope and our shield.
Surely our hearts shall rejoice in you,
for we have trusted in your holy name.
Let your merciful kindness be upon us,
even as our hope is in you.

Silence

**Loving One, moving the sun and the moon and the stars,
weave the pattern of glory to the bounds of the universe,
even in the cells of our being.**

34   God the bearer of pain

That we may trust that joy is at the heart of pain even when the pain is overwhelming, especially when there is nothing we can do for those we love.

We shall bless you, O God, at all times,
your praise opening our lips.
We shall exalt your name alone:
the afflicted will hear and be glad.
We give the Pain-bearer thanks:
we magnify the name of our God.

With the strings that are taut with pain

com - pose   new mu-sic of   joy.

Pause

I sought your help and you answered,
you freed me from all my fears.
We look towards you and are radiant:
our faces will not be ashamed.

We breathe these words out of the Silence within us, into the Silence beyond us…

Pause

The cry of the poor reaches your ears,
you saved us out of our trouble.
Your angels guard and protect us,
bringing your deliverance near.

**With the strings that are taut with pain
compose new music of joy.**

Pause

So we taste and see
how gracious and good is our God.
You meet us in the depth of our pain;
those who love you and fear you lack nothing.

Pause

Come, my children, listen to me:
I shall teach you the way of our God.
Who among you relishes life,
wants time to enjoy good things?

Pause

Let no spite defile your tongue,
no lies fall from your lips.
Renounce the ways of evil,
pursue peace with all your heart.

Pause

Your eyes, O God, turn to the humble poor,
your ears to the cry of the needy and just.
You set your face against those who do wrong,
cutting off the memory of their deeds.

Pause

When those who do no harm cry for help,
you come close to their anguish and calm them.
Gently you embrace the broken in heart,
and revive the crushed in spirit.

...in the Spirit that stirs amongst us the kaleidoscope of Jesus.

With the strings that are taut with pain
compose new music of joy.

Pause

Many are the afflictions of those who seek good,
but the pain-bearing God is with them.
You penetrate the heart of their suffering,
that they may come to no lasting harm.

Pause

Evil rebounds on itself,
those consumed with hatred come to nothing.
O God you redeem the life of your servants:
close to you, they will not be destroyed.

With the strings that are taut with pain
compose new music of joy.

Silence

Pain-bearer God, **in our affliction we sense your presence,**
moving with our sufferings to redeem them, bringing joy
out of tragedy, creating such music as the world has not
yet heard. We praise you with great praise.

35   Those who are quiet in the land

In repentance for our malice and gossip; for the calming of fear; and in solidarity with
those deeply afraid of contemptuous power.

I am angry at the proud and self-righteous,
yet I see their face in my own.
I wreak havoc in the lives of my neighbours,
seemingly concerned for the good of their souls.

Pause

By innuendo I slander a name,
prejudging the ones I dislike,
gossiping in pubs and in churches,
hypocritically enjoying the headlines.

We breathe these words out of the Silence within us, into the Silence beyond us...

Pause

Let us be put to shame and dishonour,
hawks that seek the destruction of life.
Let us be turned back and confounded,
who devise evil against our neighbours.

Pause

Let us be like chaff before the wind,
the angel of God driving us on.
Let our way be dark and slippery,
the hound of God pursuing us.

Pause

Let the nets of our devising ensnare us,
let us fall to ruin in them,
swallowed up in the pit we dug for others,
for the poor, the defenceless, the oppressed.

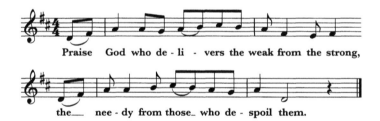

Praise God who de-li-vers the weak from the strong, the__ nee-dy from those_ who de-spoil them.

Pause

At a turn unexpected in the affairs of the world
the oppressed shall rejoice in the deliverance of God.
From the depth of their being they shall say,

**Praise God who delivers the weak from the strong,
the needy from those who despoil them.**

Pause

...in the Spirit that stirs amongst us the kaleidoscope of Jesus.

Malicious witnesses rise up,
spinning traps with their words,
making the innocent sign confessions
about things of which they know nothing.
All that is good is called evil;
even if heard the truth is not known.

Pause

And yet I prayed for my enemies,
lost in bewildered confusion.
Crumpled with grief I prayed long,
as if mourning a companion or brother.
My eyes looked to the ground,
as if I were lamenting my mother.

Pause

But when I stumbled they laughed me to scorn,
and gathered together against me.
As though I were a stranger they never knew,
they slandered me without ceasing.
When I slipped they mocked me more and more,
and hissed at me through their teeth.

Pause

How long, O God, will you look from afar?
Rescue me from the grip of their teeth,
my life from the tearing of lions.
And I shall give you thanks in the great congregation,
in the throng of the people I shall praise you.

**Praise God who delivers the weak from the strong,
the needy from those who despoil them.**

Pause

Let not the malicious triumph over their victims,
let not the mockers hate others with their eyes.
For they speak no words that make for peace,
but invent lies against those who are quiet in the land.

Pause

We breathe these words out of the Silence within us, into the Silence beyond us...

They stretch their mouths to jeer,
they rub their hands with glee,
sweeping the poor off their parcel of land,
claiming – As far as you can see, all, all is mine.

Pause

And you also have seen, O God:
do not be silent and hidden away.
Stir yourself, be awake for justice,
for the cause of the poor and oppressed.

Pause

Judge us in your righteousness,
let not the proud triumph,
let them not say, "Good, we have our heart's desire,"
let them not say, "Good, we have destroyed them."
**Praise God who delivers the weak from the strong,
the needy from those who despoil them.**

Pause

Let those who rejoice at others' hurt
be completely disgraced and confounded.
Let them be clothed with shame and dishonour
who trample the face of the needy,
exalting themselves at the expense of the poor.

Pause

But let those who long for justice
shout for joy and be glad:
let them say, "Great is God!
You delight in all those who serve you."
Then my tongue will speak of your righteous ways,
and of your praise all the day long.

**Praise God who delivers the weak from the strong,
the needy from those who despoil them.**

Silence

…in the Spirit that stirs amongst us the kaleidoscope of Jesus.

Disarm the mighty, O God, **and calm their fears. Let scales fall from their eyes, let them weep tears of repentance, that they may see their enemies as human beings, and come to know them as the only friends who bear the gift of their salvation, in Yeshua, powerless and victorious in love for us.**

36 The judge who does right

For true justice, not rough justice.

Transgression whispers to the wicked, deep in their hearts:
there is no fear of God in their eyes.
They flatter themselves with their own reflection,
imagining their wickedness is a secret for ever.

Pause

The words of their mouths are mischief and deceit:
they have ceased to act wisely and never do good.
Lying awake in the night, plotting with malice,
they set themselves on a path that is crooked,
no longer aware of the evil they do.

Pause

Your steadfast love, O God, extends through the universe,
your faithfulness to the furthest stars.
Your justice is like the high mountains,
your judgment as the great deep.

Pierce to the heart of our wick-ed-ness,
a - ban-don us not to our doom.

We breathe these words out of the Silence within us, into the Silence beyond us...

Pause

So the Judge of all the earth will do right.
You will save us, frail children of the dust:
precious indeed is your kindness and love.

Pause

The children of earth find refuge in your shade,
you entertain them to a feast in your house.
You give them water to drink from the river of delight:
for with you is the well of life,
and in your light do we see light.

**Pierce to the heart of our wickedness,
abandon us not to our doom.**

Pause

Continue your goodness to those who know you,
your saving ways to the true of heart.
Let not the foot of the proud trample us,
nor the hand of the arrogant push us aside.

Pause

Under the weight of their scheming may they crumple,
their will to do evil extinguished for ever.

**Pierce to the heart of our wickedness,
abandon us not to our doom.**

Silence

O God, **wise and discerning in all that you do, deliver us
from the delusion that we are better than others; rather
than condemning one another, may we come together and
kneel in humility, knowing only your mercy and truth.**

...in the Spirit that stirs amongst us the kaleidoscope of Jesus.

37   Dogged trust in God

For sheer plodding trust, come what may.

Part i

Fret not yourself because of the ungodly,
do not be envious of those who do evil.
For then you would become as one of them,
putting yourself in the wrong.

Pause

They will soon fade away like grass,
withering like the leaves in drought.
Simply trust in God, and do good:
we shall dwell in the land and graze safely.

In meeting the powers of evil,
let us deepen our trust in God.

Pause

Let us delight in your company, O God,
and you will give us our heart's desire.
Let us commit our lives to your goodness,
let us cast all our cares on your shoulders.

Pause

Let us trust you to act with justice,
to deliver us in your own good time.
You will make our vindication shine clear as the light,
our integrity bright as the noonday sun.

**In meeting the powers of evil,
let us deepen our trust in God.**

Pause

We breathe these words out of the Silence within us, into the Silence beyond us...

Let us be still and wait for you patiently,
bearing the tension that all is not well,
calming the restless desire to be certain,
in advance of the day of your coming.

Pause

Let us not be vexed when others prosper,
when they weave their evil designs.
May we let go of anger and rage,
refusing to let envy move us to evil.

**In meeting the powers of evil,
let us deepen our trust in God.**

Pause

For the trees of the wicked will be cut down:
those who wait for God will inherit the land.
In a while the ungodly will be shamed:
we shall look for them in their place:
we shall find it deserted, left to the wind.
The humiliated will inherit the earth,
they will enjoy the abundance of peace.

**In meeting the powers of evil,
let us deepen our trust in God.**

Silence

Part ii

Though the righteous have but a little,
it is better than the hoards of the wicked.
The strong arm of the ungodly will be broken:
God upholds those who are true of heart.

Pause

God cares for the lives of the humble poor,
and their heritage will be theirs for ever.
They will not be put to shame in evil days,
but in time of famine they will eat their fill.

Pause

...in the Spirit that stirs amongst us the kaleidoscope of Jesus.

As for the ungodly they will cease to do evil,
they will face the searing presence of God:
like fuel in a furnace they will be well nigh consumed,
all they hold dear will vanish away.

**In meeting the powers of evil,
let us deepen our trust in God.**

Pause

The ungodly borrow but never repay:
the poor are often generous and give.
Those who are blessed by God will dwell secure,
those who have neglected God's ways will wither.

Pause

If our steps are guided by God,
and if we delight in God's way,
though we stumble we shall not fall headlong,
for you, O God, will steady us with your hand.

**In meeting the powers of evil,
let us deepen our trust in God.**

Pause

Enable the powerful in these our days,
those who are the privileged few,
help them to lend their strength to the weak,
their voices to the small and the voiceless.

Pause

Help us all to sound our compassion and anger,
to strive with those who oppress the downtrodden,
showing them their greed and malice and fear,
helping them to face their enemy within,
that they may open their hearts to be generous.

Pause

May they do the same for those who exploit,
that their wickedness too may vanish away.

We breathe these words out of the Silence within us, into the Silence beyond us...

Together redeem us, long-suffering God,
bring us all to share in your peace.

Silence

Be with us, O God, **as we struggle for a more just world, yet
remind us that our actions so often tighten the mesh that
binds the oppressed. Keep us from pride in our own
strength, and keep us from despair when evil seems
entrenched. Renew our trust in your good purposes for us
all. Give us the gift of discernment, that we may know
when to strive in the power of your Spirit, and when to be
still and wait for your deliverance. Come in your good
time, but come soon.**

38   A cry in the midst of pain and guilt

*In solidarity with those who are in anguish through their own fault or the fault of
others; and in penitence for spreading gossip, slander, and rumour.*

O God, do you rebuke me in your anger?
Do you chasten me in fierce displeasure?
Is it your arrows that pierce me,
your hand come heavy upon me?
With no health in my flesh, do you punish me,
in sternness of love, for my sins?

Pause

The tide of my wrongs sweeps over my head,
their weight is a burden too heavy to bear.
My wounds stink and fester through folly,
I am bowed down with grieving all the day long.

Pause

My loins are filled with a burning pain,
there is no sound part in my flesh.
I am numbed and stricken to the ground,
I groan in the anguish of my heart.

Pause

...in the Spirit that stirs amongst us the kaleidoscope of Jesus.

The pounding of my heart comes to your ears,
my desire for love, my stumbling on the road.
My deep sighing is not hidden from you,
my longing for kindness and the touch that heals.

Pause

My heart is in tumult, my strength fails me,
even the light of my eyes has gone from me.
My companions draw back from my affliction,
my kinsfolk stare afar at my sores.

From the power of guilt and pain,
free me and heal me, O Christ.

Pause

My ears are blocked: I hear nothing;
it is as if my mouth is sealed.
I have become as one who cannot hear,
in whose mouth there is no retort.

Pause

I falter on the edge of the abyss,
my pain is with me continually.
I confess my wickedness with tears,
I shudder with sorrow for my sin.

**From the power of guilt and pain,
free me and heal me, O Christ.**

Pause

We breathe these words out of the Silence within us, into the Silence beyond us...

Those who seek my life lay their snares,
those who desire my hurt spread evil tales,
murmuring slanders all the day long.
I prayed, Let them never exult over me,
those who laugh harshly when I stumble and fall.

Pause

My enemies without cause are strong,
those who hate me wrongfully are many.
Those who repay evil for good are against me,
they blame me for what I did right.

**From the power of guilt and pain,
free me and heal me, O Christ.**

Pause

But in you, O God, I have put my trust,
and you will answer me in saving judgment.
Do not forsake me, do not go far from me;
hasten to my help, O God of my salvation.

Pause

For I know you enter the heart of our anguish,
you take to yourself the pain of the universe,
you bear the marks of our sin,
you endure and still you forgive.

**From the power of guilt and pain,
free me and heal me, O Christ.**

Pause

It is not for our sin that we suffer,
nor for the wrongs of our forebears.
Far beyond our conceiving you work out your purpose,
so that in us your glory be known.
Your vulnerable love works without ceasing,
to draw us from despair into wonder.

Silence

...in the Spirit that stirs amongst us the kaleidoscope of Jesus.

Saviour and Healer, **present in the midst of our distress, forgiving our sin and relieving our suffering, deepen our trust in your Spirit at work within us, that your love may overwhelm us with joy and your hand guide us in the dance of freedom.**

39   Anger human and divine

For a way through our anger, rage, and fury, in ourselves and in others.

I shall keep watch over my words,
so that I do not offend with my tongue.
I shall put a muzzle on my mouth,
while the wicked are in my presence.

Pause

How can I keep silent in our day,
as I see the hypocrisies around me,
the poor defrauded of land,
the dwelling place of God dishonoured?

Pause

Now that my eyes have been opened,
it is impossible not to be angry.
I cannot be aware and stay calm:
it goes against the grain of my being.

Pause

I tried to hold my tongue and say nothing,
refusing to be rash, keeping silent.
But the pain grew intolerable,
my heart burned hot within me.
While I mused the fire burst into flame,
and I spoke from the depth of my being.

Pause

Possessed by the demon of anger,
swept along by the vortex of rage,

I was an easy target for the powerful:
a well-aimed blow and I fell.

Pause

Yet I need the fire in my belly,
its heat and its light to move me,
I need it to spur me to action,
rage become love in the service of others.

Pause

Yet I know how fleeting is my life:
O God, let me remember my end, and the number of my days.
You have made my years but a handsbreadth,
my whole span is as nothing before you.

Pause

Thinking we stand secure, we are but a breath of wind,
our lives but a passing shadow.
The riches we heap are like autumn leaves,
golden and brittle to those who gather them.

My-ste-rious is___ the_ God who throws us to the ground
and con-tin-ual-ly,_ con-tin-ual-ly, rai-ses us up.

Pause

And now, O God, what is my hope?
Truly my hope is in you.
Deliver me from the trap of my sins,
do not make me the butt of fools.

Pause

I was dumb, I did not open my mouth,
silenced now by the thought of my sin.   >

...in the Spirit that stirs amongst us the kaleidoscope of Jesus.

Your arm is straightening my crookedness,
a pain not easy to bear.

**Mysterious is the God who throws us to the ground
and continually, continually, raises us up.**

Pause

With rebukes you humble me low,
you cause my fair looks to decay,
like a moth you destroy my possessions.
Surely we are but a breath,
as nothing in the sight of your eyes.

Pause

Hear my prayer and give ear to my cry:
do not be silent at my tears.
I am but a stranger with you,
a passing guest as my ancestors were.

**Mysterious is the God who throws us to the ground
and continually, continually, raises us up.**

Pause

Turn your anger away from me,
that I may breathe awhile and be glad,
before I go hence
and am no more seen.

Pause

So I rely on your kindness alone,
entrusting myself to your mercy,
even to the gates of my death,
down to the depths of the grave.

Silence

O God of mysterious anger, **may we not think of you as
destructive as we are in our rage, but r ecognize your
piercing heat and light serving the truth, your fiercely
loving anger overcoming our murdering and mortality.**

We breathe these words out of the Silence within us, into the Silence beyond us...

40   Faith rejoicing and faith struggling

In gratitude for the deepening of trust.

I waited patiently for you, my God,
and at last you heard my cry.
You lifted me out of the icy torrent,
you drew me out of the quicksand and mire.

Pause

You set my feet on solid ground,
making firm my foothold on rock.
No longer am I empty and lost:
you have given my life new meaning.

Pause

You have put a new song in my mouth,
a song of thanksgiving and praise.
Many will recognize your wondrous deeds:
they will be glad and put their trust in you.

Pause

Blessed are those who have made you their hope,
who have not turned to pride and to lying,
or to wandering in pursuit of false gods.
Great are the wonderful things you have done,
marvellous are your thoughts and desires.

Pause

There is none to be compared with you:
were I to declare everything you have done,
your deeds are more than I am able to express.

In___ the striv-ing and re-joic-ings of faith
may our search and our trust give you praise.___

...in the Spirit that stirs amongst us the kaleidoscope of Jesus.

Pause

We cannot buy your favour with bribes,
you were not pleased with the sacrifices of old.
It is the gift of my heart and my will
that you seek in your long-suffering love.

Pause

You have softened the wax in my ears,
I hear you at last and respond:
open and attentive I listen to your voice.
Dear God I long to do your will.
Your law of love delights my heart.

Pause

I have not hidden your salvation in silence,
I have told of your resurrection and glory.
I have not kept back the glad news of deliverance,
your faithfulness, justice, and truth.

In the striving and rejoicings of faith
may our search and our trust give you praise.

Pause

May your truth ever protect me,
your steadfast mercy and love ever be close –
yes, even when troubles overwhelm me,
more numerous than the hairs of my head,
when my sins overtake me and I cannot hear,
and my heart fails within me.

Pause

Let those who seek my life to take it away,
let them be put to shame and utterly confounded.
Let those who gloat with the laughter of scorn,
let them be turned back and disgraced.

In the striving and rejoicings of faith
may our search and our trust give you praise.

Pause

We breathe these words out of the Silence within us, into the Silence beyond us...

So may I turn and be glad in you,
so that those who love your salvation may say,
Great and wonderful is God.
Even in my poverty and oppression,
you are with me, caring for me.

Pause

Yes, I am assured of my faith,
and yes, I still strive to believe.
You are my helper and deliverer:
make no long delay, my Saviour, my God.

Silence

O God of truth and mercy, **whose voice we miss in the
distractions of our lives, penetrate the core of our being,
that we may hear and be glad, knowing ourselves
accepted in your love, able once again to live in your truth
and forgiveness.**

41   Who condemns?

*That we may embrace the outcast and neglected; that nobody be forced to live in
isolation; and in solidarity with children torn apart, with friends betrayed, with those
seeking asylum.*

Blessed are those who care for the poor and the helpless,
who are kind to the outcast within them.
God will deliver them in the day of their trouble,
rescuing the child who is battered and torn.
God will guard them and preserve their life.

Pause

O God, you will not give us over to the will of our enemies –
to hatred within and to blame without.
In the day of our calamity you will sustain us,
as warring turbulence threatens our life.

Pause

...in the Spirit that stirs amongst us the kaleidoscope of Jesus.

Dear God, be merciful towards me,
heal me for I have failed to be like you.
My enemies, with whisper and shout, speak evil of me:
"When will you die and your name perish for ever?"

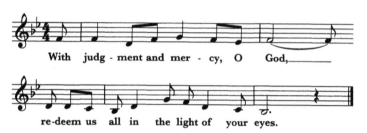

With judg - ment and mer - cy, O God,_____

re-deem us all in the light of your eyes.

Pause

They mouth empty words when they see me,
and mischief stirs in their hearts.
They talk among themselves in the street,
whispering suspicion against me.

Pause

They smile at the revealing of my sins,
gloating in triumph at my downfall,
cackling like demons that claw at me,
plucking me down to the mire.

**With judgment and mercy, O God,
redeem us all in the light of your eyes.**

Pause

"You are wracked with a deadly disease,
you will not rise again from where you lie."
Even my bosom friend whom I trusted,
who shared my bread, looks down on me.

Pause

O God, come down and raise me up,
struggling from the pit in anger and truth,

We breathe these words out of the Silence within us, into the Silence beyond us...

wrestling with my enemies in my love for them,
dependent together on your mercy.
So we shall know that you delight in us,
setting us before your face for ever.

**With judgment and mercy, O God,
redeem us all in the light of your eyes.**

Pause

Cleanse my whole being that I may see truly,
that revenge may not brood in my heart.
Keep me from believing all strangers are hostile,
let me see with the eyes of compassion.

Pause

May I think good of those who strive with me,
however full of malice seem their hearts.
Heap burning coals of love on our heads:
melt our fears with the flame of your desire.

**With judgment and mercy, O God,
redeem us all in the light of your eyes.**

Pause

Burn out from us all that breeds evil,
that we may no longer hurt or destroy.
May we follow the way of justice,
and be redeemed to your glory and joy.
Blessed be God, the God of all peoples,
at all times and all places, now and for ever.

Silence

Merciful God, **prone as we are to blame others and to hate
ourselves, take from our eyes the dust that blinds us, that
we may treat one another by the light of your compassion.**

...in the Spirit that stirs amongst us the kaleidoscope of Jesus.

42–43   Yearning for God

In solidarity with those weighed down with depression; and that we may keep moving gently and not get stuck.

As a deer longs for streams of water,
so longs my soul for you, O God.
My soul is thirsty for the living God:
when shall I draw near to see your face?

Pause

My tears have been my food in the night:
all day long they ask me, Where now is your God?
As I pour out my soul in distress,
I remember how I went to the temple of God,
with shouts and songs of thanksgiving,
a multitude keeping high festival.

Pause

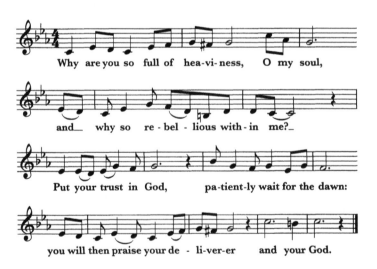

Why are you so full of hea-vi-ness, O my soul,
and why so re-bel-lious with-in me?
Put your trust in God, pa-tient-ly wait for the dawn:
you will then praise your de-li-ver-er and your God.

Pause

We breathe these words out of the Silence within us, into the Silence beyond us...

My soul is heavy within me: therefore I remember you
from the land of Jordan and from the hills of Hermon.
Deep calls to deep in the roar of the waterfalls,
all your waves and your torrents have gone over me.

Pause

Surely, O God, you will show me mercy in the daytime,
and at night I will sing your praise, O God my God.
I will say to God, my rock, Why have you forgotten me?
Why must I go like a mourner because the enemy oppresses me?
Like a sword piercing my bones, my enemies have mocked me,
asking me all day long, Where now is your God?

Pause

Why are you so full of heaviness, my soul,
and why so rebellious within me?
Put your trust in God, patiently wait for the dawn:
you will then praise your deliverer and your God.

Pause

O God, take up my cause and strive for me
with a godless people that knows no mercy.
Save me from the grip of cunning and lies,
for you are my God and my strength.

Pause

Why must you cast me away from your presence?
Why must I be clothed in rags, humiliated by my enemy?
O send out your light and your truth and let them lead me,
let them guide me to your holy hill and to your dwelling.
Then I shall go to the altar of God, the God of my joy
    and delight,
and to the harp I shall sing your praises, O God my God.

Pause

Why are you so full of heaviness, my soul,
and why so rebellious within me?
Put your trust in God, patiently wait for the dawn:
you will then praise your deliverer and your God.

...in the Spirit that stirs amongst us the kaleidoscope of Jesus.

Silence

Loving God, as we join our cries with those who are deeply depressed and in despair, renew in us the spirit of hope, the yearning for life in you alone, and the expectancy that even when every door is closed, you will surprise us with joy.

44   Cast off by God?

For allies in the struggle for the wellbeing of all; for faithfulness when God is hidden and obscure; in solidarity with explorers into God, and with those whose nightmares have yet to be calmed.

"We have heard with our ears, O God,
our ancestors have told us,
what they believed you did in their days,
how you gave them room to dwell in,
and caused them to root and to grow…

Pause

…how it was not by their swords that they did this,
nor did their own power get them victory,
but your right hand, your holy arm,
and the light of your countenance upon them.
It was out of sheer love that you did this,
out of your care and delight."

Pause

"They believed you reigned over them and their descendants,
by your power striking their enemies,
in your name alone treading them down.
They did not trust in longbow and sword,
but only in you to deliver them,
putting their adversaries to confusion.
In you alone was their boast,
giving thanks to your name without ceasing."

Pause

We breathe these words out of the Silence within us, into the Silence beyond us…

"Then came their crisis of faith:
Had you cast them off and brought them to shame,
no longer going out with their armies,
giving them as sheep to be butchered,
their foes plundering them at will,
scattering them among foreigners,
making a profitless sale?"

Pause

"They believed you had made them the scorn of their neighbours,
mocked and derided by those around them,
making them a byword among the peoples,
who dismissed them with eyes full of hatred,
their disgrace before them all the day long,
shame covering their faces,
at the voice of the slanderer and reviler,
at the sight of the enemy and avenger."

Pause

"They believed these calamities had fallen upon them,
even though they had not forgotten you.
Did they betray your covenant?
Did their hearts indeed turn away?
Had their steps strayed from your paths?"

Pause

So we take their bewilderment to heart,
sharing their anguish, doubting your presence.
Is it our fault that you seem so absent,
that the way of wickedness seems so often to triumph?

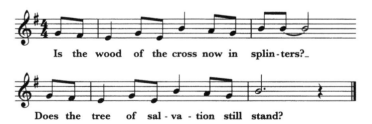

Is the wood of the cross now in splin-ters?_

Does the tree of sal-va-tion still stand?

...in the Spirit that stirs amongst us the kaleidoscope of Jesus.

Pause

With our ancestors we sense you have crushed us,
abandoning us in the haunts of jackals,
covering us with the deepest darkness.
Have we forgotten your name,
stretching out our hands to strange gods?
Do you not search us through and through,
knowing as you do the secrets of our hearts?

Pause

Yet there are those who are killed for your name,
they are counted as sheep for the slaughter.

Pause

Rouse yourself, O God, why do you sleep?
Awake, do not cast us off for ever.
Why do you hide your face
and forget our misery and oppression?

Pause

Our souls are bowed to the dust,
our bellies cleave to the ground.
Arise, O God, and help us,
and redeem us for your mercy's sake.

Is the wood of the cross now in splinters?
Does the tree of salvation still stand?

Pause

Strange how all this should surprise us –
the evil we thought was elsewhere
runs through the heart of each one of us.
No wonder we sense your eclipse, O God,
boasting you are always behind us.

Pause

Renew in us your covenant with the earth,
that we may respect one another,
even those who hate and despise us.

We breathe these words out of the Silence within us, into the Silence beyond us...

Pause

However oppressed we may be,
and must strive to disarm the oppressor,
keep hope of your forgiveness alive,
transform our thirst for revenge,
bring us home with weeping and joy.

Is the wood of the cross now in splinters?
Does the tree of salvation still stand?

Pause

Yet are we being too kind,
too easy and bland in the face of great evil?
What of the cry of the Holocaust,
of the sheep slaughtered by jackals?

Pause

What of the voice of those without name,
a number, a badge, for aliens despised?
Naked they went to the chambers of gas,
hair, clothes, and rings left behind.
Their corpses were piled into ovens,
their ashes scattered on lakes that were bitter.

Is the wood of the cross now in splinters?
Does the tree of salvation still stand?

Pause

What of those who drove the trains,
who treated so many like cattle in trucks,
who patrolled the barbed wire of the camps,
who delivered by lorry the canisters of gas?

Pause

What of those who locked the doors,
who put out the lights, melted the gold,
who turned their skin into lampshades?

Pause

...in the Spirit that stirs amongst us the kaleidoscope of Jesus.

O God, why are you silent?
Answer those who accuse you.
Why have you forgotten the wretched of the earth?
What profit do you gain from their affliction?

Is the wood of the cross now in splinters?
Does the tree of salvation still stand?

Pause

And what of the deeds of today,
of those with whom we collude?
Whose voices are raised against torture?
Who speaks for the voiceless held without charge?
Who hears the cries of women still sold into slavery,
of children abused who whimper through the night?

Is the wood of the cross now in splinters?
Does the tree of salvation still stand?

Silence

O God of love – if indeed you are love, for the howls of suffering
have hidden your face – **show us again in the crucified one
the eyes telling us that you are there, at the heart of the
desolate cries.**

45   A royal celebration

For those tempted by the trappings of power; and for justice and mercy at the forefront
of the exercise of power.

"My heart is aflame with fine phrases,
I make my song for the great king:
my tongue is the pen of a skilled writer."

Pause

"You are the fairest of the children of earth:
grace flows from your lips,
for God has blessed you for ever and ever."

Pause

We breathe these words out of the Silence within us, into the Silence beyond us...

"Take the sword to protect the weak,
defeating those who would threaten them.
Ride on in the cause of truth,
and for the sake of justice and mercy.
Your enemies will do well to tremble,
your arrows will be sharp in their hearts."

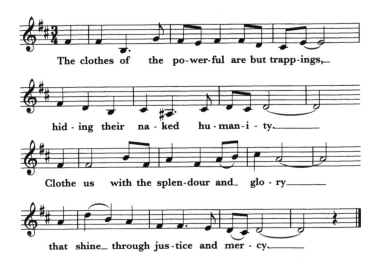

The clothes of the po-wer-ful are but trapp-ings,—
hid-ing their na-ked hu-man-i-ty.—
Clothe us with the splen-dour and— glo-ry—
that shine— through jus-tice and mer-cy.—

Pause

"Your divine throne endures for ever,
the sceptre of your realm is a sceptre of equity.
You love righteousness and hate evil:
so God has anointed you with the oil of gladness,
choosing you to serve for the sake of the people."

Pause

"Your garments are fragrant with myrrh, aloes, and cassia:
music from ivory palaces makes your heart glad.
Daughters of kings are among your noble women:
the queen is at your side in gold of Ophir."

...in the Spirit that stirs amongst us the kaleidoscope of Jesus.

**The clothes of the powerful are but trappings,
hiding their naked humanity.
Clothe us with the splendour and glory
that shine through justice and mercy.**

Pause

"Hear, O daughter, consider and incline your ear:
forget your own people and your father's house.
The king desires your beauty:
he is your lord: bow down before him."

Pause

"The richest among the people, O daughter of Tyre,
will entreat your favour with gifts.
The princess in her chamber is being robed
with garments of cloth of gold."

Pause

"In robes of brilliant colours
she is led to your presence, O king.
Her bridesmaids follow in procession,
with joy and gladness they form her train:
they enter the palace with songs of delight."

**The clothes of the powerful are but trappings,
hiding their naked humanity.
Clothe us with the splendour and glory
that shine through justice and mercy.**

Pause

So the generations pass,
as children grow strong and their elders fade.
May the old become wise and the young bring us hope.
And I will make God's name known,
whose reign has no end.
All the peoples will praise you, O God,
throughout the generations.

Pause

We breathe these words out of the Silence within us, into the Silence beyond us...

We too praise you, O God,
for the gift of yourself in the infant king:
Jesus, sovereign ruler of all,
in whom is our royal destiny too:
celebrants at the banquet of heaven,
guests at the great marriage feast,
gloriously singing in triumphal procession,
our ancestors and descendants with us,
joyful in the communion of saints.

Pause

Dear God, we offer you our lives this day,
the gift of love in our hearts and our loins,
the incense of prayer, the myrrh of our suffering,
the gold of all that we hold most dear,
that you may create, through our loyal obedience,
such wonders as pass our imagining.

Silence

Lift up our hearts, O glorious God, **and renew in us the hope of
a marvellous destiny, a life of incomparable splendour,
crowned with the love and peace that pass understanding.**

46   The God of the powers

*That we may delve the paradoxes of energy and stillness, of safety and risk; and that
we may dare to live without fortresses.*

God is our refuge and strength,
a very present help in time of trouble.
Therefore we shall not be afraid,
even though the earth be moved,
even though the mountains should crumble and fall into the sea,
even though the waters should foam and rage,
assault the cliffs and make them shudder.

…in the Spirit that stirs amongst us the kaleidoscope of Jesus.

Pause

There is a river whose streams make glad the city of God.
Here is God's dwelling place and it will stand firm.
God's rescue dawns like the morning light,
God's voice echoes through every land.
When powerful nations panic and totter
and the whole world comes crashing down,

**You are for us the God of the powers,
a safe stronghold, the God of all peoples.**

Pause

Come and see, stand in awe
at the powerful things God will do on earth,
putting an end to all war in the world,
breaking the bow, shattering the spear into splinters,
throwing our weapons on the fire.
"Be still and know that I am God:
exalted among the nations,
my name known at last on the earth."

**You are for us the God of the powers,
a safe stronghold, the God of all peoples.**

Silence

At the still centre of the turning world, **may we simply rest and
be, trusting again the promise that all shall be made new
in the bringing of the powers of this world to serve the
purposes of God's greater peace.**

We breathe these words out of the Silence within us, into the Silence beyond us...

47   The worship of the people of God

That we may use our power to serve others and enable their wellbeing.

Clap your hands, all you peoples:
cry aloud to God with shouts of joy.
Approach the presence of God with awe,
the guardian of all that is coming to be.

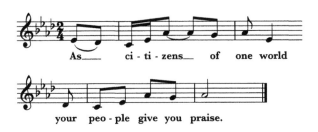

As___ ci - ti - zens___ of one world
your peo - ple give you praise.

Pause

O God you have called us to serve one another,
that we may embody your glory.
You have made us but stewards of your gifts,
that we may not boast and be proud.
You have loved us and blessed us with a goodly heritage,
overflowing with all that we need.

**As citizens of one world
your people give you praise.**

Pause

Let us join the procession in praise of your name,
with trumpets and horns and the sound of rejoicing.
We sing of our gratitude and are glad in your presence,
we your trustees take your name as our own.

Pause

For you are the guardian of the earth:
let us relish your name with well-wrought psalm.   >

...in the Spirit that stirs amongst us the kaleidoscope of Jesus.

You are the Judge of all the peoples,
wise and just in your dealings.

**As citizens of one world
your people give you praise.**

Pause

Those who give counsel gather together
as the people of the God of Abraham.
For even the mighty ones of the earth
are become the servants of God,
the God who is greatly to be praised.

**As citizens of one world
your people give you praise.**

Silence

Living, loving God, **draw the peoples of faith closer together,
ancient and ever new, that we may worship you today in
spirit and in truth.**

48   The City of God

*For the cities of the world; for Jerusalem; and for the city that influences us most
directly.*

"O God, you are greatly to be praised
in the city of your dwelling place.
High and beautiful is the holy mountain:
it is the joy of the whole earth."

Pause

"Here on Mount Zion stands the city
where you reign with just and steady hand.
Your rule is firm and secure,
strong as the walls and ramparts."

Pause

"Strangers who approach are amazed,
the powerful of the earth are dumbfounded.

We breathe these words out of the Silence within us, into the Silence beyond us...

Trembling takes hold of the proud,
anguish seizes the hostile,
like the howl of the harsh east wind
that splinters the ships on the rocks."

Pause

"We call your mercies to mind,
here in the midst of your temple.
You govern the peoples with justice,
even to the ends of the earth."

Pause

"Pilgrim, walk round the city,
count all her towers,
examine her walls with care,
consider well her strongholds."

Pause

"So may we tell those who come after,
that here they may rest secure,
for our God reigns for ever and ever,
who will guide us to all eternity."

Pause

Such was the place of your worship and dwelling,
sacred, O God, to your people of old.
Now may you dwell in each of our hearts,
may every city be the place of your dwelling.

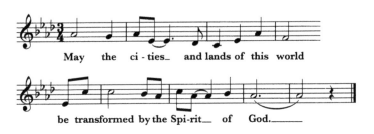

Pause

...in the Spirit that stirs amongst us the kaleidoscope of Jesus.

So may we worship you in spirit and truth,
may recognize you in streets and in squares,
in a common life of justice and peace,
in compassion and freedom under the law.

Pause

Bring the light, O God, that will one day shine
brighter than the sun and the moon and the stars,
the light of the Christ to illumine the dark.

**May the cities and lands of this world
be transformed by the Spirit of God.**

Silence

Gracious God, **calling us to the freedom of your city, so
shape our lives in the ways of justice that we may become
worthy of that citizenship that you have bestowed upon
us, in the communion of your saints and in the fellowship
of Yeshua the just.**

49   The hollowness of wealth

That we may locate true wealth and live wisely.

Hear this, all you peoples;
listen, inhabitants of the world,
all children of the earth,
both rich and poor together.

Pause

My mouth shall speak wisdom,
the thoughts of my heart be full of understanding.
I shall reveal the secret of a riddle,
unfolding a mystery to the sound of the lyre.

Pause

Why should I be afraid in times of trouble,
when the cruel and the greedy triumph,

We breathe these words out of the Silence within us, into the Silence beyond us...

those who put their trust in great wealth,
and boast of the abundance of their riches?

Where your trea-sure is,

there will your heart be al - so.

Pause

No one may ransom a sister or brother,
no one give God a price for them,
so that they may live for ever
and never see the grave:
to ransom their lives is so costly
we must abandon the idea for ever.

Pause

For we see the prosperous die,
and perish with the foolish and ignorant,
leaving their wealth to others.
The tomb is their home for ever,
their dwelling through all generations,
despite their estates named after them.
The wealthy in all their pomp –
they are just like the beasts – they perish.

**Where your treasure is,
there will your heart be also.**

Pause

This is the lot of the arrogant,
who are pleased with their words
and trust in themselves.
They are destined to die like sheep:
death is their shepherd,
they canot avoid their end.   >

...in the Spirit that stirs amongst us the kaleidoscope of Jesus.

Their good looks will fade in the tomb,
and their grandeur will follow them.

Pause

But God will ransom my life,
God will snatch me from the power of the grave.
I shall not be afraid when neighbours grow rich,
when the wealth of their households increases.
For they will take nothing away when they die,
nor will their wealth go down with them.

**Where your treasure is,
there will your heart be also.**

Pause

Though they thought highly of themselves while they lived,
and were praised for their worldly success,
they will go to the company of their ancestors,
who will never again see the sun.
The wealthy in all their pomp –
they are just like the beasts – they perish.

**Where your treasure is,
there will your heart be also.**

Silence

Living God, **may our contemplation of death free us from
envy and greed, that we may be content to travel light in
this world, undistracted by the babel of possessions and
in the Spirit of the One who had nowhere to lay his head.**

50   The judgment of God

For discerning judgment, divine and human.

From the midst of the glory of the sun,
from the mountain top of your appearing,
you come to us in perfect beauty,
the Judge of the earth doing all things well.

We breathe these words out of the Silence within us, into the Silence beyond us...

Pause

You come to us, you do not keep silent,
you sear us with the flames of your truth,
you devour the chaff of our sins:
awesome is this face of your love.

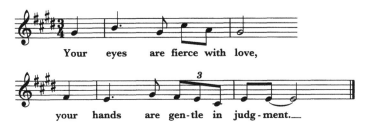

Your eyes are fierce with love,

your hands are gen-tle in judg-ment.___

Pause

We have failed to worship you in truth,
we have been disloyal to your covenant,
content with repeating mere words,
self-important in the display of our ceremonies.

Pause

We have not obeyed your will,
colluding with those who thieve and betray,
loosening our tongues in slander and gossip,
even lying against kith and kin.

Pause

Open our eyes and ears, O God,
we who have been so blind and deaf,
seduced by the glamour and dazzle around us,
lulled by the weavers of magic with words.

Your eyes are fierce with love,
your hands are gentle in judgment.

Pause

We are no better than your people of old,
who sought to please you with smoking sacrifice,   >

...in the Spirit that stirs amongst us the kaleidoscope of Jesus.

thinking you relished animals' flesh,
that this was the worship you craved.

Pause

But all the beasts of the forest are yours,
and so are the cattle on a thousand hills;
you know all the birds of the air,
the grasshoppers of the field are in your sight.

Pause

From your heart come the very gifts that we bring you,
all things come to us from out of your hand.
You give them to us to enjoy
and to share with others in need.

**Your eyes are fierce with love,
your hands are gentle in judgment.**

Pause

Sacrificial love is the altar of worship
where you touch the lives of the needy,
humbled as we are by all that you give us,
judged by those more generous than we.

Pause

Renew in us the covenant of old,
may we be faithful to the promises we made,
the vows over gifts to follow your way,
to embody your truth and your justice.

**Your eyes are fierce with love,
your hands are gentle in judgment.**

Pause

You thunder so fiercely in love for us,
you whisper so gently in judgment,
lowering the walls of defence
that surround our self-centred complaints.

Pause

We breathe these words out of the Silence within us, into the Silence beyond us...

So often we live for ourselves,
indifferent to the needs of the oppressed,
passing by the homeless under the arches,
refusing to hear how you judge us through them.

**Your eyes are fierce with love,
your hands are gentle in judgment.**

Pause

Turn us around, compassionate Judge,
show us the face of your pain:
it is we who add to your burden,
as you endure the cost of our redeeming.

Pause

In the days of our need we cry out to you,
offering our sorrowing hearts,
trusting that you will forgive us,
and refine us in the flame of your love.

**Your eyes are fierce with love,
your hands are gentle in judgment.**

Silence

Come, fierce and fiery Lover, **with burning coals and purge
our lips; come with the judgment that saves and gives us
back our sense of worth because it matters what we do;
come with passionate desire and sweep us into your arms;
come with the love that will not let us go.**

51   The utter mercy of God

For penitence with dignity; for joy through compunction.

Enfold me in your love, dear God,
yet pierce my heart with your mercy.
In the cascading of your compassion
scour away all that offends.
Wash me thoroughly from my wickedness,
and cleanse me from my sin.

...in the Spirit that stirs amongst us the kaleidoscope of Jesus.

Pause

My failures weigh heavy on my heart,
my sin confronts me at the turning of the road.
Against you alone I have sinned, my Beloved,
doing what is evil and causing more harm.
In the eyes of my victims your judgment is clear:
there is nothing I can claim in your presence.

Create in me a clean heart, O God,
and renew a right spirit within me.

Pause

I was formed in the midst of a world gone wrong,
from the moment of my conceiving I breathed my ancestors' sin.
The truths to which I am blind are hidden so deep, so secretly:
bring the light of your wisdom to the depths of my heart.

Create in me a clean heart, O God,
and renew a right spirit within me.

Pause

Bathe me in water that is fresh from the spring,
wash me and I shall be whiter than snow.
Make me hear of joy and gladness,
that the bones which you have broken may dance again.
Turn your face from my twists and deceits,
blot out all my misdeeds.

Create in me a clean heart, O God,
and renew a right spirit within me.

Pause

We breathe these words out of the Silence within us, into the Silence beyond us...

Cast me not away from your presence,
and take not your Holy Spirit from me.
Give me the comfort of your help again,
and strengthen me with your courage and hope.

**Create in me a clean heart, O God,
and renew a right spirit within me.**

Pause

Then I shall teach your ways to those around me,
and others will be converted to your path.
Deliver us all from guilt of bloodshed,
for you are the God of the world that is coming.
In health and truth we shall sing of your justice.
When you open my lips, my mouth shall sing for love
    of your name.

**Create in me a clean heart, O God,
and renew a right spirit within me.**

Pause

For you desire no animal sacrifices,
no formal gifts out of mere duty.
You do not delight in burnt offerings,
nothing from our wealth can buy your favour.
The sacrifice you ask is a troubled spirit;
it is my pride that must yield.

Pause

My broken and contrite heart I bring,
so foolish, self-centred, and vain;
and yet it is all that I have.
Even this gift you will not despise,
for I hear again that you yearn for me,
with a love I can barely imagine.

**Create in me a clean heart, O God,
and renew a right spirit within me.**

Pause

...in the Spirit that stirs amongst us the kaleidoscope of Jesus.

I give you this day the whole of my being,
dependent as I am on the gift of your grace.
Free me from the desire to dominate,
that my giving may not overwhelm or appease.
May my heart be spontaneously generous,
spreading delight and mutual embrace.
Such is the way of the city of peace,
whose walls you call us to build.

Silence

Take us to yourself, compassionate God, **we who hurt so
much in the depths of our being, caught up in the pain
of life, and so often inflicting yet more on to others,
embrace us with the hands that show the mark of the
nails, your love swallowing up all our sin and pride.
So we pray that broken bones may joy, in the dance of
Yeshua, who embodies your redeeming power.**

52   The lie and the truth

*That we may resist the temptation to deceive by a cloak of fine phrases; and in
solidarity with prophets who pull no punches.*

So often the powerful ones of the world
seem to boast of their mischief and pride.
They trust in the abundance of wealth,
they take perverse delight in their greed.

Pause

They contrive destroying slanders:
their tongues cut sharp like a razor.
In love with evil they refuse the good:
telling lies, they are far from the truth.
They love words that harm and devour,
and every deceit of the tongue.

Pause

We breathe these words out of the Silence within us, into the Silence beyond us…

They step on one another as they climb to power,
they thrust the weak to the gutter;
seducing the gullible in the magic of words,
they trample the truth in pursuit of ambition.

Pause

O God, break them down utterly,
uproot them from the land of the living,
topple them from their babel of lies,
throw them down to the dust.

Pause

Yet so often we are the powerful,
if only with family and friends.
We wound with whispers of gossip,
mockery and scorn in our hearts,
bitterness souring our lips.

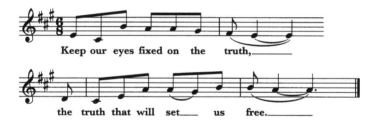

Keep our eyes fixed on the truth,
the truth that will set us free.

Pause

We have not trusted your goodness, O God,
our hearts have not been grateful.
We have not glorified your name,
either by word or by deed.

**Keep our eyes fixed on the truth,
the truth that will set us free.**

Pause

...in the Spirit that stirs amongst us the kaleidoscope of Jesus.

Too easy to call on you to destroy,
hard to be humbled by words that are true.
Even as we cry for the righting of wrongs,
for the destruction of those who harm others,
those who crush the weak and defenceless,
so we know that revenge solves nothing,
annihilation reaping more violence still.

**Keep our eyes fixed on the truth,
the truth that will set us free.**

Pause

May your Spirit go deeper within us,
purging our hearts, burning the impure.
Hold at bay our murderous words,
set us on the way of your truth and your word.
May we strive with the angel of justice,
till our faces are etched in the fierceness of love.

**Keep our eyes fixed on the truth,
the truth that will set us free.**

Pause

Keep before us the vision of a life that is whole:
may we no longer grasp at material things.
Like a green tree may we spread out our branches,
to shield the passerby from the heat,
offering the traveller refreshment and rest,
in quietness and confidence living for others,
people of truth and compassion,
oases of God in the most barren of lands.

Silence

Living One, **give us courage always to be loyal to the truth,
to follow wherever the way may lead, costly though it be,
trusting that the goal is none other than life with you.**

We breathe these words out of the Silence within us, into the Silence beyond us...

53   Flesh of our flesh

In solidarity with fools and clowns, and with those who care for the flesh — of earth,
of bodies; and for healing intimacy in the flesh.

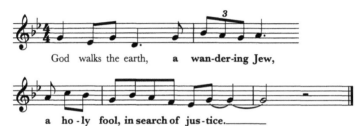

God walks the earth,   **a   wan-der-ing Jew,**

a   ho - ly   fool, in search of jus-tice.

Pause

Acid in the rain shrivels the leaves,
the wind rattles in the city's throat,
cancerous fish float down the rivers,
even the innocent grass is corrupted.

Pause

We have become as appetites in nightmares,
as horses of apocalypse with thundering hooves,
like monsters with ravening jaws,
devouring what was given us to cherish.

Pause

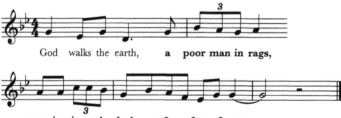

God walks the earth,   **a   poor man in rags,**

peer-ing in-to the dark-ness for a face of trust.

Pause

We have raped the good earth and her peoples,
tearing them apart to satisfy greed.   >

...in the Spirit that stirs amongst us the kaleidoscope of Jesus.

We have relished the flesh of our neighbours,
like lions tearing their prey.

Pause

The powerful prepare a cannibal feast,
harsh eyes glint in the sharpening knives.
They have become as flesh-eating gods;
we, blind consumers, we follow them.

Pause

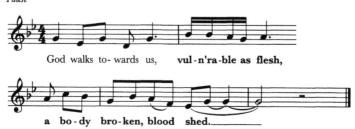

God walks to-wards us,   **vul-n'ra-ble as flesh,**

a bo-dy bro-ken, blood shed.

Pause

Weighed down with bloodlust our footing slips,
we begin to drown in the floods of despair.
O God, grasp the hand stretched out in panic,
before we vanish for ever and are no more seen.

Pause

Forgetting the early days of our pain,
afraid of the intimacy we desperately crave,
we have speared the flesh of our neighbour,
refusing to draw near in healing embrace.

Silence

**Intimate God, flesh of our flesh, earth of our earth, reveal to
us the anger and malice, the greed and pride, that mask our
pain; enable us to withdraw the spear of our revenge from
the flesh of others, and from your flesh, O God. Enclose our
hurt in your side that we have wounded, and draw us closer
to one another in compassion and forgiveness, dependent
utterly on your mercy and acceptance.**

We breathe these words out of the Silence within us, into the Silence beyond us...

54   A cry of complaint

For the right use of power; for honesty in protest and complaint; and in solidarity with those struggling for dignity whose lives have been diminished by the powerful.

Helpless, hemmed in, we are trapped by the powerful;
the insolent lash out with their tongue.
The ruthless sweep away what we thought were our homes,
the ignorant blame us because we are poor.

Pause

O God, are you not more powerful than they?
Why do you not speed them down to their doom?
Sweep them away who would treat us as worthless,
that we may feast our eyes on their fall.

O— God,— act soon,—
O— God,— act soon.

Pause

What kind of God are you, my helper?
Why do you not show the strength of your arm?
You have promised to put an end to their power,
yet the promise remains unfulfilled.

O God, act soon. *(If sung, repeat.)*

Pause

Just once we have seen the world overturned,
your chosen One vulnerable yet strong,
absorbing the evil thrown by the powerful,
triumphant through death in the ways of your love.

Pause

...in the Spirit that stirs amongst us the kaleidoscope of Jesus.

To keep trust with you taxes our faith:
How can we praise you with hearts that are sad?
Why do you let the powerful still trample us down?
How can we believe when a child screams with pain?

O God, act soon. (*If sung, repeat.*)

Pause

Yet still we desire the face of your love,
to praise you in wonder for all that you do,
to know the scales fall from our eyes,
to dance the way of freedom hand in hand with the powerful.

Silence

Spirit of the living God, **deftly and quickly probe the
diseased heart of our world, and dissolve the evil
encrusted there, that healed of our wounds and rescued
from our wrong, we may no longer oppress but set one
another free, after the pattern of the One who brought
liberation and meaning to humankind.**

55   Days of betrayal in the city

*In solidarity with those suffering the pain of betrayal; and for the restoration of broken
friendships.*

In these days of turmoil,
of restlessness and complaint,
we accuse and betray one another,
lashing out in the fury of pain.

Pause

We set on one another with greed,
we persecute with baying and clamour.
We see slaughter, and our hearts writhe,
the horrors of dying overwhelm us.

Pause

We breathe these words out of the Silence within us, into the Silence beyond us…

Violence reigns in the streets of the city,
vicious dogs snarl at the stranger.
Fraud flits through the market place,
greed wins softly behind baize doors.

Pause

My eyes flash wild with horror,
my limbs quake and I cannot still them.
My heart grows cold through fear,
the ice of death grips me.

Pause

I said, O for the wings of a dove,
that I might fly away and be at rest.
I yearn to flee to the mountains,
to make my dwelling in the wilderness.

Pause

O for a refuge of peace,
out of the blast of slander,
far from the tempest of calumny,
from the harsh wind of the double-tongued.

Pause

For it was not an enemy who taunted me,
or I might have been able to bear it.
It was not a foe who was so insolent,
or I might have hidden myself away.

Pause

But it was you, my equal,
my companion, my familiar friend.
Ours was a pleasant harmony
as we walked side by side to the house of our God.

Pause

You have not kept your word,
you have no love of God in your heart,   >

...in the Spirit that stirs amongst us the kaleidoscope of Jesus.

you have broken the covenant you have sworn,
deserting those who were at peace with you.

Pause

Your mouth is smooth as butter,
yet war is in your heart.
Your words are softer than oil,
yet your sword flashes in the dark.

Pause

My heart cries out in anguish and grief,
Get out of my sight, you hypocrite!
Go down in terror to your grave, you betrayer,
for you have worked treachery among us.

Pause

Yet how I yearn for the healing of pain,
for a love grown cold to kindle again.
I pray to you, God, that we may be reconciled,
drawn again to the way of your justice.

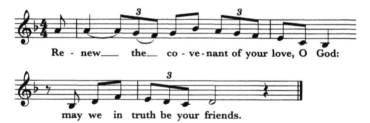

Re - new___ the___ co - ve - nant of your love, O God:
may we in truth be your friends.

Pause

Humble the pride in us all,
your love and your power consistent forever.
May we lift the weight of oppression,
may our enemies release the spring of their traps.

Renew the covenant of your love, O God:
may we in truth be your friends.

Pause

We breathe these words out of the Silence within us, into the Silence beyond us...

I cast my burden on you, O God,
and you will sustain and encourage me.
I shall call from the midst of my groaning,
you will redeem me to healing and peace.

Renew the covenant of your love, O God:
may we in truth be your friends.

Pause

My heart has been so constricted,
my affections so easily hurt.
Yet your arms are wide and welcoming,
in your presence we are relaxed,
and feel most strangely at home.

Renew the covenant of your love, O God:
may we in truth be your friends.

Silence

Living God, **whose love has been betrayed and denied over**
and over again, whose covenants have been torn apart,
forgive our lack of trust and loyalty, and call us to yourself
again, we who bear the marks of Judas and of Cain.

56   Empty and afraid, yet trusting

In solidarity with those betrayed before they were born; and for trust in the only One
who does not know how not to love.

How can I put my trust in you, O God?

How can I praise you when I   do not feel your pre-sence?

How can   I trust and not be a - fraid?   >

...in the Spirit that stirs amongst us the kaleidoscope of Jesus.

What more— can my mor-tal flesh suf - fer?

Pause

The echo of the infant sounds,
the unwanted child cries for affection.
The giver of my life is my adversary,
persistently pressing upon me.

Pause

I feel nothing but hatred towards me,
I stand on no ground of my worth.
Are my tears counted in your flask,
are my hurts noted in your book?

Pause

I feel I am dying before I am born,
my feet slip from under me.
Empty and distressed, I am nothing,
yet I yearn for life to the full.
From the midst of my wasteland of needs never met,
knowing my emptiness, I wait to be filled.

Pause

Rain on the desert of my terror,
fill my empty soul to overflowing,
that I may delight in the life that you give,
a river that will flow to those who are parched.

Pause

I shall put my trust in you, O God,

I shall praise— you— for—— your— pre - sence.

We breathe these words out of the Silence within us, into the Silence beyond us...

I shall trust and not be a - fraid:

what can mor-tal flesh__ do to__ me?

Silence

As Mary opened her will, her heart, and her womb, **giving her emptiness to be filled with your living presence, that the beloved of your heart might be born through her, so, giver of life, fill us with trust and expectancy, that we may dare to be empty and open before you, that, being born in us, you may displace all our fear and distress.**

57   Identity in the city

In solidarity with those under stress in the city; and that we may have a welcoming heart for strangers.

The crowds on the pavement jostle me,
the drone of the traffic wearies me.
In the shadow of your wings I find refuge,
beneath your hovering presence I find peace.

Be ex - al - ted, O God,__ in your lit-tle ones,__

let your glo - ry shine in our streets.__

Pause

...in the Spirit that stirs amongst us the kaleidoscope of Jesus.

The faces of strangers stare through me;
aimless I wander, there is nowhere I belong.
In the compassion of your face I find mercy,
in you and you alone do I know who I am.

Be exalted, O God, in your little ones,
let your glory shine in our streets.

Pause

I fear the hard glint in their eyes,
whose teeth snap from behind locked doors.
In the faithfulness of your promise I trust,
giving us freedom and wide open space.

Be exalted, O God, in your little ones,
let your glory shine in our streets.

Pause

Their faces look careworn and hollow,
grey like the evening and houses around.
Let melody break through the gloom,
the trumpet and flute to awaken the morning.

Be exalted, O God, in your little ones,
let your glory shine in our streets.

Pause

Compassion and care is locked in each one of us,
faithful and kind we all long to be.
Melt the fear in our hearts of the stranger we meet,
that we may open our arms in vulnerable embrace.

Silence

God of freedom, **unlock the hearts of your people who strive**
to be human in the city, that your love may cast out fear,
that we may know again that we belong to one another
and to you.

We breathe these words out of the Silence within us, into the Silence beyond us...

58   The justice of vengeance or of restoration?

That we may recognize the depths of our rage; that those who have suffered at others'
hands may in time offer forgiveness; and that the power of anger may be channelled in
work for justice.

Rage rises within me as I look at our world,
at the evil, the pain, the death all around me.
Rulers of the nations, do you decree what is just?
Do you judge the peoples of the earth with justice?
No, you are swayed too often by power and by greed,
you do not repent the violence you have wrought.

Pause

The wicked are estranged even from the womb,
they are liars that go astray from the day of their birth.
They are poisonous with the venom of snakes,
like the deaf asp that stops its ears,
that will not heed the voice of the charmers,
though the binder of spells be skilful.

Pause

"Break their teeth, O God, in their mouths,
shatter the jaws of the young lions, O God.
Let them vanish like water that drains away,
let them be trodden down and wither like grass,
like a woman's miscarriage that passes away,
like an abortive birth that sees not the sun."

Pause

"Let them be cut down like thorns before they know it,
like brambles swept angrily aside.
The just shall rejoice when they see your vengeance,
they will wash their feet in the blood of the wicked.
People will say, There is a reward for the virtuous,
for the wicked there comes the judgment of God."

Pause

Purify me, refine me, scour me, implacable God,
take away my malice and hatred, my bitterness of memory.   >

...in the Spirit that stirs amongst us the kaleidoscope of Jesus.

Stop my rejoicing at the pain of their doom,
even the worst of those who oppress me.

Pause

Only so can I hope to stand in your presence,
for you read all my ways and my heart,
all its murky unease and its fickleness.
We are all unjust, disordered, and lawless,
hardly sensing the lure of your love:
we can but know it as wrath.

The fa-ces of___ the down-trod-den ac-cuse us:___
on - ly the des - ti - tute can re - deem.

Pause

Withhold your light – it will blind us,
yet let us not perish in the dark and the cold.
Tenderly warm the hearts that are frozen,
till the depths of the darkness dazzle.

**The faces of the downtrodden accuse us:
only the destitute can redeem.**

Pause

Have mercy upon us, have mercy,
criminals and judges with the roughest of justice.
No plea can we enter before you.
It is the deprived and homeless, ragged and shivering,
who stand in the court to accuse us.

**The faces of the downtrodden accuse us:
only the destitute can redeem.**

Pause

We breathe these words out of the Silence within us, into the Silence beyond us...

Those on the edge, unkempt, unacceptable,
they are the ones who show us your face.
And, deep within, is a child who is shunned,
whom we treat as our enemy, battered and bruised.

**The faces of the downtrodden accuse us:
only the destitute can redeem.**

Pause

O when will we learn to stretch out our arms,
to receive from the outcasts and scapegoats
the redeeming embrace and the melting of tears:
in them and them only is our last dying hope.

Silence

Living God, whose holiness in our midst is known as justice,
**harness the seething power of our anger, the whirlpools of
rage, the waves of indignation, and channel this awesome
energy in the ways of your justice, in Yeshua the just, our
doom and our deliverance.**

59   For the imprisoned and tortured

*In solidarity with those in pain inflicted by torturers; and with those who work for the
release of the unjustly imprisoned.*

Cruel men roam the streets in the darkness;
howling like dogs, they prowl round the city.
They snarl and snap as they seize their prey,
they growl if their desire is frustrated.

Judge and sa-viour of the world,

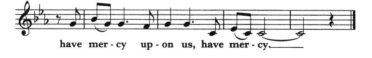

have mer-cy up-on us, have mer-cy.

...in the Spirit that stirs amongst us the kaleidoscope of Jesus.

Pause

I pray for the tortured and victims of malice,
for those imprisoned for no fault of their own.
My feelings run high – God forgive my excess –
but why is your mercy and justice delayed?

**Judge and saviour of the world,
have mercy upon us, have mercy.**

Pause

Deliver the oppressed from the terrors of evil,
free them from those who relish their pain.
For the savage stir up violence against them,
waiting to knock at the door before dawn.

**Judge and saviour of the world,
have mercy upon us, have mercy.**

Pause

They keep the peacemakers distracted and tense,
breaking their spirit, mauling their flesh,
and all for no sin or transgression,
or any crime of which they are guilty.

**Judge and saviour of the world,
have mercy upon us, have mercy.**

Pause

The oppressed look to you, God their strength:
arise from your sleep and do not delay.
May your eyes flash with judgment and truth,
silencing the treacherous and false.

**Judge and saviour of the world,
have mercy upon us, have mercy.**

Pause

Show them the height of their pride,
reveal to them the lie they have lived.
Bind them so that their power is removed,
bring to their eyes the tears of repentance.

We breathe these words out of the Silence within us, into the Silence beyond us...

**Judge and saviour of the world,
have mercy upon us, have mercy.**

Pause

In your great love run to meet those who suffer,
show them the ruin of those who oppressed them.
Yet slay not the wicked, copying their ways:
make them powerless to harm, and bring them to truth.

**Judge and saviour of the world,
have mercy upon us, have mercy.**

Pause

O God, from the depth of your pain-bearing love,
break the cycle of our wraths and our sorrows.
For you are not a God who destroys,
you seek always to redeem and renew.

**Judge and saviour of the world,
have mercy upon us, have mercy.**

Pause

So I shall sing of your love and your power,
I shall sing in the morning and tell of your goodness.
For you have been our strong tower,
a sure refuge in the day of distress.
I shall sing your praise, O God my strength,
for you are my kraal for ever.

Silence

O God, **seeking always to create at the heart of our evil
and pain, sustaining life in all your creatures and present
with them in their distress, let us not fall beyond your
reach, and raise us by forgiveness and healing to a new
love for one another and for you.**

...in the Spirit that stirs amongst us the kaleidoscope of Jesus.

60   The war of the unholy

*That fanatics may laugh; that the military mind may be sober; that we may never treat
our opponents as less than human; and that the human race may grow in wisdom.*

Echoes of warriors sound through the years:
"We are zealous for God, holy our war.
We shout for you, our God, resplendent in armour,
your banner unfurled as we sweep into battle."

Pause

"The fleet sails and our eyes shine;
our cause is just, our God is with us.
You are angry, O God, with our enemies –
we can slaughter them all, feeling no shame."

Pause

"O God, do not be lukewarm and bland:
be provoked still by our enemies.
Do not storm out of sight through the dust,
leaving us to tremble in fear."

Pause

"Yet you vanished from our sight: where were you?
You betrayed your promise to be with us.
Wounded and weary, we limp back defeated;
bewildered, we cling to your flag."

Turn us, O God, from our slaugh-ter,
yet keep us striv-ing for truth.

Pause

We breathe these words out of the Silence within us, into the Silence beyond us…

Are we far from the cry of the zealot,
from the mob who follow the drumbeat?
So easy to spit out the slogans of hate,
to become like those who oppose us.

Pause

So easy to swoop on the spoil,
to claim another parcel of land,
to grind the poor to submission,
to be drunk on the shedding of blood.

**Turn us, O God, from our slaughter,
yet keep us striving for truth.**

Pause

Though we cling to belief in your blessing,
you are the God of island and continent,
and we but one race spread over the earth,
not one of us favoured above all the rest.

Pause

Our common greed and our fear of each other,
our desire for mammon grown to excess,
our zeal for being right and others so wrong:
these are our enemies now.

**Turn us, O God, from our slaughter,
yet keep us striving for truth.**

Pause

We shall endure by your name alone,
content to be trustees of the earth,
to live in justice with our neighbours,
the power of the fanatic taken away.

Silence

Forgive us, O God, **for stubbornly continuing to picture you
with iron fist, for claiming that you are always on our side.
Renew the vision of you as a wise and just guardian of
the people, curbing the power of those who would harm,**

...in the Spirit that stirs amongst us the kaleidoscope of Jesus.

bearing in yourself what is unresolved. **Keep us steady and true, that those we now perceive as our enemies may come to be our partners in the work of your creating.**

61   Hope in God alone

That we may let go of the trivial, the delusory, and all self-centred desires; and that we may be open to the truth of the living God.

I stand on a rock at the edge of the sea,
the wind hurls the spray at my face.
The depths of the ocean swell heavy with menace,
tides of despair drown my heart in the deep.

In our des - pair   give us   hope;

in our death   give us   life.

Pause

I collapse by a rock in the wastes of the desert,
the noonday sun scorches my skin.
Waves of heat beat upon my weary heart,
my eyes stare at the dry bones around me.

**In our despair give us hope;
in our death give us life.**

Pause

The spirit has gone out of me,
my self-centred desires are as nothing.
I have come to the brink of inner death,
I descend to the depths of my doom.

We breathe these words out of the Silence within us, into the Silence beyond us...

In our despair give us hope;
in our death give us life.

Pause

Rescue me, O God, pity the pitiful,
lend me the strength of your tower of rock.
Succour me under your hovering wings,
welcome me into your hospitable home.

In our despair give us hope;
in our death give us life.

Pause

My vows lie broken, yet I would serve you,
my heart's desire is to love your name.
May the angels of mercy and truth stand by me,
the hand of deliverance heal me.

In our despair give us hope;
in our death give us life.

Pause

With a glimmer of hope I remember your love,
the love that finds me even as I search.
You have entered the void of my despair,
meeting me in the very place of your absence.

In our despair give us hope;
in our death give us life.

Pause

The music of praise sounds again in my heart,
the words of rejoicing take shape on my lips.
You renew my strength to fulfil what I promise,
the name that you give me endures through the years.

Silence

Implacable God, **face us with the truth that we have no**
power of ourselves, raise us from the depths of exhaustion
and despair, and renew in us the spirit of life and hope.

...in the Spirit that stirs amongst us the kaleidoscope of Jesus.

62   Holding steadily to God

*For steady hands for delicate work; that we may be weaned from addiction to money;
and that we may be invigorated with a love of truth.*

In the depths of my being I become quiet and still:
I wait for you, my God, source of my salvation.
You are a sure and steady rock, watching over me,
so that I shall not fall to my doom.

Pause

I am afraid of the powerful who overwhelm me,
bullies who encircle me, towering above me.
They are like a battering ram to a crumbling wall,
they exult in their lust for destruction.

Pause

Their delight is only in lies;
the truth is far from their hearts.
They utter words that are softer than butter;
inwardly they do but curse.

Keep our eyes____ fixed on the goal,
Christ in us,____ the hope of our glo - ry.____

Pause

Nevertheless, I hold steadily to you:
you are my hope, my rock, my salvation.
In the stillness I wait for your presence:
you watch over me, I shall not fall to my doom.

Pause

We breathe these words out of the Silence within us, into the Silence beyond us...

In you, O God, is my health and glory,
the rock of my faith; in you is my trust.
I pour out my whole being in your presence:
in you I place all my hope.

Keep our eyes fixed on the goal,
Christ in us, the hope of our glory.

Pause

In very truth we are but a breath of wind:
faithless and fearful, we have betrayed you.
Put us in the balance and we can only rise:
we are lighter than a feather in the wind.

Pause

Let us not trust in extortion and robbery,
let us not put on the masks of vanity.
When riches and possessions increase,
let us not set our hearts upon them.

Keep our eyes fixed on the goal,
Christ in us, the hope of our glory.

Pause

Keep us from lusting for power,
betraying you again with our love of money,
trampling the face of the poor in the mire,
holding on to wealth by means of the lie.

Pause

Teach me again the truth of your name:
to you alone belongs power,
in you alone we find mercy,
in you alone is our hope.

Keep our eyes fixed on the goal,
Christ in us, the hope of our glory.

Silence

...in the Spirit that stirs amongst us the kaleidoscope of Jesus.

May the powerful of the land know their own failings and fears, **and recognize their need for forgiveness, that they may empower the oppressed, temper the law with mercy, and work for the common good, always holding before them the vision of the commonwealth of God.**

63   The city-dweller's desert

For contentment with simple things; for the befriending of the creatures of the night; and in solidarity with those in dry and dark places.

In the depths of my being you are my God,
at the rising of the sun I seek your face.
My heart thirsts for you, my flesh longs for you,
in a barren and dry land where no water is.

Pause

I search for you in unexpected places,
at the edges of the known, in the language of dreams,
in the wilderness of the city streets,
in the shacks where the destitute dwell.

**Sustain me through the dry places,
bring me to the beautiful country.**

Pause

We breathe these words out of the Silence within us, into the Silence beyond us...

There may I look long and lovingly,
there may I listen for the word beyond words,
there may I wait for a glimpse of your glory,
there may I utter strange songs of your praise.

**Sustain me through the dry places,
bring me to the beautiful country.**

Pause

For your love endures to the end,
it is better even than life itself.
So my lips will praise you,
and I shall lift up my hands in your name.

**Sustain me through the dry places,
bring me to the beautiful country.**

Pause

With food, shelter, and clothing we shall be content;
with simple dignity we shall be rich in friends.
The streets and squares of the city will be our meeting place,
among the trees of the parks we shall breathe free and play.

**Sustain me through the dry places,
bring me to the beautiful country.**

Pause

With manna in my exile you feed me,
with water springing up from parched land.
I am satisfied with a sumptuous feast,
my whole being resounds with murmurs of joy

**Sustain me through the dry places,
bring me to the beautiful country.**

Silence

Courage have I found to face the creatures of the night,
the terrible faces masking cries of abandonment,
swords that glint in the darkness protecting the weak,
jackals that swoop on those who dare near.

...in the Spirit that stirs amongst us the kaleidoscope of Jesus.

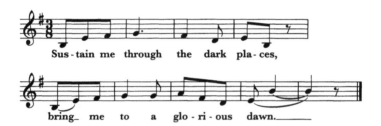

Pause

I am bewildered by mirrors distorting the truth,
lost before hallucinations spun in the heat.
Yet I shall trust you through the blindness of light,
through the delusions that threaten to destroy me.

**Sustain me through the dark places,
bring me to a glorious dawn.**

Pause

I hear your voice, "Do not be afraid."
You sustain me in the watches of the night.
Your hovering wings give me shade on my journey.
I stumble yet I trust you not to let go.

**Sustain me through the dark places,
bring me to a glorious dawn.**

Pause

The faces of terror will prove my friends yet,
guarding as they do my fragile soul-self,
waiting the calm word of the approach of true love,
wanting to be named as faithful and true.

**Sustain me through the dark places,
bring me to a glorious dawn.**

Pause

So I shall emerge to the place of rejoicing,
the child and the adult linked arm in arm.

We breathe these words out of the Silence within us, into the Silence beyond us...

We shall see your face in all your creatures,
we shall know the truth in our hearts.

Silence

Pioneer of the living way, **give us cour age to traverse the
waste and barren places, trusting that we shall come at
the last to our true home and to the city of our God.**

64   Bewildered by cruelty

*That we may recognize our wicked deeds and our hidden collusions; that we may
become aware of the motives we keep secret from ourselves; and in solidarity with the
makers and users of all kinds of surveillance, that the revelations of the camera may
serve justice and truth.*

Hear me, O God, from the depths of my being,
fearful as I am of being destroyed.
Who are these enemies that swirl around me,
who conspire against me in a hostile world?

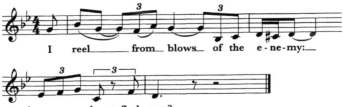

Pause

How have I released this torrent of abuse?
Whence come these arrows of bitter words?
Those whom I thought were my friends
pile all my faults on my tired spirit.

**I reel from blows of the enemy:
where can my heart find ease?**

Pause

...in the Spirit that stirs amongst us the kaleidoscope of Jesus.

No innocence, O God, would I pretend,
my failure and guilt are too real.
But it feels they were planning in secret,
ready to pounce from a place unseen.

**I reel from blows of the enemy:
where can my heart find ease?**

Pause

Through the years they smiled and spoke tenderly:
now the lash of their tongues is unleashed.
They have laid their mines with such skill –
they have even forgotten they did so –
and they blame me for stepping upon them.

**I reel from blows of the enemy:
where can my heart find ease?**

Silence

Perhaps they did not even know what they did,
so dark and deep is the human heart.
They dare not face the truth of their pain:
they seek revenge for hurts unremembered.

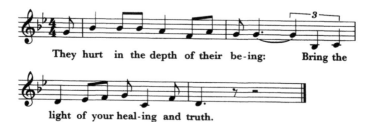

Pause

Deliver us, O God, from the paralysis of fear,
from the confusions of our minds and the turmoil of our hearts.
We are consumed with anxiety and dread,
the hovering unknown fills us with terror.

We breathe these words out of the Silence within us, into the Silence beyond us...

They hurt in the depth of their being:
Bring the light of your healing and truth.

Pause

The sky seems full of probing eyes,
an unseen lens orbits the earth,
ears hide in dim corners of the room,
the wavelengths carry our secret thoughts.

They hurt in the depth of their being:
Bring the light of your healing and truth.

Pause

Reveal them to themselves, O God,
bring them down for the evil they have spoken,
those who say they hate only my sin,
but who slay me in the name of your justice.

They hurt in the depth of their being:
Bring the light of your healing and truth.

Pause

Let the devices of our hearts be made known,
your arrows of truth piercing our confusions.
Reveal us in scorching light to one another,
that we may lay down our weapons and forgive.

They hurt in the depth of their being:
Bring the light of your healing and truth.

Pause

Even now we rejoice and give thanks to your name,
the distortions of our being are eased gently through judgment,
the fierceness of your love is holding us upright,
the light of your eyes shines with compassion and justice.

Silence

Dear God, **we bring to you everything of which we are**
unaware, the unknown murky devices of our fearful
hearts, the untapped sources of generosity and laughter,
the forgotten confusions and hurts from which come our

...in the Spirit that stirs amongst us the kaleidoscope of Jesus.

excessive anger, the unrealized capacity for truth and forbearance. Reveal us to ourselves and reassure us in the true humanity of Yeshua the just.

65   In gratitude for the generosity of God

That the hungry be satisfied; that the harvest be abundant; and that all humanity may reflect the generosity of God.

We praise you in your city, O God of justice;
we renew our vows in the sacred places.
For you meet us in the depth of our being,
when we come to confess all that is true of us.
When our misdeeds haunt us with their power,
your generous love sweeps them aside.

Let the peo - ple praise you,   O God:

let all cre - a - tion   praise you.

Pause

Blessed are those whom you choose as your friends,
who lodge with you in your house.
You empower them with talents and gifts,
you crown them with an abundance of life.

Pause

In dread deeds you will deliver us,
O God of our salvation,
for you are the hope of the ends of the earth,
and of the distant seas.

We breathe these words out of the Silence within us, into the Silence beyond us...

Let the people praise you, O God:
let all creation praise you.

Pause

By your strength you make the mountains rise,
by your power you gouge the valleys deep.
You still the raging of the seas,
the roaring of the waves,
and the tumult of the peoples.

Pause

Those who dwell at the ends of the earth
are held in awe at your wonders:
the dawn and the evening sing your praise,

Let the people praise you, O God:
let all creation praise you.

Pause

You tend the earth and you till it,
you make it rich and fertile.
Your clouds are full of water,
they provide rain for the swelling of grain.

Pause

You drench the furrows,
you level the ridges between,
you soften the soil with showers
and bless its early growth.

Let the people praise you, O God:
let all creation praise you.

Pause

You refresh hearts withered and dry,
you bring to life the land parched with drought.
You crown our years with good gifts,
the fruit trees drip with abundance.

Pause

...in the Spirit that stirs amongst us the kaleidoscope of Jesus.

The alpine pastures shimmer with green,
the hills are wreathed with dancing clouds.
The meadows are clothed with sheep,
and the valleys mantled with corn.

Let the people praise you, O God:
let all creation praise you.

Silence

Loving God, **ceaselessly redeeming and creating, astonish**
us with your abundant generosity, and still our hearts in
awe and wonder.

66   Symphony of praise

That praise be stirred in the human heart; and that God and humanity recognize each
other in the fellowship of pain.

Let the earth give praise to you, our Creator,
let all the peoples of the world give you praise.

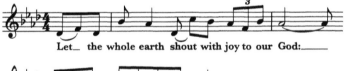

Let_ the whole earth shout with joy to our God:___

let all the peo-ple sing your praise.

Pause

Let psalms ring out to your glory,
for awesome indeed are your works.
Those who would defy you are brought low,
and the people fall silent in your presence.

Pause

Let the people you have redeemed give you praise:
marvellous are the deeds you have wrought for us.

We breathe these words out of the Silence within us, into the Silence beyond us...

**Let the whole earth shout with joy to our God:
let all the people sing your praise.**

Pause

You turned the water into dry land,
and we passed through the sea on foot.
So we rejoiced in your strength:
your redeeming power has no end.
Even though the rebellious rise,
your quiet strength quells them.

Pause

Let the people you have rescued give you praise,
let the sound of singing voices carry far.

**Let the whole earth shout with joy to our God:
let all the people sing your praise.**

Pause

You established us where we now dwell,
you keep us from all lasting harm.
Yet you test us as silver is tried,
you catch us in the nets of our weaving,
you let others ride over us roughshod,
you lay sharp torment on our loins.

Pause

There is no wealth or worldly applause
as we go through fire and water.
But you have borne our pain with us,
bringing us into a place both broad and free.

Pause

I too will add my morsel of praise
as I thank you for all you have done.

**Let the whole earth shout with joy to our God:
let all the people sing your praise.**

Pause

...in the Spirit that stirs amongst us the kaleidoscope of Jesus.

I have kept my vows in the teeth of distress,
tempted to hold back my offering.
But I bring my best gifts to your presence,
my possessions and talents, all of them are yours.

Pause

When I cherished evil you brought me low,
and turned my twisted heart to face you again.
You heard the deepest voice of my being,
faint as it was, unknown to my clamour,
and you responded with grace unpredictable,
you never ceased in your love and your care.

Silence

Let the wordless cries of creation, **and the shaped voices of
the people, let the deep sighs of each heart, and the
testimony of faithful lips, let all be joined in a harmony
of exultant praise to you, beloved God, for ever creating
and redeeming us.**

67   God's abundant blessings

That justice be done, and that the earth bring forth an abundance of harvest.

God, be gracious to us and bless us,
and show us the light of your countenance
and be merciful to us,
that your way may be known on earth,
your saving health among all nations.

We breathe these words out of the Silence within us, into the Silence beyond us...

Pause

Let the nations rejoice and be glad,
for you judge the people with wisdom,
and you guide the nations upon earth.

**Let the people praise you, O God,
let all the people praise you.**

Pause

Then will the earth bring forth the harvest,
and God, even our own God, will give us great blessing.
Dear God, you will bless us indeed,
and all the ends of the earth will praise your holy name.

**Let the people praise you, O God,
let all the people praise you.**

Silence

O God of wise judgment, **accepting us as we are and guiding
us in your ways, enable us so to appreciate your gifts
of the harvest that we may know them as a pledge of
abundant life and thank you as the source and goal of all
that is good.**

68 What kind of power?

*In solidarity with those bereaved of parents or partners; with the destitute and desolate;
and with those imprisoned.*

O God, humble and truthful,
scatter falsehood and bloated pride.
By the fierce light of your eyes
shrivel the power of the powers.

Pause

As smoke vanishes in the wind,
so they will be dispersed.
As wax sizzles in the flame,
so evil will squirm in your presence. >

…in the Spirit that stirs amongst us the kaleidoscope of Jesus.

But justice and truth will be glad,
they will exult and rejoice.

We— praise you, O God, for your power,
the power of the way of Christ,
we praise you, O God.

Pause

We sing to you, O God, we sing praise to your name.
We give you the glory in the midst of our desert.
You come with living water to dry and thirsty ground.
You are the father of the fatherless,
you are the mother of the orphans,
you uphold the cause of the widow,
you give voice to the cries of the poor.

Pause

You give the desolate a home to dwell in,
you bring prisoners out of the dungeon.
Only those who complain and rebel,
who resent second place to the outcast,
know the storms of the desert within them,
feel the sun scorching their pride.

Pause

Like your people of old we delight in you,
glad of the home and the land which you give us,
which you put in our hands to care for.

Pause

We breathe these words out of the Silence within us, into the Silence beyond us...

Marching out as you do in the wilderness,
still leading us on by the pillar of fire,
you stride on always before us,
preparing a place for your dwelling.

Pause

We bless you and give you thanks,
for you bear us as your burden.
You are to us a God who saves,
by your power we escape the pangs of death.

**We praise you, O God, for your power,
the power of the way of Christ,
we praise you, O God.**

Pause

Even the snow-capped mountains shrink in your presence,
all the wealth of the nations is as nothing before you.
The power of the haughty is a broken reed,
our silver and gold worthless on your scales.
You quieten our shouts of triumph and victory,
as we see your rain refreshing our enemies.

**We praise you, O God, for your power,
the power of the way of Christ,
we praise you, O God.**

Pause

Sing to God, far places of the earth,
sing praises to the God of the heavens,
who rides on the stormy wind,
whose voice thunders through the skies.

Pause

O God, you are awesome and terrible,
your light blinds even through clouds.
You give strength and power to your people,
to resist and scatter the relishers of war.

...in the Spirit that stirs amongst us the kaleidoscope of Jesus.

**We praise you, O God, for your power,
the power of the way of Christ,
we praise you, O God.**

Pause

Exuberant is our victory song,
yet we are no better than those who oppose us.
We too are greedy for spoil,
we too are self-righteous in slaughter.

Pause

Let us see you again as you came to us,
contracted to the span of a child,
helpless in the arms of his mother,
compassionate in bearing while pinned to a cross,
taking the trampling of blood
deep in the heart of your being,
breaking the barrier of death
to new and glorious life.

**We praise you, O God, for your power,
the power of the way of Christ,
we praise you, O God.**

Pause

We fall silent before the mystery of love,
this renouncing of power familiar so long,
this reversal of power that none can defeat,
this wonder we can scarcely believe.

Silence

Living God, **as we struggle to understand and use aright the
power that you entrust to us, set before us again the way
of Yeshua, and work through us in your Spirit, that we
may steward our power in ways that do not bind others
but free them to take their share in the inheritance of life.
May we grow tall but humble.**

We breathe these words out of the Silence within us, into the Silence beyond us...

69   Any hope for the earth?

In solidarity with those who heal the damage we do to planet earth; and that we may
willingly and graciously simplify our lives.

Save us, O God: we are perishing.
The seas are swelling and flooding the land.
The rivers sweep away the soil laid bare,
the algae thickens off the summer coasts.

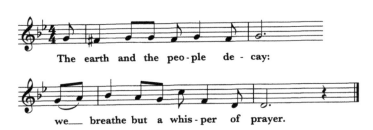

The earth and the peo-ple de - cay:
we__ breathe but a whis-per of prayer.

Pause

What is this weariness that grips us,
this cry of alarm that sticks in our throat,
the eye of conscience that no longer sees you,
the snap of hatred in those we thought wise?

The earth and the people decay:
we breathe but a whisper of prayer.

Pause

We shame and disgrace our ancestors,
we betray those who come after us,
we rape the earth who mothered us,
we mock the few who stand for truth,
we have become as strangers to our children,
we are like aliens from a planet far away.

The earth and the people decay:
we breathe but a whisper of prayer.

Pause

...in the Spirit that stirs amongst us the kaleidoscope of Jesus.

No longer is our word our bond;
we destroy trust by rumours and lies;
we find fault wherever we go,
we pillory those who are different.

The earth and the people decay:
we breathe but a whisper of prayer.

Pause

We throw all the blame on to foreigners,
or on those in positions of power.
In truth there are few who are innocent –
the humble, the needy, the oppressed –
and vengeance is a luxury now.
The bombs and guns of our fear
now destroy the earth and our neighbour.

The earth and the people decay:
we breathe but a whisper of prayer.

Pause

In despair we are trapped and brought low,
unaware and unable to change.
We have even forgotten there may be a God,
a power beyond our own to whom we could cry.

The earth and the people decay:
we breathe but a whisper of prayer.

Pause

In this our critical time,
is there a God who is good?
What price deliverance now,
as the very earth and the seas turn upon us?

The earth and the people decay:
we breathe but a whisper of prayer.

Pause

Pride, greed, and malice all mock at us:
inordinate selfishness cries out in triumph.

We breathe these words out of the Silence within us, into the Silence beyond us...

With insults we break others' hearts,
we trample the weak to the ground.

The earth and the people decay:
we breathe but a whisper of prayer.

Pause

We poison the food of our children,
the wine on our tables turns to vinegar.
We toss aside those we pretend we have loved,
our loins shake with disease.

The earth and the people decay:
we breathe but a whisper of prayer.

Pause

The streets of our cities are deserted,
the rich and strong have flown to the hills.
The flowers of the parks turn to weeds,
the slides of the children rust.

The earth and the people decay:
we breathe but a whisper of prayer.

Silence

We croak from the mire of the pit:
Let the echo of the walls be our prayer.
Let the menace of the waves turn to laughter.
Let the currents of the rivers dance.

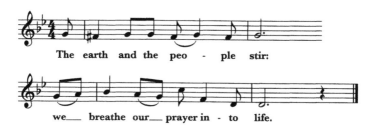

The earth and the peo - ple stir:
we__ breathe our__ prayer in - to life.

Pause

...in the Spirit that stirs amongst us the kaleidoscope of Jesus.

From deep underground let the waters rise,
let them float us out of the caverns of darkness.
Let seeds of the trees be planted again,
let the clouds rain with pure water.

The earth and the people stir:
we breathe our prayer into life.

Pause

High on a cross a man hangs parched,
forsaken by friends and by God,
taking to himself their suffering and pain.
He dies with a cry – a whisper or howl? –
yet trusting the One who seems absent.

The earth and the people stir:
we breathe our prayer into life.

Pause

Open our eyes again that we may see,
unfold our hearts to be open to your love.
May we greet our neighbours in trust,
and rebuild the walls of the city.

The earth and the people stir:
we breathe our prayer into life.

Pause

Be for us, O God, a deliverer still,
a God of compassion and joy.
Then our mouths will discover praise:
we shall glorify you with thankful hearts.

The earth and the people stir:
we breathe our prayer into life.

Silence

Strange and terrible God, **so often silent and hidden, rescue**
us from the brink of our doom, and renew the scarred face
of the earth.

We breathe these words out of the Silence within us, into the Silence beyond us…

70   Faith stripped bare

That we may live with patience and trust through the decay of old forms of faith;
and that we may keep awake in the darkness of doubt.

The ruthless seek to destroy,
they hurt beyond repair.
Gaunt and hollow-eyed,
their victims limp to the grave.

Pause

Refused even their dignity,
they have no voice of their own.
Their faces press to the window,
they slink starving away.

Pause

The cruel are oblivious:
Surely they would be appalled
by a conscience revived,
by eyes that were opened?

Pause

The cries of the needy are drowned
by their baying taunts of mockery.
Blind to the needs of the weak,
they dismiss them as merely a number.

Pause

The needy cry to the heavens,
to the eagle with piercing eye.
But the skies are empty and cold,
no deliverer descends in our day.

Pause

Is there a God of compassion?
Is there a God of justice?
Is there One yearning in love?
Is there a God who can save?

...in the Spirit that stirs amongst us the kaleidoscope of Jesus.

Hold___ to___ the God who is ab-sent,

trust___ in the God who with-draws.

Pause

Why do you delay your appearing?
Why do you keep us nailed to our pain?
Why do you harden the hearts of the cruel?
Why is our sense of you slipping away?

**Hold to the God who is absent,
trust in the God who withdraws.**

Silence

God, hard to believe in, **bring us through dark nights of
doubt to the joy in which our ancestors danced your
praise.**

71   A prayer of old age

In solidarity with those entering the time of diminishment.

You have been the source of my strength, O God,
from before the day I was born.
You brought me forth from the womb,
you sustained me before ever I knew you.
You were the confidence of my heedless youth,
you gave me my hope and my courage.

Pause

When I strove with the evil in my heart,
when I fought the enemies of your truth,
you refreshed me in the heat of the battle,
you were the rock in whose shade I recovered.

We breathe these words out of the Silence within us, into the Silence beyond us...

You were my stronghold on the mountain crag,
you were my refuge in the homes of my friends.

Pause

I have seen the eyes of the pitiless and cruel,
I have been wounded by words and by deeds.
I have been ignored and neglected by the powerful,
they passed over my name for promotion.
They have gossiped with glee at my failings,
they delight in rumour and lies.

Pause

My fate has filled many with awe:
I have become as a warning and portent.
And now I contend with old age,
withdrawing my eyes and my ears.
Few and grey are the hairs of my head –
no problem in numbering them now.

As the winds of___ win-ter ga - ther,___
do not for-sake me, O God.___

Pause

In this new testing of faith,
still would I praise you, my God.
I long for you still with hope,
and I shall praise you more and more.
My mouth will tell of your ways
to the generations taking my place.

Pause

Yes, you have brought me through deep waters,
through trials bitter and troublesome.   >

...in the Spirit that stirs amongst us the kaleidoscope of Jesus.

You have burdened me yet given me strength,
you have raised me up from the depths.
Bless me now in the days of my fading,
turn to me again and give me your comfort.

**As the winds of winter gather,
do not forsake me, O God.**

Pause

Your just ways, O God, spread through the world –
great is the tale of your wonders.
I shall make music in praise of your faithfulness,
through the days of my life and beyond.
I shall sing of the mystery of love,
my being soul-deep will rejoice in your name.

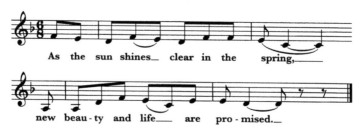

As the sun shines clear in the spring,
new beauty and life are promised.

Pause

Even through the waters of death you will bring me,
keeping at bay my terror of drowning.
My lungs will fill with the breath of new life,
and I shall praise you in the garden of delight.
We shall dance as the poor enriched,
we shall sing as the oppressed redeemed.

**As the sun shines clear in the spring,
new beauty and life are promised.**

Pause

Those who knew not what they did,
and those who relished their malice,
even our enemies, through their shame and disgrace,

We breathe these words out of the Silence within us, into the Silence beyond us...

will be lured by the beauty of love,
will weep at the music they spurned,
will at last speak the truth from their hearts.

**As the sun shines clear in the spring,
new beauty and life are promised.**

Silence

As trust and doubt, **delight and distress, success and failure,
wax and wane through the years, keep our eyes fixed on
you, dear God, and give us courage to face the trials and
temptations that have yet to come our way.**

72   A prayer for just and wise rulers

For lawmakers; and for the protection of the vulnerable.

O God, give wisdom to those who govern us,
a sense of justice to those who wield power,
that they may frame laws that are life-giving,
that the poor and weak may breathe freely.
May they defend the cause of the needy,
save the abandoned and orphans,
disarm the rebellious and violent.

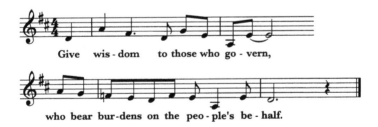

Give   wis - dom   to those who go - vern,

who bear bur-dens on the peo - ple's be - half.

Pause

May such wisdom endure like the sun and moon,
giving light from one age to the next.   >

...in the Spirit that stirs amongst us the kaleidoscope of Jesus.

May justice rain down like showers
that water the new-sown fields.
May justice flourish in our days,
and abundance of peace till the moon be no more.

Give wisdom to those who govern,
who bear burdens on the people's behalf.

Pause

May wisdom reign from sea to sea,
following the great rivers to the ends of the earth.
May folly bow down to truth,
the enemies of justice lick the dust.
May the rulers of the peoples seek wisdom,
the nations serve the ways of justice and truth.

Give wisdom to those who govern,
who bear burdens on the people's behalf.

Pause

The wise deliver the needy when they call,
the weak who have no one to speak for them.
They will be rescued from oppression and violence,
for their lives are precious in God's sight.

Give wisdom to those who govern,
who bear burdens on the people's behalf.

Pause

So may there be abundance of grain in the land,
to the tops of the hills may it wave.
Let the mountains be laden with peace,
with the prosperity that follows from justice.
May the corn swell with the gentle rains,
the sheaves thicken like the grass of the meadows.

Give wisdom to those who govern,
who bear burdens on the people's behalf.

Pause

We breathe these words out of the Silence within us, into the Silence beyond us...

May prayer be made for those in high office,
that they may bear their burdens with wisdom.
May blessings be invoked on them day by day,
may they be heartened by the prayers of the people.

Give wisdom to those who govern,
who bear burdens on the people's behalf.

Pause

Blessed be the God of all the earth,
who alone is all wisdom and justice,
who alone does great wonders.
Blessed be the glorious name of God:
may the universe be filled with God's glory.
Let the Amen echo with praise.

Silence

God of wisdom and justice, **hearing the cry of our prayer**
and knowing the reality of our politics, renew in all of
us a thirst for justice. May we cherish the earth and the
oceans, teach us the wisdom of restraint, and give us a
deep desire for the common good.

73   Perplexity unresolved but transformed

In solidarity with those who despair of meaning; and with those who have lost track
of their story.

To the loyal and loving and faithful,
God indeed is pure goodness.
And yet I was losing my foothold,
slipping and slithering from faith.
For I was envious of the boast of sinners:
without God they were entirely content.

Pause

...in the Spirit that stirs amongst us the kaleidoscope of Jesus.

They suffer no pains that I can see:
they look ever so healthy and sleek.
They never seem plunged into grief,
never harassed or thrown off course.
Pride is the signet ring on their finger,
craving for power fits them like a glove.

Pause

Their eyes gleam through folds of fat,
mirror of their empty minds.
Their faces ooze malice and greed,
their hearts brim over with the basest of thoughts,
with mocking laughter and cynical scorn,
overwhelming with menace and threats.
Their slanders are raised against heaven,
their tongue plies to and fro on the earth.

Pause

Of course they carry the mob with them,
lapping up their words like cheap wine –
What has God to do with us?
Are you still there?
Do you take any notice?
They go their godless way with a will,
untroubled they grow ever more wealthy.

Pause

Why did I ever keep faith with you,
why did I keep my conscience alert?
Every day is a punishment to me,
every morning I wake feeling beaten.

Pause

I have often thought, Do like those others.
But then I would betray the best that I know,
I would deny the faith of my ancestors.
So I am tossed backwards and forwards,
perplexed, desperate, baffled by it all.

We breathe these words out of the Silence within us, into the Silence beyond us...

Let   us   delve___   the deep-est ques-tions,___

liv - ing   their my - ste - ry.

Pause

Then I turned to worship you, O God,
and I pierced the heart of the mystery.
I began to see you with a sword in your side,
I began to see life in the light of your future.

Pause

The life of the unheeding totters on quicksand,
keeling over and falling to ruin.
They are in one fell moment destroyed.
They are living in the shadow of nightmares,
evil dreams that haunt in the morning,
dreams that are suddenly ended,
as they fall to their doom, unmourned and forgotten.

**Let us delve the deepest questions,
living their mystery.**

Pause

Yes, the struggle for faith has cost me dear:
like Jacob I limp in the sunrise.
With the heart's blood alone is victory wrought,
the price of the whole of my being.

Pause

You have embraced me in the ocean wastes,
a bird whose wings are trapped in black oil.
You weave all my doubts and distress
to a pattern of dancing joy.

...in the Spirit that stirs amongst us the kaleidoscope of Jesus.

**Let us delve the deepest questions,
living their mystery.**

Pause

It was a bitter heart that made me rebellious,
I was hurt in the depth of my being.
Distraught, I hammered away at you:
deranged, I vented my fury.

Pause

Nevertheless you absorbed my rage,
you embraced me and held me,
drawing the poison out of my heart,
giving me rest, calming my distress.

Pause

I do not see you, yet I deepen my trust.
No wisdom or strength dare I claim as my own.
Yet still you uphold me, and receive me in glory.

**Let us delve the deepest questions,
living their mystery.**

Pause

Though my flesh is falling apart,
though my heart is strained to breaking,
though my bones ache in the winter,
though my blood runs thin in my veins,
nevertheless still you are my God,
you are the future that waits for me.

Pause

How this can be is hidden from me,
you are the mystery giving no answers.
Yet I look to no one else in the universe,
with you I am well content.

**Let us delve the deepest questions,
living their mystery.**

Pause

We breathe these words out of the Silence within us, into the Silence beyond us...

Those who abandon you are doomed.
To break faith with you is to be lost.
True joy lies in drawing closer to God,
to the suffering, the mystery, the awesome love.

Pause

In you I believe that all will be well.
So I shall speak of your name and your ways,
not with a shout that covers my doubts,
but a whisper that sounds the depths of enduring.

Silence

And yes, the questions trouble us still, perplexing God. Is there no
way the pride of the powerful can be punctured? Can we not learn
to share the good things of the earth? Do we not project our unrecognized nastiness on others? Do we not collude with those who
are unjust? Do we not compensate too glibly with the promise of
good things after death?

Into the silence we hurl all that is unresolved. Nevertheless, in
the midst of our questions, **deepen our trust**, in the midst of our
trust, **keep our questions alive**.

**Cleanse the eye of our perception and purify our hearts
that we may will one thing, that your way indeed be
followed through and beyond the perplexities we cannot
escape.**

Glorify your name, O God, and justify your ways!

74   The sea of faith?

That we may wait and work for new unfoldings of faith.

The more we are aware, O God,
the harder does faith become.
The more we contemplate the desolation,
the further you seem to withdraw.

Pause

...in the Spirit that stirs amongst us the kaleidoscope of Jesus.

Millions die in the labour camps,
a child's scream pierces the night.
The chainsaws screech through the forests,
an elm withers in the meadow.

Pause

The desert sands creep onward,
acid rain crumbles the statues,
chemicals choke the rivers and lakes,
nuclear waste stores wrath in the earth.

The tide of faith__ still__ ebbs:
dare we work and wait for its turn - ing?__

Pause

Beautiful buildings decay into ruin,
exquisite carvings crumble to dust.
The places of prayer are too heavy for faith,
their very doors oppressive with weight.

Pause

You have deserted the altars, O God,
the faithful few ignore their decadence,
maintaining at extraordinary expense
that from which the meaning has departed.

Pause

Faith retreats into privacies,
or clashes with violent fervour.
The sensitive shudder and whisper,
the bullies shout and trample.

We breathe these words out of the Silence within us, into the Silence beyond us…

The tide of faith still ebbs:
dare we work and wait for its turning?

Pause

The grass of the arenas is scarred,
games turn to battles, the injured hobble.
New domes rise up from industrial waste,
temples for consumers at worship.

Pause

The voice of the prophet is thrown to the wind,
the springs of sacrifice run dry.
Service of others is measured by money,
those who would guide lack all sense of direction.

The tide of faith still ebbs:
dare we work and wait for its turning?

Pause

The tales of faith falter,
the memory of God grows dim.
Did you really swoop down to rescue,
do you truly care for Jerusalem?

Pause

Did your hand strike the rocks of the desert,
and make the waters flow?
Do you care for the sparrows' brood?
Do you give us manna in our wilderness?

The tide of faith still ebbs:
dare we work and wait for its turning?

Pause

Look on this earth of your creating,
see the billowing of corruption,
listen to the trudge of the weary,
open your ears to the taunts of the mindless.

Pause

...in the Spirit that stirs amongst us the kaleidoscope of Jesus.

Dare we praise you, O God, do you hear our cry,
meeting it in the depths of your being,
giving yourself for us and all people,
a love that costs all across aeons of time?

**The tide of faith still ebbs:
dare we work and wait for its turning?**

Pause

To the mystery of a cross we throw our questions,
and doggedly worry away at our doubts.
Yes, you absorb the wastes of our wraths and sorrows,
turning pain to glory in the vortex of love.

Silence

O God of our ancestors' faith, **fading from view as our
own sight grows dim, work still in us and through your
world, till our eyes open to a strange and shocking light, a
scarcely believable new dawn.**

75   Sure judgment

That we may lower our defences against the refining power of love.

Love flashes like lightning,
cuts through the heart of evil,
shows up pride in its ghastly light,
surprises our hidden boasting.

Pause

Love thunders in judgment,
sounding from horizon to horizon,
searching the depths of our being,
proclaiming the truth from the rooftops.

We breathe these words out of the Silence within us, into the Silence beyond us…

Come with the judg-ment that chas-tens,

come with the wounds that heal.

Pause

In awe and wonder we look to you, O God,
creating anew through your judgment,
sovereign and free in discernment,
at last making things right.

**Come with the judgment that chastens,
come with the wounds that heal.**

Pause

You hold a strange cup in your hands,
foaming with wine, astringent with spices.
You give it to us to drink,
to test the extent of our wickedness.
We drain it down to the dregs,
and see ourselves as we are.

Pause

The wine like liquid flame
burns through the layers of evil.
Like a hammer to the skull,
it breaks the crusts of habit.

**Come with the judgment that chastens,
come with the wounds that heal.**

Pause

Drained of our evil we tremble,
empty and naked before you.
We would be glad of the rags of the starving,
so defenceless do we feel.

...in the Spirit that stirs amongst us the kaleidoscope of Jesus.

Pause

The oppressed and the dying look into our eyes,
stretch out their hands in their weakness,
not to receive – we have nothing –
but to lift us out of fear and despair.

**Come with the judgment that chastens,
come with the wounds that heal.**

Pause

In them do we see you, O Christ.
eyes so clear and compassionate,
forgiving our wrong at the cost of your life,
with wounded palms embracing us.

Pause

We praise you, dear God, we give you the glory.
We shall tell of your wonders, of your judgment and mercy.

Silence

Living flame, **refine us in the truth, burn out all that is
impure with the fiery eye of clarity, and warm into life the
frozen battered child that longs to live again.**

76   The lion's wrath

*That swords be beaten into ploughshares; that warmongers be restrained; and that
forces of law use the minimum of force.*

Heraldic you stand on the battlements,
radiant in the dawn of the day –
Lion of Judah, powerful and just,
more majestic than snow-capped mountains.

With   dread__ deeds save   us,

We breathe these words out of the Silence within us, into the Silence beyond us...

with fierce__ love em-brace us.__

Pause

Jerusalem you claim as your own,
scattering the haughty and proud,
at a stroke snapping their arrows,
silencing their rebellion with a roar.

**With dread deeds save us,
with fierce love embrace us.**

Pause

The men of war tremble,
there is no strength in their arms;
they stand aghast, helpless;
dumbfounded, they cannot speak.

**With dread deeds save us,
with fierce love embrace us.**

Pause

You beat our swords into ploughshares,
you defeat all the wiles of our warring,
you restrain those who use terror,
the powerless and oppressed having nothing to fear.

**With dread deeds save us,
with fierce love embrace us.**

Pause

Our human wraths hurt and destroy:
your wrath is clear in its justice,
an awesome love that drums in our ears,
insistent, compelling, triumphant.

**With dread deeds save us,
with fierce love embrace us.**

Pause

...in the Spirit that stirs amongst us the kaleidoscope of Jesus.

Marvellous is your promise to love us,
terrifying is the response you seek from us.
Our weapons of war lie broken before you:
your vow is fulfilled in our sight.

Silence

Lion of wrath, **we would cower from the prowling of your love, we would slink into the prison we have made for ourselves. Give us your courage to face our fear. Break down our iron bars. In one bound rescue us despite ourselves.**

77   Past mercies, present despair, future hope

In solidarity with the fevered and delirious; with those paralyzed by fear; and with the sick in soul; and that we may remember the times of unexpected goodness.

In anxiety I murmur towards you,
in distress I cry out from my heart.
I call but hear only my echo:
Is God wrapped in silence for ever?

Pause

My eyes stream tears of sorrow,
groaning wells up from within.
Despair grips my heart like ice,
there is no breath in my lungs.

Keep the me-mo-ry___ of your good-ness a - live,

fan in - to flame the___ em-bers of hope.

Pause

We breathe these words out of the Silence within us, into the Silence beyond us...

Drenched in sweat I lie on my bed,
in the grip of delirium and fever.
There is nothing to cool me and comfort,
a terrible darkness descends.

Pause

I stretch out my hands and my soul,
yearning towards you from the depth of the night.
I think on your name but see nothing:
exhausted, my spirit faints.

**Keep the memory of your goodness alive,
fan into flame the embers of hope.**

Pause

Disconsolate, I pluck at the strings,
unable to hear the music we made,
eye to eye loving each other,
with melody in our hearts.

Pause

Paralyzed in terror, my eyes stare wild:
gripped by fear, I am weighted to the ground.
Like a rabbit dazzled by headlamps
I am dazed and cannot flee.

**Keep the memory of your goodness alive,
fan into flame the embers of hope.**

Pause

Will you cast me away for ever?
Will you no longer surprise me with joy?
Is your mercy vanished for ever?
Have your promises come to end?

Pause

Have you forgotten to be gracious?
Have you closed your heart to pity?
Have you broken that strong right arm?
Has your love no power to endure?

...in the Spirit that stirs amongst us the kaleidoscope of Jesus.

**Keep the memory of your goodness alive,
fan into flame the embers of hope.**

Pause

I suffer a sickness of soul:
I demand you live up to my image.
But you are no idol to serve my desires:
Thou art Thou, living, mysterious, and free.

Pause

With numbed fingers I hold on to you yet,
like a climber on the face of a mountain.
Though the waves of the sea crash over me,
like a limpet I cling to the rock.

**Keep the memory of your goodness alive,
fan into flame the embers of hope.**

Pause

Dogged and grim, yet I remember the past,
the wonders of rescue, the God who acts.
You made known your power among the peoples,
by great deeds you redeemed your own.
You brought the children of Jacob and Joseph
from bondage to the promise of freedom.

**Keep the memory of your goodness alive,
fan into flame the embers of hope.**

Pause

The waters of the sea cowered back before you,
the voice of your thunder was heard in the whirlwind,
your lightning lit up the horizon,
the clouds poured down rain at your bidding.

Pause

Your path was through the Sea of Reeds,
and on through the trackless wastes.
The earth shuddered at your passing,
though your footsteps were not seen.

We breathe these words out of the Silence within us, into the Silence beyond us...

Pause

By the hand of Moses and Aaron,
you led your people out of slavery.
By the wounds of your Beloved on a cross,
you led them through the pangs of death.

**Keep the memory of your goodness alive,
fan into flame the embers of hope.**

Pause

In times of exhaustion you lifted us up,
through closed doors you surprised us with joy.
Through the words of friends you have encouraged us,
through intimate touch you come close again.

Pause

And yes, you are holy indeed,
leading us beyond all that comforts us.
Of course we must expect not to see you
when you leave no trace of your passing.

**Keep the memory of your goodness alive,
fan into flame the embers of hope.**

Pause

Narrow is the path, no room for another,
thin is the air, no breath to name you,
thick is the cloud, there is nothing we can see,
lonely is the way, no companions now.

Pause

Veiled in mystery, yet you are God.
Dark is the night, yet your glory transforms it.
Revealed in Yeshua, yet a stranger so often.
The Unknown That Shall Be, yet the hope of our future.

Silence

...in the Spirit that stirs amongst us the kaleidoscope of Jesus.

O God, the same yesterday, today, and for ever, **though we sense your absence in a bleak despairing time, focus our minds and hearts on memories of grace surprising us, that faith may be kept alive and hope rekindled.**

78   Riddles of history

That we may ponder the riddles of history; that we may not lose our memories and our stories; that we may be spiritually sustained by the stories of God at work among our ancestors.

Part i

Listen to my teaching, O my people:
incline your ears to the words of my mouth.
For I shall open my lips in a parable,
and expound the mysteries of former times.

Pause

"What we have heard and known,
all that our ancestors told us,
we shall not hide from our children,
but declare to a generation to come
the praiseworthy acts of God,
God's powerful and wonderful works."

Pause

"O God, you established a law for your people,
you witnessed to your ways in Israel,
which you commanded our ancestors
to teach to their children,
that future generations might know you,
and children yet to be born,
that they in their turn might teach it,
that their daughters and sons might trust you,
that they might keep your commandments
and not forget your works –"

Pause

We breathe these words out of the Silence within us, into the Silence beyond us...

"– as did their ancestors,
a rebellious and stubborn generation,
a generation whose heart was warped,
whose spirit was not faithful to God."

De - lu - ded, re - bel - lious, es - tranged,

we know nei - ther our - selves nor our God,

the God whose ways are my - ste - ri - ous,_____

an e - nig - ma, a ques - tion, a rid - dle.

Pause

"The children of Ephraim armed with the bow
turned back in the day of their battle.
They did not keep your covenant, O God,
they refused to walk in your law:
they forgot what you had done,
and the wonders you had shown them."

Pause

"You worked marvels in the sight of their forebears,
in the land of Egypt, in the country of Zoan.
You divided the sea and let them pass,
you made the waters pile up in a heap."

Pause

...in the Spirit that stirs amongst us the kaleidoscope of Jesus.

"In the daytime you led them with a cloud,
and all night long with the pillar of fire.
You cleft rocks in the wilderness,
and gave them drink in abundance."

Pause

"You made streams flow out of the rock,
you caused the waters to tumble like rivers.
But for all this they sinned against you,
and rebelled against their God in the desert."

**Deluded, rebellious, estranged,
we know neither ourselves nor our God,
the God whose ways are mysterious,
an enigma, a question, a riddle.**

Pause

"They wilfully put you to the test,
and demanded food for their appetite.
They spoke against you and said,
'Can you prepare a table in the wilderness?
You indeed struck the rock and the water flowed,
but can you also give bread and meat for your people?' "

Pause

"When you heard it you were angry
and a fire was kindled against Jacob,
your wrath blazing against Israel.
For they put no trust in you,
nor would they believe your power to save."

Pause

"Then you commanded the clouds above,
and opened the doors of heaven.
You rained down manna for them to eat,
and gave them the bread of heaven.
Mere mortals ate the food of angels,
which you gave to them in abundance."

Pause

We breathe these words out of the Silence within us, into the Silence beyond us...

"You stirred up the south east wind
and guided it by your power.
You rained down meat on them thick as dust,
and winged birds like the sands of the sea.
You made them fall in the midst of their camp,
and all about their tents."

Pause

"So they ate and were well filled,
for you had given them what they desired.
But before they had satisfied their craving,
while the food was still in their mouths,
your anger blazed up against them
and you slew their strongest men
and laid low the youth of Israel."

**Deluded, rebellious, estranged,
we know neither ourselves nor our God,
the God whose ways are mysterious,
an enigma, a question, a riddle.**

Pause

"But for all this they sinned yet more,
and put no faith in your wonders.
So you ended their days like a breath,
and their years with sudden terror."

Pause

"When you struck them down they sought you,
they turned and searched eagerly for their God.
They remembered that God was their rock,
their strength and their redeemer."

Pause

"But they lied to you with their mouths,
and dissembled with their tongues,
for their hearts were not fixed upon you,
nor were they true to your covenant.

Pause

...in the Spirit that stirs amongst us the kaleidoscope of Jesus.

"Yet being merciful you forgave their iniquity,
and withheld your hand from destroying them.
Many times you turned your anger aside
and would not wholly arouse your fury.
You remembered that they were but flesh,
like a wind that passes and does not return."

Deluded, rebellious, estranged,
we know neither ourselves nor our God,
the God whose ways are mysterious,
an enigma, a question, a riddle.

Silence

Part ii

"How often they grieved you in the wilderness,
and rebelled against you in the desert.
Again and again they put you to the test,
trying your loyalty and patience."

Pause

"They did not remember your power,
or the day when you rescued them,
how you wrought your signs in Egypt,
your wonders in the country of Zoan."

Pause

"For you turned their rivers into blood,
so that they could not drink from the streams.
You sent swarms of flies that devoured them,
and frogs that laid them waste."

Pause

"You gave their crops to the locust,
and the fruits of their labours to the grasshopper.
You struck down their vines with hailstones,
and their sycamore trees with frost."

Pause

We breathe these words out of the Silence within us, into the Silence beyond us...

"You gave up their cattle to hail,
and their flocks to the flash of lightning.
You loosed on them a terrible anger,
a fierce indignation, your distress and your fury."

Pause

"You would not spare them from death,
but gave up their lives to the pestilence.
You struck down the firstborn of Egypt,
the firstfruits of the womb in the dwelling of Ham."

De - lu - ded, re - bel - lious, es - tranged,

we know nei - ther our-selves nor our God,

the God whose ways are my - ste - ri - ous,____

an e - nig - ma, a ques - tion, a rid - dle.

Pause

"As for your own people you led them out like sheep,
and guided them in the wilderness like a flock.
You led them to safety and they were not afraid,
but the sea overwhelmed their enemies."

Pause

"You brought them to the land of the promise,
to the mountains your right hand had won.
You drove out the tribes before you,
and gave their lands to your people."

...in the Spirit that stirs amongst us the kaleidoscope of Jesus.

Pause

"You settled the tribes of Israel in their tents.
But they rebelled against you, O God of deliverance,
and put you to the test:
they would not obey your commandments."

Pause

"They turned back and were treacherous again.
they turned aside, slack as an unstrung bow.
They provoked you to anger at heathen shrines,
moved you to jealousy with their carved idols."

Pause

"You heard and were angry, you utterly rejected them,
you forsook the tabernacle at Shiloh,
the tent where you dwelt among the people.
You gave the ark of your power into captivity,
your glory into the hands of the enemy."

Pause

"You delivered your people to the sword,
and were enraged against them.
Fire devoured the young men,
there was no one to bewail the young women.
Their priests fell by the sword,
and there was none to mourn for the widows."

**Deluded, rebellious, estranged,
we know neither ourselves nor our God,
the God whose ways are mysterious,
an enigma, a question, a riddle.**

Pause

"Then, O God, you awoke from sleep,
like a warrior inflamed with wine.
You struck the backsides of your enemies,
bringing them down to their shame."

Pause

We breathe these words out of the Silence within us, into the Silence beyond us...

"You rejected the family of Joseph,
you refused the tribe of Ephraim.
But you chose the tribe of Judah,
and the hill of Zion which you loved."

Pause

"You built the sanctuary high as the heavens,
and as firm as the earth which you founded.
You chose David the youngest as your servant,
and plucked him away from the sheepfold."

Pause

"You took him from guiding the flocks,
to be the shepherd of your people Jacob,
and of Israel your own possession.
He tended them with a true and faithful heart,
and guided them with skilful hands."

**Deluded, rebellious, estranged,
we know neither ourselves nor our God,
the God whose ways are mysterious,
an enigma, a question, a riddle.**

Pause

And so the story unfolded,
the mystery ever deepening,
a kingdom split apart,
a people carried off into exile.

Pause

Even the clue of a cross
has left us many a puzzle.
Our loyalty ebbs and flows,
our sense of your presence too.

Pause

Those in high office betray you,
integrity crumbles in gossip.
The obscure are so often submerged,
the powerful far beyond love.

...in the Spirit that stirs amongst us the kaleidoscope of Jesus.

Pause

The stones of the churches decay,
your agelong Spirit moves on.
We have become so timid and fearful,
we refuse to enter the unknown.

Pause

We desperately cling to our comforts,
one by one you take them away.
We resent you stripping us bare,
untrusting of this prelude to glory.

**Deluded, rebellious, estranged,
we know neither ourselves nor our God,
the God whose ways are mysterious,
an enigma, a question, a riddle.**

Silence

Mysterious God, **choosing the small, the unnoticed, the
obscure, to renew the ways of your covenant when your
followers wander and fail you, strive yet with our intractable clay, and open us to the love you revealed to us in
Yeshua, emptied of power, untouched by delusion, dying
unrecognized, yet for those with eyes to see the decisive
clue to the mystery of your being.**

79   The body of God

*That water, air, and soil be cared for; that more trees be planted than uprooted; that
we may not be violent but tender towards one another; and that we may cherish beauty
in nature, buildings, and people.*

We neglect, we ravage the body.
We rape the earth, your temple.
We pollute the rivers, the oceans.
We care not for the soil that sustains us.

Pause

We breathe these words out of the Silence within us, into the Silence beyond us...

And the earth cries out in pain.
The algae fills the creeks,
sucking down the unwary,
releasing its poisonous fumes.

O God, we wound your bo - dy:
come quick - ly, heal and save us.

Pause

We neglect, we ravage the body.
We take our pleasures with violence.
We forget the language of reverence.
We care not for the weak and the vulnerable.

Pause

And the people cry out in pain.
Their anger rises in vengeance:
they pass on the needles infected,
they delight in spreading disease.

O God, we wound your body:
come quickly, heal and save us.

Pause

We neglect, we ravage the body.
We flatten the beautiful cities.
We ransack the places of prayer.
We care not for beauty, for peace.

Pause

And the land cries out in pain.
The contorted ruins smoulder.   >

...in the Spirit that stirs amongst us the kaleidoscope of Jesus.

The survivors stumble in shock,
their children inherit their wounds.

**O God, we wound your body:
come quickly, heal and save us.**

Pause

We neglect, we ravage the body.
Radiation drifts on the wind.
Waste is dumped in the oceans.
We care not for fish or for bird.

Pause

And the trees cry out in pain,
sprouting misshapen leaves.
An earthquake in the depths of the sea
splits open the canisters of doom.

**O God, we wound your body:
come quickly, heal and save us.**

Silence

O God, forgive our murderous deeds and blind, unthinking rage.
**Give us your Spirit of compassionate anger, that we may
live and work in harmony with you for the healing of the
body of this planet, gasping for air, sores weeping on its
skin. Make us a people of one earth, our bodies no longer
violated, but cherished and loved.**

80   The face of God

*That we be not slothful but energetic; that we be not fickle but constant; and that our
impress on the world be creative and kindly.*

Radiant and glorious God,
shining through the universe,
lighting our tortuous landscape,
guiding your troublesome peoples,
straighten the path of your coming,
stride forth to meet us and save us.

We breathe these words out of the Silence within us, into the Silence beyond us...

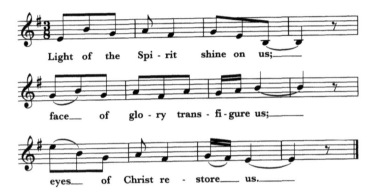

Light of the Spi - rit shine on us;____

face____ of glo - ry trans - fi - gure us;____

eyes____ of Christ re - store____ us.____

Pause

Radiant and glorious God,
shining through a human face,
illuminate our blinded eyes,
guide us with an inner light,
feed us who gasp by the wayside,
lift us up with nurturing hand.

Light of the Spirit shine on us;
face of glory transfigure us;
eyes of Christ restore us.

Pause

We have misused the freedom you gave us,
we have felt the anger of your love.
You have fed us with the bread of tears,
and given us many a bitter drink.

Pause

You cared for us like a young vine,
clearing the ground and planting us in.
You nourished the soil for our roots to deepen,
you sent us the warmth of the sun and the rain.

Pause

…in the Spirit that stirs amongst us the kaleidoscope of Jesus.

We flourished and grew strong,
our boughs were like those of the cedar.
Our branches stretched out to the sea,
our tender shoots to the great river.

Pause

Why then have you sent us drought?
Why do the locusts devour our fruit?
Why does the wind tear our branches?
Why do the boars of the forest uproot us?
O God, no longer do we see your face,
no longer do we hear your voice.

**Light of the Spirit shine on us;
face of glory transfigure us;
eyes of Christ restore us.**

Pause

With the eyes of your compassion look upon us.
Prune us if need be, but do not destroy.
We are a fickle and cowardly people:
strengthen our wills and heal our wounds.

Pause

Let all that is wilful perish at your word,
let all that is slothful be burned.
Empower us again to follow your way,
give us life and we shall delight in your name.

**Light of the Spirit shine on us;
face of glory transfigure us;
eyes of Christ restore us.**

Silence

Living God, **whose face no one can look upon and live,
sustain our faith in the human face of Christ, revealing the
infinite depths of your justice and compassion. So shine
upon us with the light of your Spirit that we may recognize
you in the faces of one another, and realize the presence of
your glory among us.**

We breathe these words out of the Silence within us, into the Silence beyond us…

81   The God who yearns to save

*That we may deeply believe that God yearns for us, loves us, and passionately cares
about us; and that those who trade in evil be brought to their senses.*

"The people of God sang for joy,
the people of the God of Jacob.
They beat the drum, they plucked the strings,
they blew the horn of the ram, and the people gathered.
At the phases of the moon they held their festivals,
even as their ancestors from their time in Egypt."

Pause

"God spoke to the people in a voice not known:
I eased your shoulders of burdens,
your hands were freed from the load.
You called to me and I rescued you,
I answered from the place of secret thunder,
I tested you at the waters of Meribah."

O God who saved a small peo - ple

from sla - ve - ry, op - pres- sion, and fear,

de - li - ver us, peo - ples of one earth,

from our im - pri-son-ment one of a - no - ther.

Pause

...in the Spirit that stirs amongst us the kaleidoscope of Jesus.

"My people, listen to my charge.
Israel, if only you would hear me!
Do not bow down to alien gods,
let there be no strange gods among you."

Pause

"I am your God and your Saviour,
who brought you out of the land of Egypt.
Open your mouth wide and I shall satisfy you:
filled with my presence you will live in my truth."

Pause

"But you would not listen to my voice,
you would have nothing to do with me.
So I gave you up to your stubborn hearts,
to walk according to your own designs."

Pause

"If only you would listen to me,
if only you would walk in my ways,
I would soon defeat your enemies,
and lift you free of your oppressors."

Pause

"Those who despise me would cringe before me,
they would be trapped in their fate for ever.
But I would feed you with the finest wheat,
with honey from the rock I would satisfy you."

**O God who saved a small people
from slavery, oppression, and fear,
deliver us, peoples of one earth,
from our imprisonment one of another.**

Pause

Like our ancestors, O God, we would worship you,
we would be glad and sing for joy.
To us as to them you would speak,
reminding us of your yearning and care.

We breathe these words out of the Silence within us, into the Silence beyond us...

Pause

In the moment of prayer we are one with them,
our past is alive and so is the future.
You would warn and admonish us still,
for we also wander from your way.

Pause

We lay burdens upon one another:
oppressed, we oppress in our turn.
Release the traps we have laid,
deliver us from the compulsion to punish.
Do not imprison us for ever,
even those we see as our enemies.

**O God who saved a small people
from slavery, oppression, and fear,
deliver us, peoples of one earth,
from our imprisonment one of another.**

Pause

Do not exalt us who are far from deserving it,
at the expense of hell for our enemies.
The people of earth are your people now.

Pause

Work in us all your deeds of deliverance,
even in those who abuse and enslave,
in those who traffic in terror or drugs,
in those who dictate the slaughter of innocents.

Pause

If they are so thoroughly wicked,
that they dissolve into dust at your sight,
so let it be, your design come to nothing.
But would not your love have failed?
Inscrutable God, is that not so?

Silence

...in the Spirit that stirs amongst us the kaleidoscope of Jesus.

Dear God, **yearning for us to realize how trapped we are, giving us freedom to ch oose to be imprisoned, yet compelling us with your insistent love, turn our hearts and wills without our knowing it, and kindle in us the desire for true freedom. Deliver us in love's most costly way, and give us the courage to bear it, at one with Yeshua, for whom such love was the weight of glory.**

82   The false promises of idols

That we may see through the lies of singers and politicians, gurus and televangelists; and that they may be silent and so begin to listen to the truth.

They seem to be as gods,
those who promise utopias.
Fickle as a crowd we gawp,
cheering the latest idolatry:

Pause

romantic illusions of singers,
false pledges of politicians,
slippery words of the gurus,
sleek suits of the televangelists.

Pause

From your pedestals you no longer see,
high above the weak and oppressed.
You say nothing about the orphaned and widowed,
never touch the lives of the silenced.

We breathe these words out of the Silence within us, into the Silence beyond us...

Pause

You say nothing of the toughness of love,
you promise no just laws for the poor,
your words pass over the stricken,
your mouthings stir up irrational guilt.

Down to the dust, vain idols!
Come, living God of justice.

Pause

You proclaim a false god of terror,
by threats you hold on to your power,
you never show the true God,
wounded by love, embracing the failure.

Pause

Indeed you are lost, you crumble,
you wander about in the darkness,
you stumble, you do not understand,
your name will vanish into dust.

Down to the dust, vain idols!
Come, living God of justice.

Pause

O God, make your promises true,
imbue us with your Spirit of justice.
Favour the oppressed, humble the oppressor,
bring laughter and love to our eyes.

Silence

O God, living God, **if you are the living God, justify your**
ways to your people, and let not our cry for justice echo in
silence. We cling to our trust in your promises. Fulfil
them. Do not betray us. Do not be to us a false god.

83   The enemies of God

That the apathetic may be stirred to action; that the unseeing may have their eyes opened; that the fanatic may be blessed with a sense of humour; and that those who collude may have courage to refuse.

A small people, in a small land,
surrounded by tribes that were hostile,
threatened by empires expanding,
cried out to their God to protect them.

Pause

Their enemies made their alliances,
whispering, conspiring, plotting together.
They schemed against those whom God cherished,
they seized on the pastures of God.

Pause

Who are your enemies now, O God?
A people apathetic who do not care,
those who sit at ease while millions slave,
those who eat their fill while children starve.

Pause

And those who wage war in the name of their God,
and those who supply them with weapons;
those who poison the rivers and seas,
and those who spread lies through our minds.

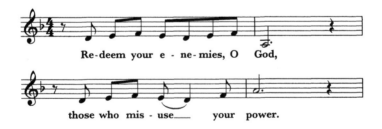

Re-deem your e - ne- mies, O   God,
those who mis - use___ your   power.

We breathe these words out of the Silence within us, into the Silence beyond us...

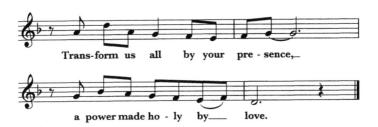

Trans-form us all by your pre - sence,—

a power made ho - ly by—— love.

Pause

Destroy them, O God, who poison the land,
let their remains become dung for the earth.
Make them like chaff before the wind,
as insubstantial as thistledown.

Pause

May they cower backwards in fear,
flattened by the fury of your wind,
shrivelled by the heat of your fire,
the flame that sets hillsides ablaze.

Pause

Let them be disgraced and dismayed for ever,
and those who collude – like ourselves.
Wild-eyed, bewildered, let us tremble,
in a moment of dread and of truth.

**Redeem your enemies, O God,
those who misuse your power.
Transform us all by your presence,
a power made holy by love.**

Pause

Yes, we yearn for an omnipotent king,
the ruler who gives life to the people,
who leads out his armies to lay waste and destroy.

Pause

...in the Spirit that stirs amongst us the kaleidoscope of Jesus.

Such a king was an ikon of God,
but a king on a cross shows a power that is humbling,
an awesome love that endures through the pain,
that takes our rage and our venom to heart,
dissolving our evil in the power of your goodness.

Redeem your enemies, O God,
those who misuse your power.
Transform us all by your presence,
a power made holy by love.

Pause

May we turn from our hatreds and face you,
burned clean by the eye of your love,
that you may forgive our destruction and greed,
and our naming of strangers as enemies.

Pause

In your Spirit let us care for the earth,
in compassion one for another.
Let us welcome the strangers and share what we have,
enjoying the wealth of justice and friendship.

Silence

All-embracing One, **ease the paranoia from our hearts,**
grown cold in a time of fear. Remind us of the truth that
even those who terrify us – eyes harsh and vengeful – are
created and loved by you. Show us how to be reconciled
and so to live in peace.

84   On pilgrimage

That pilgrims may discover on their journey the God who is always and everywhere
present.

How lovely are your dwellings, O God,
how beautiful are the holy places.
In the days of my pilgrimage I yearn for them:
they are the temples of your living presence.

We breathe these words out of the Silence within us, into the Silence beyond us…

I have a desire and longing to enter my true home:
my heart and my flesh rejoice in the living God.

The end is glimpsed___ in the midst of the jour-ney:

the ful-fil-ment is be - yond our i-ma-gin-ing.___

Pause

For the sparrow has found a house for herself,
and the swallow a nest to lay her young.
Even so are those who dwell in your house –
they will always be praising you.
And your Spirit makes a home deep within us:
let us welcome and delight in your presence.

The end is glimpsed in the midst of the journey:
the fulfilment is beyond our imagining.

Pause

Blessed are those whose strength is in you,
in whose heart are your ways,
who trudging through the plains of misery
find in them an unexpected spring,
a well from deep below the barren ground,
and the pools are filled with water.

Pause

They become springs of healing for others,
reservoirs of compassion to those who are bruised.
Strengthened themselves they give courage to others,
and God will be there at the end of their journey.

The end is glimpsed in the midst of the journey:
the fulfilment is beyond our imagining.

...in the Spirit that stirs amongst us the kaleidoscope of Jesus.

Pause

O God of our ancestors, hear my prayer:
guide me as you did your servants of old.
Bless those who govern on the people's behalf,
keep us close to your will and your ways.

Pause

One day lived in your presence
is better than a thousand in my own dwelling.
I had rather beg in the burning sun
on the threshold of the house of my God
than sit in cool courtyards
of luxury and worldly success.

**The end is glimpsed in the midst of the journey:
the fulfilment is beyond our imagining.**

Pause

For you are my light and my shield,
you will give me your grace and your glory.
You are ready with bountiful gifts,
overflowing to those who follow you.
Living God of love,
blessed are those who put their trust in you.

Silence

O God of the desert pilgrims, **we who are wearied by
monotonous days of sun or cloud, who are battered by
the monstrous whirling winds, surprise us yet with a
monstrance of wonder, a revelation of love, an oasis of
refreshment, a taste of the harvest, a moment of grace.**

We breathe these words out of the Silence within us, into the Silence beyond us...

85   Rooted in one land?

For a deeper love of the local, the particular place where we live; for a generous patriotism; and for a sense of belonging together on one earth.

We thank you, O God, for the land where we dwell,
for a country to cherish and honour,
for farms and cities to care for,
gardens and houses to dwell in.

Pause

You chose a particular people,
you gave land to a wandering tribe,
that they might learn to follow your way,
and give light to the peoples around them.

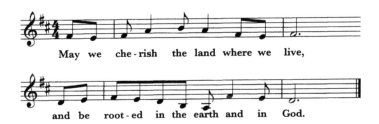

May we che-rish the land where we live,
and be root-ed in the earth and in God.

Pause

So often the light was dimmed by their failures,
as they turned aside from your path.
You led them through the mourning of exile,
and they knew you as the God of creation.

Pause

Then you filled the life of one particular man,
born of your people, brought up in that land,
whose name has spread over the earth,
calling us all to be neighbours.

May we cherish the land where we live,
and be rooted in the earth and in God.

...in the Spirit that stirs amongst us the kaleidoscope of Jesus.

Pause

Still does your love strive with our waywardness,
reaching across the abyss that is wrath,
opening our eyes to the needs of the hidden ones,
compelling us to cherish an earth that is fragile.

Pause

We look upon the world and its peoples,
and there seem few grounds for our faith.
Yet we sense the ground of our being,
and you meet us with riches of grace.

**May we cherish the land where we live,
and be rooted in the earth and in God.**

Pause

So you give us life yet again,
and we your people sing and rejoice,
speaking your praise on behalf of the creatures,
claiming our inheritance as stewards of the earth.

Pause

Indeed you will speak peace to your people,
to your faithful ones who have turned their hearts.
Truly your salvation is near those who fear you,
and your glory will shine on our earth.

**May we cherish the land where we live,
and be rooted in the earth and in God.**

Pause

Mercy and truth have met together,
righteousness and peace have kissed each other.
Faithfulness will spring up from the earth,
and justice leap to meet it from heaven.

Pause

O God, you will give us all that is good,
and our lands will yield their plenty.

We breathe these words out of the Silence within us, into the Silence beyond us...

For righteousness will go before you,
and clear the way for your appearing.

**May we cherish the land where we live,
and be rooted in the earth and in God.**

Silence

God of the whole earth and God of each land, **so guide us in
your Spirit that we may not betray our country for the
sake of fanatical ideals, nor betray our earth out of fearful
and blinkered loyalties, but with a steady and faithful
endurance build at least the tents of justice.**

86   God is God

That we may relate to one another with persistence, faithfulness, and constancy.

Like the sun through the heavens,
and the moon through its phases,
like the rivers that flow,
and the seas that welcome them,
so are you, God of the universe,

Per - si - stant in   faith-ful- ness,

con - stant   in   love.

Pause

Like the humble of heart,
and the kindly of soul,
like the ones who forgive
and are no longer bitter,
so are you, God of compassion,

...in the Spirit that stirs amongst us the kaleidoscope of Jesus.

**persistent in faithfulness,
constant in love.**

Pause

You hear the cry of the afflicted,
you listen to the howl of the lonely,
you continually search for the lost,
you heal the hurts of the wounded,
for you are a God of yearning,

**persistent in faithfulness,
constant in love.**

Pause

You gladden the human heart,
you lift the burdens of the depressed,
you give new hope to the despairing,
you reach to the depths of the grave,
for you are a God of rejoicing,

**persistent in faithfulness,
constant in love.**

Pause

You bind the rebellious,
you quieten the strident,
you draw the fangs of the ruthless,
you silence the bullying dictators,
for you are a God of justice,

**persistent in faithfulness,
constant in love.**

Pause

You welcome the stranger,
you embrace the outcast,
you bear our pain,
you strive with our evil,
for you are a God crucified and risen,

We breathe these words out of the Silence within us, into the Silence beyond us...

**persistent in faithfulness,
constant in love.**

Pause

Abiding is your love,
enduring is your patience,
everlasting are your truths,
eternal is your glory,
O God, you are God,

**persistent in faithfulness,
constant in love.**

Silence

God of mystery and revelation, **at the extremes of our distress
and despair, when you are the only hope left, let us hear
your name again, and so take courage on the journey:**

I Am Who I Am,
I Shall Be Who I Shall Be,
That Which I Am I Shall Be,
That Which I Shall Be I Am.

I shall be there
as the one who I there shall be,
I am with you always
as I always choose to be with you.

I shall be there
**in the encounter you cannot predict,
but there you will meet me,**
and I shall be for you
as the one who there shall be.

...in the Spirit that stirs amongst us the kaleidoscope of Jesus.

87   Cities of pilgrimage

*In solidarity with the people of the great cities; with the people of the places of
pilgrimage; and with all the peoples of faith.*

Egypt, the old enslaver,
Babylon, the ancient foe,
Philistines over the border,
Phoenicians from the shores of the sea,
Ethiopians from over the mountains,
those who once were our enemies
now worship God in Jerusalem.

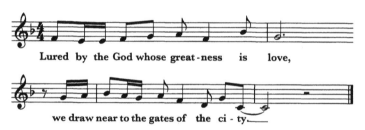

Lured by the God whose great-ness is love,
we draw near to the gates of the ci-ty.

Pause

The eye of faith looks to the dawn,
to the day of peace universal,
to a new age of the salvation of God,
to an earth transfigured, made new.
The dancers dance; the singers make melody;
the fountains of God enliven the city.

Pause

The peoples are widely scattered
over the earth and across the sea.
A poet with vision broods
as the pilgrims draw near to Jerusalem,
to the God who draws them together
to give praise on the holy mountain.

Pause

We breathe these words out of the Silence within us, into the Silence beyond us...

The peoples of another time,
citizens of far-flung cities,
the powerful – and the powerless –
of Washington, of Moscow, and Beijing,
the powerless – and the powerful –
of Sao Paulo, of Soweto, and Calcutta,
all the peoples give you praise.

**Lured by the God whose greatness is love,
we draw near to the gates of the city.**

Pause

Pilgrims to Jerusalem,
to Mecca and to Rome:
faithful of Canterbury,
of Geneva and Byzantium:
gatherers to the rivers,
to the Naranjara and the Ganges:
markers of the journey
through the deserts and the mountains:
they celebrate in gratitude,
in wonder and rejoicing.

**Lured by the God whose greatness is love,
we draw near to the gates of the city.**

Pause

No room for the aloof and arrogant,
for the divisive and superior spirit:
God is greater than the idols of nations,
deeper in mystery than any faith.

Pause

Like a people of old, small, obscure,
stretched beyond fear to a wider belief,
so are God's people today
challenged by a love that is awesome,
drawn to the gates of the city of God,
whose name is yet to be known.

Silence

…in the Spirit that stirs amongst us the kaleidoscope of Jesus.

Living mysterious God, **greater than the human heart, greater than all the peoples of the world, greater than the faiths that try to cage you, shatter the idols which we make to keep us safe, to claim you for ourselves, to portray you in superior ways. Humble us, living God, and draw us by the magnet of your love into the glory of your presence and the harmony of a new Jerusalem.**

88 In bleak despair

In solidarity with the despairing and the suicidal; and that our prayer may breathe them hope.

The praise of your salvation, O God,
has died on lips that are parched.
The story of your wonders towards us
has turned hollow, bitter, and sour.
I doubt any prayer can enter your heart,
your ear is deaf to my cry.

There is drought in the depths of my being, no rain, no water, no life.

Pause

Soul-deep I am full of troubles,
and my life draws near to the grave.
I totter on the edge of the abyss,
ghostly, ghastly, shrivelled.
I am like the wounded in war that stagger,
like a corpse strewn on the battlefield.

**There is drought in the depths of my being,
no rain, no water, no life.**

We breathe these words out of the Silence within us, into the Silence beyond us...

Pause

I belong no more to my people,
I am cut off from your presence, O God.
You have put me in the lowest of dungeons,
in a pit of scurrying rats.
To a wall that drips with water I am chained,
my feet sink into mud.

**There is drought in the depths of my being,
no rain, no water, no life.**

Pause

I feel nothing but your pounding in my head,
surges of pain overwhelm me.
I cannot endure this suffering,
this furious onslaught, so searing.
I can remember no time without terror,
without turmoil and trouble of mind.

**There is drought in the depths of my being,
no rain, no water, no life.**

Pause

I have been dying since the day of my birth:
O God, have I ever really existed?
I have never known who I am,
and even my friends who once loved me,
who gave me some sense of belonging,
have drawn back in horror and left me.

**There is drought in the depths of my being,
no rain, no water, no life.**

Pause

My sight fails me because of my trouble;
there is no light in the place of deep dark.
I am alone, bewildered, and lost;
yet I cannot abandon you, O God.
Day after day I cry out to you,
early in the morning I pray in your absence.

...in the Spirit that stirs amongst us the kaleidoscope of Jesus.

**There is drought in the depths of my being,
no rain, no water, no life.**

Pause

Do you work wonders among the tombs?
Shall the dead rise up and praise you?
Will your loving kindness reach to the grave,
your faithfulness to the place of destruction?
Are the stories of old an illusion?
Will you again do what is right in the land?

Silence

In times of despair, O God, **rain showers of gentleness upon
us, that we may be kindly to one another and also to
ourselves. Renew in us the spirit of hope. Even in the
depths of the darkness, may we hear the approach of the
One who harrows hell and greets even Judas with a kiss.**

89   The promise

*That we may question and puzzle and argue our way faithfully with the One who
promises when so much remains unfulfilled.*

Part i

We cannot know the depths of your being, O God,
you are to us a mystery profound.
Revealed as a love that is selfless,
still do we touch but a fringe of your being.
Your promises of love are steady and sure,
yet in perplexity we doubt them.

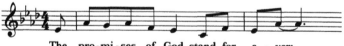

The pro-mi-ses of God stand for   e - ver:___

We breathe these words out of the Silence within us, into the Silence beyond us...

when will we   see them   ful-filled?

Pause

Your people of old called you 'king of high heaven':
they thought of you praised by the holy ones,
by the inner council who held you in awe,
who praised your wonders and deeds.

Pause

They bowed down to the king who was just,
whose promises they believed to be sure.
Justice was the foundation of your reign,
loving kindness and faithfulness your closest attendants.

The promises of God stand for ever:
when will we see them fulfilled?

Pause

They praised you as the God of power:
no other gods could stand in your way.
They believed in your strength and your faithfulness,
that you were in charge of the powers of creation:

Pause

stilling the surging of the sea,
reining in the monsters of chaos.
When floods drowned them in their thousands,
they believed you were punishing them for their evil.

The promises of God stand for ever:
when will we see them fulfilled?

Pause

A particular people believed that you favoured them,
promising them a land of their own,
rescuing them from slavery in Egypt,
bringing them safe through the wilderness.

...in the Spirit that stirs amongst us the kaleidoscope of Jesus.

Pause

With joy they shouted in triumph,
and walked in the light of your countenance.
You were their glory and strength,
their heads lifted high by your favour.

**The promises of God stand for ever:
when will we see them fulfilled?**

Pause

They believed you made a covenant with David your servant,
promising to be with him for ever,
to establish his house and his throne,
to build it up for all generations,

Pause

choosing a mere youth, no warrior,
the youngest of brothers, not the eldest,
promising to scatter his enemies,
to enlarge the bounds of his kingdom.

Pause

He called to you as his father,
his God, and the rock of his salvation.
They believed you made him your firstborn son,
highest among the rulers of earth.

**The promises of God stand for ever:
when will we see them fulfilled?**

Pause

When he wandered away from your path,
when his children forsook your law,
they believed you punished their rebellion
and gave strength to their enemies.

Pause

Yet they held on to your promise,
that you would not betray or be disloyal,

We breathe these words out of the Silence within us, into the Silence beyond us...

once and for all vowing your faithfulness,
that you would not prove false to David.

The promises of God stand for ever:
when will we see them fulfilled?

Silence

Part ii

Yet it seemed as if the promise lay shattered,
that in your wrath you had rejected your anointed,
spurning the covenant with your servant,
defiling his crown in the dust,
breaking down the walls of the city,
making his strongholds desolate.

Pause

The scavengers swooped down to plunder,
the king was scorned by his neighbours.
The power of his enemies grew,
they humiliated him with their mockery.
His bright sword lay tarnished and broken,
no longer will he stand firm in battle.
His glory was brought to an end,
his throne was cast to the ground.

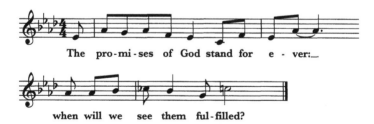

The pro-mi-ses of God stand for e - ver:_
when will we see them ful-filled?

Pause

For centuries the seed of the promise was buried,
unnoticed in the sands of the desert.   >

...in the Spirit that stirs amongst us the kaleidoscope of Jesus.

Yet human hearts cherished the hope,
waiting and yearning through oppression and exile.
At last the young and the humble heard your voice,
Mary responded to the grace of your word.
The carpenter Joseph accepted the dream,
and the promise to David burst into life.

Pause

Spirit seized the being of Yeshua,
anointing him in grace and in power.
The poor heard the news of acceptance and love,
the bolts of the prisoners slid back.
The blind recovered their sight,
the wounds of the victims were healed.

Pause

But the challenge of the promise was too great:
they drew back from love's fierce demands.
The incarnate of God was left quite alone,
the promise seemed broken by the wood of a cross.

**The promises of God stand for ever:
when will we see them fulfilled?**

Pause

But the flame that had been lit was not extinguished,
from death's very tombs was the promise renewed.
Love in its grief went to care for a corpse,
and returned full of terror and joy.
He was alive in their hearts and their wills,
and his Spirit leapt through the land.

Pause

They expected him soon to return,
that the day of your glory would dawn.
Yet again did their hopes fade away,
and the centuries began to roll by.

Pause

We breathe these words out of the Silence within us, into the Silence beyond us...

The promise was obscured by worldly success,
the corruptions of power, the slither of compromise.
The sufferings of children still cry aloud,
terror and greed freeze the heart still.

**The promises of God stand for ever:
when will we see them fulfilled?**

Silence

O God of the promise, **but fleetingly fulfilled among us, test
us not beyond our endurance, keep hope alive, and hasten
the day when we shall know the promise has been kept.**

90   Time and eternity

In solidarity with those who are dying; and with those who will take our place after us.

God of eternity, God beyond time,
our refuge and hope from one generation to another:
before the mountains rose from the sea,
before the rivers carved the valleys,
before time itself began, you are God, eternal.

Pause

From dust we came, to dust we return.
"Be shaped from clay, be crumbled to earth."
Creator of life, of death, so did you order our ways.
A thousand years in your sight are as yesterday.
As a watch in the night comes quickly to an end,
so the years pass before you, in a flicker of the eye.

A - midst   the___ con - fu - sions of time,___

may we hear   e - ter - ni -ty's heart - beat.

...in the Spirit that stirs amongst us the kaleidoscope of Jesus.

Pause

The years are like the grass,
which in the morning is green,
and by evening is dried up and withered.
As the grass shrivels in the smoke,
so is our pride consumed in your fire:
we are afraid of the burning of the dross.

Pause

All our misdeeds and deceits
are brought to light before your eyes,
all our secret sins made clear in the light of your truth.
When you are angry, our days are as nothing:
our years come to an end, vanishing with a sigh.

**Amidst the confusions of time,
may we hear eternity's heartbeat.**

Pause

The decades soon pass, no more than a handful.
Some show vigour in age, yet even they are soon gone.
So much of our span is wearisome, full of labour and sorrow.

Pause

O the speed of it all,
and the vanity of the years:
all I have done is like straw,
and most of it forgotten already.
Success crumbles into dust:
there is nothing to pay love's account.

**Amidst the confusions of time,
may we hear eternity's heartbeat.**

Pause

Who is even aware
of the purging of your wrath?
Who pays a moment's attention
to the fierceness of your love?

We breathe these words out of the Silence within us, into the Silence beyond us…

Teach us to number our days,
and apply our hearts to wisdom.

**Amidst the confusions of time,
may we hear eternity's heartbeat.**

Pause

Turn again, O God, do not delay:
give grace to your servants.
Satisfy us in the morning
with your lovingkindness.
So we shall rejoice and be glad
all the days of our life.

**Amidst the confusions of time,
may we hear eternity's heartbeat.**

Pause

Give us days of gladness
to make up for those of affliction,
for the years of adversity.
Show your servants your deeds,
and your glory to our children.

Pause

May your grace be upon us:
fill us with the Spirit of love.
For in the evening of our days
when we come to be judged,
we shall be known only by love,
delivered only by love.

Silence

Eternal God, **thank you for your gift of time and the
measure death gives to our days. They pass so quickly
as to dent our pride. May we neither rely on our
achievements nor be downcast at our failures. Keep us
but faithful to your love, and dependent on your grace
alone. We ask this in the Spirit of the One who died a
human failure, and died so young.**

…in the Spirit that stirs amongst us the kaleidoscope of Jesus.

91   Unshakeable trust in God

That our laws may protect the vulnerable; and that we may trust one another with our vulnerability.

At nightfall I come to an inn on my journey,
a place of refuge, of your presence, O God,
a sanctuary, a temple, the tent of your dwelling,
where I lie down to sleep in safety.
Under the shade of your hovering wings
I have no fear of the unknown in the dark.

You are trust - wor - thy   and   true, my   God,

hold-ing fast   to your co - ve - nant of   love.____

Pause

You have set me free from the snare of the hunter,
from the depth of the pit of snakes.
My trust in you keeps me from terror,
they sense no need to attack me.

Pause

You overshadow me with your wings,
I am safe under your feathers.
As a mother protects her brood,
so are you tender and strong towards me.
With your faithfulness as shield and defence,
I have courage to face any danger.

**You are trustworthy and true, my God,
holding fast to your covenant of love.**

Pause

We breathe these words out of the Silence within us, into the Silence beyond us...

In the dead of night I have no terror to fear,
neither dread in the daytime the plunge of the dagger,
nor fear the plague that stalks in the darkness,
nor the fever that strikes in the heat of the day.

Pause

Though a thousand fall beside me in battle,
ten thousand at my right hand,
even though faith has endured to the limit,
still do I reach to the God who saves.

**You are trustworthy and true, my God,
holding fast to your covenant of love.**

Pause

Yes, with a faith that moves mountains
still do I trust in my God.
I shall never know lasting harm,
whatever the testing ordeal.
With my own eyes I shall see
your judgment and mercy, O God.

**You are trustworthy and true, my God,
holding fast to your covenant of love.**

Pause

Because I have said,
"O God, you are my hope:
you are my refuge and stronghold,"
no great evil will overwhelm me,
no final destruction crush me.

Pause

For you will command your angels
to keep me in your narrow ways:
they will bear me up in their hands
lest I dash my foot against a stone.

Pause

...in the Spirit that stirs amongst us the kaleidoscope of Jesus.

I may step upon cobra and adder,
but even the snakes I shall tread underfoot.
In the strength of my God, in impossible faith,
I will bind the powers that rebel.

**You are trustworthy and true, my God,
holding fast to your covenant of love.**

Pause

"Because I am bound to you in love,
therefore I shall deliver you.
I shall lift you out of danger
because you hold on to my name.
You know me in intimate trust,
in your inner heart you are loyal and true."

Pause

"In your anguish and need I am with you,
I shall set you free and clothe you with glory.
You will live to be full of years,
you will know the abundance of my salvation."

Silence

Open our eyes, O God of marvel and of wonder, **beyond the
puzzling reflections in the mirror, beyond the brutal
images of violence, beyond the fading of the years, that we
may see the wide open spaces of promised freedom, may
glimpse the communion of saints and brush the wings of
angels, may recognize for a moment the glory of the
universe, where darkness and doubt dissolve, where the
gash of the wound shines, where death and destruction
have vanished for ever.**

We breathe these words out of the Silence within us, into the Silence beyond us...

92   The steadiness of God

For steadiness in times of turmoil and for contentment in the present moment; that
oppressors be shamed by tenderness and laughter; and in solidarity with those who have
nobody to turn to.

How precious a thing it is to give thanks to you, O God.
How good and beautiful to sing your name, most beloved,
to receive your love in our hearts
at the rising of the sun in the morning,
to sing of your faithfulness in the watches of the night,
on the strings of the harp and the lyre.

Stea - dy and sure is the pulse of your heart,
quiet- ening, calm- ing, all our dis - tress.

Pause

In everything you have done you make me glad,
I sing for joy at the beauty of creation.
The depths of your thoughts I cannot comprehend,
the wonder of the universe I shall never fathom.

Pause

Everything that happens impinges on your heart,
in wisdom and love you hold us and heal us.
The wounds of the broken-hearted you bind,
you patiently stitch the severed limbs of your body.

Steady and sure is the pulse of your heart,
quietening, calming, all our distress.

Pause

The brutal do not understand your ways,
the cruel add to the pain that you suffer.   >

...in the Spirit that stirs amongst us the kaleidoscope of Jesus.

Because of the freedom you give us,
wickedness can sprout like the grass in spring.

Pause

But in the drought of summer those who do evil
in their need have no one to turn to.
Cut off from the flow of companionship
they wither, decay, and die.
The fruits of their wrongdoing shrivel,
burnt up in the heat of your fire.

**Steady and sure is the pulse of your heart,
quietening, calming, all our distress.**

Pause

Those who have rebelled against you
will scatter their arms as they flee.
Lost and bewildered they will cower in fear,
at the mercy of those they betrayed,
whose eyes now look down on their enemies,
whose ears hear the crash of their fall.

Pause

Yet the oppressed draw near in compassion,
with water to slake their enemies' thirst.
Their deeds are as a lingering fragrance,
a perfume with which you anoint them.

Pause

With their quiet and dignified presence
they will shame their enemies to silence.
Vibrant with life, they will invite them to dance,
their eyes glistening with laughter and joy.

Pause

Those who keep faith will flourish like the palm tree,
like the spreading cedar of Lebanon.
Planted firm in the earth of your courtyard, O God,
they will mature and give fruit for your house.

We breathe these words out of the Silence within us, into the Silence beyond us...

Pause

To old age they will be vigorous and fresh,
sturdy and laden with branches.
Like the trees and the mountains strong,
they will confirm your patient endurance.

**Steady and sure is the pulse of your heart,
quietening, calming, all our distress.**

Silence

God of infinite pains and patience, **in these our turbulent
days take from us the stress of seeking for security in
force of arms and luxury of comfort, and give us the quiet
confidence of those who have enough for today and who
trust you for tomorrow.**

93   A calm authority

*That with divine wisdom we may sufficiently contain the energies we have unleashed;
and that those with inner chaos and fury may find peace.*

In the silence of the night your word was spoken,
a calm creative word in the heavens.
It was but a whisper of your voice,
the faint rustling of your robes of glory.
Light of the universe, yet did you hide yourself,
so that your beams might not dazzle and shrivel us.

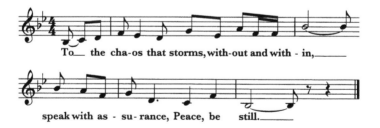

To__ the cha-os that storms, with-out and with - in,____

speak with as - su - rance, Peace, be   still.____

Pause

...in the Spirit that stirs amongst us the kaleidoscope of Jesus.

In quiet ways you hold the world together,
chaos contained by your compassionate power.
When the seas hurl their pounding waves,
when the hurricane howls across the ocean,
when the tornado rips through the farmland,
when the rivers rage through city streets,
you set a limit to their power,
that they may not overwhelm us for ever.

**To the chaos that storms, without and within,
speak with assurance, Peace, be still.**

Pause

The surges of chaos pound through our heads,
a murderous fury rises within us;
wrenched apart by the sobbing of grief,
we are lost and bewildered, tossed to and fro.

Pause

A relentless pain throbs through our bones,
we scream in the night at the faces of terror.
Yet even as we plunge in the fearful abyss,
the face of the crucified is there in the void.

**To the chaos that storms, without and within,
speak with assurance, Peace, be still.**

Pause

For where do we best see your power?
Nowhere else but a man who is stricken,
deserted and betrayed by his friends,
killed by his people, an outcast, unclean.

Pause

The chaos they dared not face in themselves
they hurled with abuse and the nails.
They hid from their pain in the thicket of laws,
and refused to allow their wounds to be healed.
They defended themselves in self-righteous armour,
and refused the calm word of forgiveness and love.

We breathe these words out of the Silence within us, into the Silence beyond us...

**To the chaos that storms, without and within,
speak with assurance, Peace, be still.**

Pause

The material world looked so solid around us,
we never even dreamed of the chaos in matter.
As the cloud mushroomed high in the desert,
we were stunned by the force we'd unleashed.
The power of apocalypse is now in our hands:
is the calm word of God lost for ever?

Silence

Creator God, **woven into the very fabric of the universe, for
ever committed to bringing harmony out of chaos, assure
us of your presence in the midst of our perplexities and
fears, that you will endure with us and speak the calm
word of a deeper and more lasting peace.**

94   That justice be done

*For the repentance of the cruel; in solidarity with those cowering indoors and afraid to
walk the streets; and that we may not allow evil to spread by saying and doing nothing.*

A child is murdered in the street,
a widow is mugged for a meagre purse,
a stone shatters the bedroom window
of a couple whose skin is strange.
A violent spirit runs amok,
the powerless are the first to suffer.

Hun-gry for jus-tice, thir-sty for mer-cy,
fierce is our cry: Put___ right what is wrong.

...in the Spirit that stirs amongst us the kaleidoscope of Jesus.

Pause

Masked gunmen, why do you kill?
Arrogant fool, why do you trample?
Drunken gang, why have your hearts
become the very stones that you throw?
What is this rampaging spirit
that sweeps the mob to such fury?

**Hungry for justice, thirsty for mercy,
fierce is our cry: Put right what is wrong.**

Pause

No wonder the widower weeps;
no wonder the mother howls;
no wonder they shrink back in fear;
no wonder they cry, Revenge.
O God, stop these too-familiar horrors,
this wasteland of our killing fields.

**Hungry for justice, thirsty for mercy,
fierce is our cry: Put right what is wrong.**

Pause

How long will the ways of violence triumph?
How long will cruel words pierce the air?
How long will the arrogant boast of their conquests?
How long will prejudice keep us apart?
O God, do you not hear, do you not see?
Will you not chasten? Where is your justice?

**Hungry for justice, thirsty for mercy,
fierce is our cry: Put right what is wrong.**

Pause

Arise, Judge of all the earth.
May your justice be seen to be done.
Lift the burdens of oppression,
heal the crushed in mind and spirit,
bind up the wounds of the injured,
bend the necks that are stiffened with pride.

We breathe these words out of the Silence within us, into the Silence beyond us...

**Hungry for justice, thirsty for mercy,
fierce is our cry: Put right what is wrong.**

Pause

You know the thoughts of all our hearts,
you know that each of us is no more than a breath.
Yet you will not cast us away, people of the earth,
you will not forsake those you have created.
Justice will be seen to flourish again,
vindicating those who are true of heart.

**Hungry for justice, thirsty for mercy,
fierce is our cry: Put right what is wrong.**

Pause

Take up the cause of the weak and helpless,
speak for those overpowered by words,
bring to light the corruptions of justice,
bind those who spread evil by means of the law,
expose the conspiracies of silence,
let not the innocent be condemned.

**Hungry for justice, thirsty for mercy,
fierce is our cry: Put right what is wrong.**

Pause

If you had not been our helper,
we would have lost our way in the mists.
When our feet slipped on the narrow path
you held us firm in your merciful strength.
In all the anxieties of our minds
your peace steadied and calmed us.
In all the doubtings of our hearts
your presence sustained and consoled us.

**Hungry for justice, thirsty for mercy,
fierce is our cry: Put right what is wrong.**

Pause

...in the Spirit that stirs amongst us the kaleidoscope of Jesus.

Humble those who work evil,
silence those whose words weave corruption,
gently withdraw the sting of their violence:
with healing ointment may their poison dissolve.
Remove the power of those who wreak havoc,
put them to tasks of service and care.

**Hungry for justice, thirsty for mercy,
fierce is our cry: Put right what is wrong.**

Pause

In your good time bring us face to face,
oppressors and victims who often collude.
None of us has words of defence in your presence,
we are silenced by the power of your truth and your love.

Pause

May the victims among us stretch out our hands
to touch those who would now shrink away,
gently to turn their faces towards us,
that our eyes may fill with mercy and wonder.

Pause

So may we look with confidence towards you,
loving God, so awesome in mercy,
fierce in compassion and judgment,
yearning for reconciliation and peace,
bearing the pain with a heartfelt cry,
in which grief and joy become one.

Silence

Spirit of the living God, **in communion with you and with the
cries of those who suffer injustice, work in and through us
new deeds of discerning wisdom and true judgment, that
we may know among us the fulfilment of your promises,
even the firstfruits of your rule of justice.**

We breathe these words out of the Silence within us, into the Silence beyond us...

95   Encountering the redeeming Creator

For places of bitterness and quarrel; for a reassuring glimpse of the sheer power of divine love; for a deepening of commitments made; for the making good of what has gone wrong.

Let us sing to the God who is creating us,
let us rejoice in the rock of our salvation.

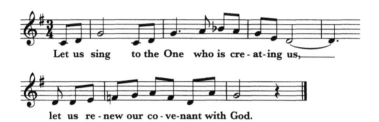

Let us sing   to the One   who is cre - at-ing us,_____

let us re - new our co - ve-nant with God.

Pause

Dear God, we celebrate your presence with thanksgiving,
and with our whole heart sing psalms of praise.
We greet you with love, Creator of the universe,
Spirit who strives with the chaos of the world.

Pause

With your finger you shape the mountains of the earth,
and the depths of the valleys are scoured by your power.
The wings of your Spirit brood over the seas,
and your hands mould the dry land.

**Let us sing to the One who is creating us,
let us renew our covenant with God.**

Pause

Not one of the threatening powers escapes you,
the thundering of the gods on the cloud-capped mountains,
the rumbling of demons as the earth quakes,
the faces that loom in the dreams of the night,
the punishing voices from our helpless past.   >

...in the Spirit that stirs amongst us the kaleidoscope of Jesus.

The power of your love reaches so far
that nothing and no-one is beyond your redemption.

Pause

O come let us worship and lift our hearts high
and adore our God, our Creator.
For you indeed are God, and we are your people,
crafted by the skill of your hands.

Silence

"Listen to my voice this day
and harden not your hearts.
Do not be like your ancestors
who saw the great deeds I had done,
yet put me to the test in the desert,
at the place of 'Bitterness' and 'Quarrel'."

Pause

"They were wayward in their hearts,
they were ignorant of my ways.
So they could sense my love only as wrath,
they were lost in their restless wandering."

Pause

If we listen to your voice deep within us,
we shall know the mercy and grace of your love.
We shall meet you as you sit in wise judgment,
doing right in the sight of all peoples,
discerning us in your faithfulness,
quelling our rebellious strife.

**Let us sing to the One who is creating us,
let us renew our covenant with God.**

Pause

Spirit of Christ, take shape among us,
Spirit of the One who fulfilled God's promise.
Humble us in awe at your presence:
let us adore you in the silence of love.

We breathe these words out of the Silence within us, into the Silence beyond us...

Deepen our gratitude in obedience and trust,
in your covenant made sure for ever.

Silence

**To the beauty and bounty of your creation and grace, we have
responded, O God, with desecration and greed. We have
presumed upon the constant renewal of your gifts. Give us
penitent hearts and the will to cherish the earth, that we
may know you again as our redeeming Creator, bringing
good from our wastes and sorrows.**

96   Joy in God

*In solidarity with musicians; and with all who work with others from discord to
harmony.*

Sing to the great God a new song,
sing to the Creator, sing the whole earth.

Pause

We sing to you, God, and praise your name,
telling of your salvation from day to day,
declaring your glory to those who do not know you,
and your wonders to the peoples of the earth.

Pause

Marvellous God, you are greatly to be praised,
more to be honoured than all the powers.   >

...in the Spirit that stirs amongst us the kaleidoscope of Jesus.

Glory and worship are before you,
power and honour are in your sanctuary.

Sing to the great God a new song,
sing to the Creator, sing the whole earth.

**Let nature and peoples join in harmony
to sing praise, to sing praise, to the God of glory.**

Pause

May we, the household of your people,
ascribe to you worship and glory,
giving you the honour due to your name,
bringing presents as we come into your house.
We worship you in the beauty of holiness:
let the whole earth stand in awe of you.

Pause

Let us tell it out among the peoples that you are God,
and that you are making the round world so sure,
held within the bounds of your love,
and that you will judge the people righteously.

Sing to the great God a new song,
sing to the Creator, sing the whole earth.

**Let nature and peoples join in harmony
to sing praise, to sing praise, to the God of glory.**

Pause

Let the heavens rejoice and let the earth be glad:
let the sea roar, and all its creatures delight;
let the fields be joyful, and all that is in them:
then shall the trees of the wood shout for joy.

Pause

For you come to judge the earth,
with justice to make right what is wrong,
to judge the people with your truth.

Sing to the great God a new song,
sing to the Creator, sing the whole earth.

We breathe these words out of the Silence within us, into the Silence beyond us...

**Let nature and peoples join in harmony
to sing praise, to sing praise, to the God of glory.**

Pause

All creatures of the earth will sing your praise,
for you are a God who is faithful,
for ever loyal to your covenant,
creating out of discord a harmony rare.

Silence

God of glory and splendour, **whose bright radiance we see in
glimpses of wonder, both rare and everyday, open our
eyes and hearts, alert the nerve ends of our being, that in
trembling and rapture all our fears may dissolve into joy.**

97   The old order turned upside down

*That our thirst for justice be quenched, but not in the old religious mindset of us against
them; that the world's powerful may restrain their use of force, repent of their own
complicity in murky deeds, act to constrain evil without ever believing they can root it
out for ever; and that we may steadily believe that God's restorative justice will prevail.*

The foundations of your reign are rarely seen, O God,
salvation and justice are hidden away.
Clouds and darkness deepen the mystery:
faith hears but a possible cry.

Pause

The God of justice comes: the thunder rolls,
the lightnings flash, the earth quakes.
Evil is burnt up by fire,
the mountains melt like wax;
the flames consume corruption,
the falling rocks hiss in the sea.

Pause

...in the Spirit that stirs amongst us the kaleidoscope of Jesus.

We have served vain idols,
and we are ashamed:
awed by the searing truth,
in fear and trembling we are brought to our knees.
Your glory lights up our faces,
and our eyes are blinded.

Pause

We have put lovers and leaders before you,
we have bowed down to our petty gods,
we have gloried in mere nothings:
like them we crumble to the dust.

Pause

The city of peace hears its God,
and all its inhabitants rejoice.
In your judgment, O God, the poor are lifted high,
the burdens of oppression slide from their backs.

Pause

For you love those who resist evil,
you guard the life of the faithful,
you sustain them when held in the grip
of the cruel and greedy and hateful.

God reigns:_ the gen-tle peo-ple_ in-he-rit the earth,
the lit-tle is-lands re-joice_____ to see the day.
God reigns! God_ reigns!_

We breathe these words out of the Silence within us, into the Silence beyond us...

Pause

Your promised day dawns, O God,
a day of gladness for the true of heart.
Your domain spreads fair before us,
like a banquet prepared for a homecoming.

Pause

Those who love truth flourish in your presence,
their faces glow in the light of your welcome.
The courageous and faithful sing for joy,
and give thanks to your glorious name.

**God reigns: the gentle people inherit the earth,
the little islands rejoice to see the day.
God reigns! God reigns!**

Silence

In the day of your vindication, O God, **we shall laugh and sing
as we never have before. From our bellies will flow the
ripples of joy, the living water that makes the desert
bloom and the true of heart delight in one another's love.**

98   The song of a renewed creation

*In solidarity with judges, lawyers, political leaders, parliaments; and that we may
enact God's justice on earth.*

We praise you, O God, with a new song,
for you have done marvellous things.
With the strength of endurance
and the folly of weakness,
with the wisdom of justice
and the power of gentleness,
you have won the greatest of victories,
bringing triumph from the midst of defeat.
The rebellious powers lay down their arms,
the people of the earth rejoice in your will.

...in the Spirit that stirs amongst us the kaleidoscope of Jesus.

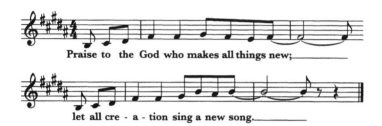

Praise to the God who makes all things new;

let all cre - a - tion sing a new song.

Pause

So you have declared your salvation,
wide-ranging freedom for your people.
You have fulfilled your promise to be faithful
towards the house of Israel;
your healing and peace have shone forth,
even to the far-flung islands of the world.

**Praise to the God who makes all things new;
let all creation sing a new song.**

Pause

Show yourselves joyful in God, all you peoples,
sing, rejoice, and give thanks.
We praise you, O God, upon the harp,
singing a psalm of thanksgiving,
with trumpets and echoing horns,
showing ourselves joyful in your presence.

**Praise to the God who makes all things new;
let all creation sing a new song.**

Pause

Let the sea roar, and all its creatures,
the round earth, and those who dwell on it.
Let the streams clap their hands,
and let the hills be joyful before you.

Pause

We breathe these words out of the Silence within us, into the Silence beyond us...

For you have come to judge the earth,
at last making all things well.
You restore all the people with justice,
with wisdom and mercy beyond our comparing,
O holy, compassionate, and most loving God.

**Praise to the God who makes all things new;
let all creation sing a new song.**

Silence

Faithful Creator, **ever striving with your creation, with
nature, with your people, with the One who embodied
your will, bringing new and unexpected life out of despair
and death, work still in these our days, that we may sing a
new song to your glory.**

99   Holy is God

For courage to make holy the least likely places.

Holy God, reigning throughout the universe,
serving as a ruler humble and just,
kneeling before us as a healer with wounds,
touching our foreheads as a woman who is wise:
Creatures of light and darkness surround you,
eyes glistening with tears of thanksgiving.

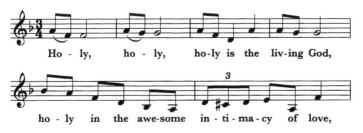

Ho - ly, ho - ly, ho-ly is the liv-ing God,
ho - ly in the awe-some in - ti - ma - cy of love,

...in the Spirit that stirs amongst us the kaleidoscope of Jesus.

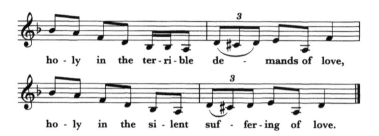

ho - ly in the ter - ri - ble de - mands of love,

ho - ly in the si - lent suf - fer - ing of love.

Pause

Yours is the power that holds all things in being,
the power of justice and love.
Yours is the holiness that sears,
bringing to light our falsehoods.

Pause

The prophets, the priests, and the wise,
Moses and Aaron, Samuel and Solomon,
they called assured upon your name,
knowing that you would teach them.

Pause

You showed them how to lead the people,
burning into them your holiness,
never yielding the commandment to love,
refusing to let any of us sink deep
into the mire and oblivion of sin.

**Holy, holy, holy is the living God,
holy in the awesome intimacy of love,
holy in the terrible demands of love,
holy in the silent suffering of love.**

Pause

Holy is your presence in the love of your Christ,
always in places the pious rejected,
born in a cave among a people oppressed,
suffering the hidden cost of forgiveness,
embracing the outcast who were deemed impure,

We breathe these words out of the Silence within us, into the Silence beyond us...

dying disgraced and disfigured:
yet even a cross became holy and hopeful.

Holy, holy, holy is the living God,
holy in the awesome intimacy of love,
holy in the terrible demands of love,
holy in the silent suffering of love.

Silence

Holy God, **teach us not to be afraid of anything you have**
created, however threatened or repelled we may be. Fill us
with your Holy Spirit, the Spirit that makes us a holy
people who may then draw near to transform whatever we
meet, the Spirit that finds its home in our flesh and blood.

100   A joyful people

That joy may rest at the centre of all human beings.

Let the whole earth be joyful in you, O God,
greet you with gladness,
and celebrate your presence with a song.

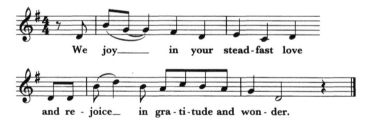

We joy___ in your stead-fast love
and re-joice__ in gra-ti-tude and won-der.

Pause

For we know that you are creating us,
you are alive in us and we belong to you.
You are weaving us into a marvellous tapestry,
a people of diverse threads and colours.

We joy in your steadfast love
and rejoice in gratitude and wonder.

...in the Spirit that stirs amongst us the kaleidoscope of Jesus.

Pause

We enter your gates, a motley procession,
with heartfelt thanksgiving and joy.
We dance with delight and bless one another,
in the Spirit of your love, intimate and just.
For you are gracious and courteous, compassionate in embrace,
faithful through all generations.

**We joy in your steadfast love
and rejoice in gratitude and wonder.**

Silence

Living, loving, holy Mystery, **our joy rests in you and comes
from you, for we are indeed content to be your people, and
we are humbled by your care for us. You are God and there
is none other. You are steadfast, faithful, loyal, and kind.
We would seek to embody your will on earth, and to trust
you for all that is to come.**

101   The single eye

*That we may encourage those in power to exercise restraint, to serve the common good,
to make the best compromises they can; that we may spend more time encouraging than
blaming; and that we may be accurate, kindly, and constructive in our criticisms.*

Take from us, O God, the burden of pretence,
the lie that we and our leaders are just.
Let songs of wisdom sound from our lips;
keep self-righteousness far from our hearts.

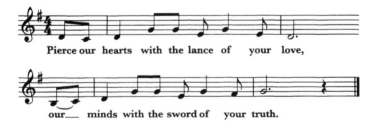

Pierce our hearts with the lance of your love,
our minds with the sword of your truth.

We breathe these words out of the Silence within us, into the Silence beyond us...

Pause

So often we pretend to be innocent,
blameless and free of all guilt.
Open our eyes that we may see clear:
there is no escaping our crookedness.

**Pierce our hearts with the lance of your love,
our minds with the sword of your truth.**

Pause

So often we slander our neighbours,
afraid of their class or colour or creed.
Expose to the light the projections of our minds:
it is ourselves we should see in their mirror.

**Pierce our hearts with the lance of your love,
our minds with the sword of your truth.**

Pause

So often we are angry with the greedy and proud,
the arrogant who are deaf to the cries of the poor.
Keep our eye single; give us hearts that are pure,
lest we trample without knowing what we do.

**Pierce our hearts with the lance of your love,
our minds with the sword of your truth.**

Pause

So often we grumble at people with power,
calling them deceitful and corrupt in their ways.
Humble us all whose eyes are so blurred:
dishonest we are, we discern not the truth.

**Pierce our hearts with the lance of your love,
our minds with the sword of your truth.**

Pause

So often we fail to take account of our wealth,
the power of body, possessions, or talent.
May the light that shines from the eyes of the humble
burn out the corruption to which we are blind.

...in the Spirit that stirs amongst us the kaleidoscope of Jesus.

Pierce our hearts with the lance of your love,
our minds with the sword of your truth.

Silence

God of truth, **hold before our eyes a vision of your com-**
monwealth, your rule of integrity and wisdom, justice and
mercy. Give to those in public life minds that are true and
hearts that are compassionate. May they be humbled by
those who pass by.

102   Resurrection promise

In solidarity with those whose faith falters; that we may welcome a generous vision
of God.

We live through a night of deep trouble,
of dreams that disturb, of collapse and decay.
We restore the façades of our heritage;
they are hollow within, the meaning has gone.

Pause

Even the stones turn to dust,
as the beauty of the ages departs.
The lines of power strut the landscape:
the energy that feeds them fails.

Pause

To the One who has dis - ap - peared,
to the pre-sence we know___ as ab - sence,

We breathe these words out of the Silence within us, into the Silence beyond us...

we wave with the shreds of our faith,

Is the power of death o - ver - turned?

Pause

The smoke of my days rises in the twilight,
curls in the air and is gone.
Already my bones blaze in the furnace,
reduced to the ash that soon they will be.

Pause

My heart is scorched and shrivels,
pounded like grass in the summer heat.
The groans of my throat shrink to a croak,
my skin is glued to my bones.

Pause

**To the One who has disappeared,
to the presence we know as absence,
we wave with the shreds of our faith,
Is the power of death overturned?**

Pause

Like a bird that is trapped by midwinter,
I find no food in the frozen waste.
Anxiously I look all around me,
afraid of the swoop of my enemies.

Pause

Chattering and restless I flit to and fro,
screeching through the desolate silence.
Exhausted, I limp through the snow;
I sink to the earth, shot through by the wind.

...in the Spirit that stirs amongst us the kaleidoscope of Jesus.

Pause

To the One who has disappeared,
to the presence we know as absence,
we wave with the shreds of our faith,
Is the power of death overturned?

Pause

Slowly, steadily, I turn to you, my hope,
daring still to whisper your name.
Surely your heart moves with pity,
even to the grey streaks of my hair?

Pause

Your name has been known by my ancestors,
my children will seek and will find.
The nations will at last sing your praise,
the rulers of the peoples give you glory.

Pause

To the One who has disappeared,
to the presence we know as absence,
we wave with the shreds of our faith,
Is the power of death overturned?

Pause

Your heart must surely hear the cry of the destitute,
you cannot despise your little ones.
The wounded you embrace with compassion,
you slide back the bolts of the prisoners.

Pause

Oh, it sounds so glib – though we say it in faith –
so nearly like vain repetition.
We desperately want to believe it is true,
that those yet unborn may give you the praise.

Pause

We breathe these words out of the Silence within us, into the Silence beyond us...

To the One who has disappeared,
to the presence we know as absence,
we wave with the shreds of our faith,
Is the power of death overturned?

Pause

You have broken my strength before my time,
the very days cut short, their gift snatched away.
Soon I shall perish, and yet you endure,
my clothes become rags, yet your years never fail.

Pause

A comfort perhaps – but the children still die,
and the barren know nothing but dust.
Can the young man who died give us hope?
The cry of the night be answered with joy?

Pause

To the One who has disappeared,
to the presence we know as absence,
we wave with the shreds of our faith,
Is the power of death overturned?

Pause

Where is the language of words that catch fire?
Where is the wonder of a birth that is new?
Where is the savour of salt on the breeze?
Where is the bouquet of the freshest of wines?
Where is the confounding of the powers in the land?
Where is the community indifferent to threat?
Where are the alert, the wise and compassionate?
Where are the gifts whose giving does not end?

Silence

Your promises, O God, stand for ever, **yet our hearts are**
torn when we see them unfulfilled; even the crumbs of
reassurance fail to fall, and we are shrivelled by perplexity
and doubt. Keep us faithful through our winter. May the
slender thread hold.

...in the Spirit that stirs amongst us the kaleidoscope of Jesus.

103   Unfathomable love

That people of faith may recognize that God is for all humanity, not only for the like-minded; and that we may grow in patience, endurance, faithfulness, and forgiveness.

From the deep places of my soul I praise you, O God:
I lift up my heart and glorify your holy name.
From the deep places of my soul I praise you, O God:
how can I forget all your goodness towards me?

Pause

You forgive all my sin, you heal all my weakness,
you rescue me from the brink of disaster,
you crown me with mercy and compassion.
You satisfy my being with good things,
so that my youth is renewed like an eagle's.

There is no end to your mer - cy,

en - dur-ing and in-fi - nite is your love.____

Pause

You fulfil all that you promise,
justice for all the oppressed.
You made known your ways to Moses,
and all the people saw your deeds.

Pause

You are full of forgiveness and grace,
endlessly patient, faithful in love.
You do not haunt us with our sins,
or nurse grievances against us.
You do not repay evil with evil,
for you are greater than our sins.

We breathe these words out of the Silence within us, into the Silence beyond us...

Pause

As vast as the heavens are in comparison with the earth,
so great is your love to those who trust you.
As far as the east is from the west,
so far do you fling our sins from us.

**There is no end to your mercy,
enduring and infinite is your love.**

Pause

Just as parents are merciful to their children,
so are you merciful and kind towards us.
For you know how fragile we are,
that we are made of the dust of the earth.

Pause

Our days are like the grass,
they bloom like the flowers of the field:
the wind blows over them and they are gone,
and no-one can tell where they stood.

Pause

Only your merciful goodness endures;
age after age you act justly
towards all who hold on to your covenant,
who take your words to heart and fulfil them.

**There is no end to your mercy,
enduring and infinite is your love.**

Silence

For you have triumphed over the power of death,
and draw us to your presence with songs of joy.
We hear the echo of your angels praising you,
and the whole communion of your saints,
those who have walked in your narrow ways,
and heard the voice of your yearning,
whose food is to do your will,
and in whom you take great delight.

…in the Spirit that stirs amongst us the kaleidoscope of Jesus.

Pause

From the widest bounds of the universe
to the depths of my very being
the whispers and cries of joy
vibrate to a shining glory,
O God, our beginning and our end.

Silence

**Creator God, as we contemplate the vast universe of which
we are so small a part, swamping us with fear and despair
and our insignificance, deepen our trust that the meaning
of it all is love, beyond whose reach it is impossible to fall.**

104   Exuberant wonder

*That we may become still and contemplate the natural world; that we may recognize
that human life is bound up with nature; that we may be responsible in the changes we
make to the basic structures of life; and that we may wonder and adore.*

Part i

Light from the dawn of the cosmos,
reaching out over billions of years;
the sun so familiar and steady,
spun off from that ancient fireball:

Pause

the primal explosion murmurs,
we hear the hiss of the aeons,
whispering insistent relic
of the original moment of time.

Pause

The beginning was all flame,
and the flame was unfurled into time;
all that has come into being
began at the heart of the flame.

Pause

We breathe these words out of the Silence within us, into the Silence beyond us...

Slowly the fire cooled,
the storm of particles ceased,
combed into structures of matter,
clouds and clusters of galaxies.

Pause

The cosmic dust was scattered –
a heart bursting into stars:
truly strange is our ancestor –
we ride on its pulsing still.

Pause

Mar - vel - lous   and   vi - gor - ous,

splen - did - ly   un -   fold   - ing,

the   won - ders   of   cre   -   a   - tion

we con - tem - plate   with   awe.

Praise be   to   the Cre - a - tor:___

fresh   e - ner - gy   di - vine___   >

...in the Spirit that stirs amongst us the kaleidoscope of Jesus.

with   pas - sion and with ten - der - ness

brings beau - ty new   to   birth.

Pause

Alone we seem in the darkness,
puppets of impersonal forces,
at best a mere flicker of light,
extinguished against the night sky.

Pause

But look at the world of the atom,
a minute yet infinite space,
where the unpredictable happens,
place of the improbably new.

Pause

Innumerable fragments that scattered
our consciousness begins to make whole,
mysteriously linked to our minds,
synapses by the billion in our brains.

Pause

Sounds stir through our bodies,
themselves fashioned by the stars,
bound up with the smallest particles.
Each of us seems like a universe.

Pause

Do we see deep in your mind,
more incredible still, our Creator?
To and fro have you ceaselessly woven
this web of matter and energy?

We breathe these words out of the Silence within us, into the Silence beyond us...

Pause

**Marvellous and vigorous,
splendidly unfolding,
the wonders of creation
we contemplate with awe.
Praise be to the Creator:
fresh energy divine
with passion and with tenderness
brings beauty new to birth.**

Silence

Part ii

We stand on a cliff top and watch,
gazing out over infinite seas,
whence our ancestors lately emerged,
obeying the call to a more complex life.

Pause

And still in the teeming oceans
swim the marvellous creatures,
the vital plankton sustaining them,
on which we also depend.

Pause

There go the whales and the dolphins,
even, it is rumoured, Leviathan,
that great monster of the deep,
the delight and sport of our God!

Pause

The heat of the sun draws the moisture
up from the seas to the turbulent skies,
where the wind blows the rain-bearing clouds
to fall on the mountains and valleys.

Pause

...in the Spirit that stirs amongst us the kaleidoscope of Jesus.

Thence spring the rivers and streams
watering the brown of the earth into green,
quenching the thirst of the animals,
bearing the people in trade and in play.

Pause

Mar - vel - lous   and   vi - gor - ous,

splen - did - ly   un - fold - ing,

the   won - ders   of   cre - a - tion

we con - tem - plate   with   awe.

Praise be   to   the Cre - a - tor:___

fresh   e - ner - gy   di - vine___

with   pas - sion and with   ten - der - ness

brings beau - ty   new   to   birth.

We breathe these words out of the Silence within us, into the Silence beyond us...

Pause

The eyes of the satellites roam,
the soaring balloons hover,
the gliders smoothly range,
they see the mosaics of earth.

Pause

There in the tangle of rain forests
is the clicking of insects, the slither of snakes,
the screech of parrots, the blanket of rain,
and numberless species yet to be named.

Pause

There jostle the shining mountains,
lands of the long white clouds,
eagles soaring to their eyries,
snow leopards ruling the heights.

Pause

There ripple the sands of the desert,
where the barren flowers at the touch of rain,
where the fennec fox watches and listens,
through the deep silence that falls with the night.

Pause

The lions of the savannahs roar,
the cedars of Lebanon spread their branches,
the cattle graze in the pastures,
the cats curl up in the sun.

Pause

Marvellous and vigorous,
splendidly unfolding,
the wonders of creation
we contemplate with awe.
Praise be to the Creator:
fresh energy divine
with passion and with tenderness
brings beauty new to birth.

...in the Spirit that stirs amongst us the kaleidoscope of Jesus.

Pause

We harvest the goodness of earth,
we reap the wheat and the maize,
we pluck the grapes from the vine,
the olives from the gnarled branches.

Pause

You give us an abundance to share,
the loaves of life for the table,
wine to gladden our hearts,
oil to lighten our skin.

Pause

Yet the sun can scorch the corn,
the lava snap the trees,
the hurricane flatten the houses,
the tidal waves and river floods drown.

Pause

The meteors hurtle through space,
the stars explode and vanish,
the violence our hearts abhor,
yet playing its vital part.

Pause

We may believe your Spirit created
and renews the face of the earth:
the destruction tempers our praise,
darkened by pain and perplexity.

Silence

Creator God, **we celebrate a new unfolding of the universe
this day, in us and in everything around us. We listen to the
silence and we hear the rustling of our breath, the hum of
engines, the cries of birds...We question and we adore...
we wonder...we trust...**

We breathe these words out of the Silence within us, into the Silence beyond us...

105   The covenants of God

That we may ponder our history; that we may make new covenants among the people of the world; and that we may honour the covenants we make.

Part i

Let us give thanks, O God, and call upon your name;
let us tell among the peoples the things you have done.
We sing to you, we sing your praise,
and tell of all your marvellous works.

Pause

We exult in your holy name;
even in seeking your wisdom and strength,
we long for the compassion of your face.
Let us call to mind the wonders you have done,
your marvellous acts and your discerning judgments.

Give praise to the God of the promise,
who keeps faith with the earth for ever.

Pause

"Time was when we were but a few,
small in number and aliens in the land.
We wandered from valley to valley,
from one oasis and people to another."

Pause

"Even then you protected us,
keeping at bay those who would harm us.
Then you called down a famine on the land,
and destroyed the bread that we needed."

...in the Spirit that stirs amongst us the kaleidoscope of Jesus.

Pause

"But you sent on a man ahead of us,
Joseph who was sold into slavery,
whose feet the Egyptians fastened with fetters,
and they thrust his neck into a hoop of iron.
He was tested to the limit by his captors,
until the time when his words proved true."

Pause

"Then the pharaoh sent word to release him,
to become steward of all his household,
to order his officers at will,
and to teach his counsellors wisdom."

**Give praise to the God of the promise,
who keeps faith with the earth for ever.**

Pause

"Then Israel came into Egypt,
and Jacob dwelt in the land of Ham.
There you made your people fruitful,
too numerous for those who opposed us,
whose hearts you turned to hate us
and deal deceitfully with your servants."

Pause

"Then you sent Moses your servant,
and Aaron whom you had chosen.
Through them you worked your signs,
and your wonders in the land of Ham.
You sent darkness to cover the land,
the darkness of your ways that we do not understand."

Pause

"You turned their waters into blood,
and the fish rose dead to the surface.
Their country swarmed with frogs,
even into the house of the pharaoh.

We breathe these words out of the Silence within us, into the Silence beyond us...

You spoke the word and there came swarms of flies,
and gnats within all their borders.
You sent them storms of hail,
and darts of lightning into their land."

Pause

"You struck their vines and their fig trees,
you sent locusts to devour their crops.
Death and decay spread their misery,
even to the firstborn of each family."

**Give praise to the God of the promise,
who keeps faith with the earth for ever.**

Pause

"You brought Israel out with silver and gold,
and not one of our tribes was seen to stumble.
Egypt was glad at our going,
for dread of Israel had fallen upon them."

Pause

"You spread out a cloud for our covering,
and fire to lighten the night.
The people asked and you brought us quails,
and satisfied us with manna from your hand."

Pause

"You opened a rock so that the waters gushed,
and ran in the parched land like a river.
For you had remembered your holy word,
the promise to Abraham your servant."

Pause

"So you led out your people with rejoicing,
your chosen ones with shouts of joy.
You gave us the land you had promised,
and we inherited the toil of others,
so that we might keep the gift of your law,
and faithfully fulfil your covenant."

...in the Spirit that stirs amongst us the kaleidoscope of Jesus.

Give praise to the God of the promise,
who keeps faith with the earth for ever.

Silence

Part ii

So we remember our ancestors' story,
how they knew you as the God of the promise.
Out of your limitless love
you have chosen, O God, to be bound
within the limits of body and time
to the earth and all its people.
For you renew the covenants of old,
ever deepening your promise to love.

Pause

In the covenant with Abraham and Isaac,
with Jacob and their descendants for ever,
you vowed your loyalty to them,
giving them the land of the promise,
and requiring the response of their hearts,
a steady will to trust and obey.

Pause

In the covenant of exodus from Egypt
you brought the people out of slavery.
In the covenant of Sinai with Moses
you gave shape and meaning to their lives.

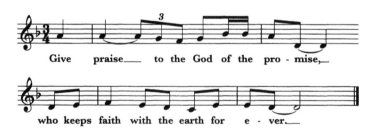

We breathe these words out of the Silence within us, into the Silence beyond us...

Pause

You sustain your covenant with Noah,
with the living creatures of earth,
that never again will you destroy them,
with a flood laying waste to the world.
Your love is for the whole of our planet,
a vow of restraint and protection for ever.

Pause

Again and again you renew your promise,
putting a new heart and spirit within us,
through a covenant sealed with your lifeblood,
your last will and testament for us.

**Give praise to the God of the promise,
who keeps faith with the earth for ever.**

Pause

You demand no unthinking obedience,
a loyalty blind and correct.
You do not try to control us,
you seek the pledge of our wills and our hearts.

Pause

You are the one who endures our betrayals,
with a precarious and vulnerable love.
You keep faith with us and humble us,
and so renew us in hope.

Pause

You laid down the power of coercion,
and gave of yourself with generous love.
Our hearts burst out with gratitude,
in awe at the wonder of your goodness.

Pause

You have bound yourself to us – we belong to you,
and to one another – there is no way to escape.   >

...in the Spirit that stirs amongst us the kaleidoscope of Jesus.

Keep us responding in friendship and service,
giving and receiving your presence among us,
protecting those who are weak and in need,
trust deepening in sacraments of love.

**Give praise to the God of the promise,
who keeps faith with the earth for ever.**

Silence

In the mystery of divine love, **we become gifts to one another,
bound together in the covenants of God. In the paradox of
our free will and destiny let us embrace one another,
choosing in friendship to share our being and becoming.
And with that divine love, and in the spirit of that love, let
us promise to be steady and reliable in our loving, to work
for our mutual well-being and the cherishing of our earth,
to honour one another as God's dwelling place, and to
keep loyal and full of faith, our life-day long.**

106   As our ancestors did

*That we may respect ancient forms of belief but not be bound by them; in penitence for
rigidity in religion, and for repeating cycles of projection, scapegoating, and destruction.*

Part i

O God of our ancestors we praise you
for your goodness and mercy for ever.
We can but stammer our gratitude,
so marvellous and mysterious are your ways.
Only the just and humble of heart
can sound the depths of the story.

Pause

In remembering the times that are past,
renew us in penitence and hope.
Come alive in us with the power that heals
that we may share in your freedom and love.
Let your shalom spread over the world:
let us rejoice that we belong with you for ever.

We breathe these words out of the Silence within us, into the Silence beyond us...

Pause

O - pen our eyes that we may see
the harm we have done in the world.
O - pen our ears that we may hear
your word__ of warn-ing and mer - cy.
Draw us through the nar - row - est of gates
to the wide o - pen space of the pro-mise.__

Pause

We disobey you as our ancestors did:
we act perversely and do what is wrong.
We are glad in our moments of freedom,
whenever you deliver us from slavery.
But soon we forget the wealth of your love,
unaware our opponents are also your people.

Pause

Our ancestors believed that you cleared their way,
parting the reeds of the marsh for the fleet of foot.   >

...in the Spirit that stirs amongst us the kaleidoscope of Jesus.

Though their pursuers were their enemies,
yet you grieved for all who died that day.
For those who sank in their chariots
were also created by you.
You wept with those who were waiting at home,
grieving in war as so many still do.

Pause

Bowed down by oppressions of self and of others
we cry out for help and you bear the load with us.
Lighter of step we go on our path,
whispering your love, pondering your ways.

Pause

**Open our eyes that we may see
the harm we have done in the world.
Open our ears that we may hear
your word of warning and mercy.
Draw us through the narrowest of gates
to the wide open space of the promise.**

Pause

It takes but a moment to forget you:
we blunder along and wait not for your counsel.
We cannot face how empty we are,
and greed takes hold in the desert.

Pause

In our craving we put you to the test,
and you give what we say we desire.
But envy and bitterness seize us,
and the loathing we have for ourselves
we project on to those who are holy,
like Moses and Aaron of old.

Pause

Faction and quarrel spread unchecked,
we are secretly glad when our neighbours fall.
"Let the earth itself swallow them up;

We breathe these words out of the Silence within us, into the Silence beyond us...

let fire burn our rivals even as they sleep."
Forgive us, O God, our cycles of vengeance,
bring us face to face with our enemies.

Pause

Open our eyes that we may see
the harm we have done in the world.
Open our ears that we may hear
your word of warning and mercy.
Draw us through the narrowest of gates
to the wide open space of the promise.

Pause

Many are the idols we have made as our gods,
golden calves of comfort and money.
Again and again we exchange your glory
for the pursuit of the utterly worthless.
So easily do we forget what you have done
to bring us out of enslavement.

Pause

We need the holy ones we scapegoat
who can bear the fierceness of your love,
the fiery anger that we fear would consume us,
did Moses not stand in the breach.

Pause

Open our eyes that we may see
the harm we have done in the world.
Open our ears that we may hear
your word of warning and mercy.
Draw us through the narrowest of gates
to the wide open space of the promise.

Pause

We refuse to recognize the gifts that you give,
our faith in your promise evaporates.
We grumble and murmur in our tents
and refuse to listen to your voice.

...in the Spirit that stirs amongst us the kaleidoscope of Jesus.

Pause

You lift up your hand against us,
to scatter us through the wilderness,
our children losing their respect,
and vanishing far and wide.

Pause

We turn to the many false comforters,
wanting change without cost to ourselves.
We still eat the food of the dead,
though it is but ashes in our mouths.
We provoke you to anger by our foolishness,
and the body starts breaking apart.

Pause

Open our eyes that we may see
the harm we have done in the world.
Open our ears that we may hear
your word of warning and mercy.
Draw us through the narrowest of gates
to the wide open space of the promise.

Silence

Part ii

Plagues rage around the world,
and few there are with the courage
to sacrifice their own comforts and wealth,
to take to themselves the wraths and the sorrows,
standing firm as the beacons of hope.

Pause

And yes, we embitter our leaders,
who in turn become fatherless and rash.
Did Moses suffer for our misdeeds,
when you were angry at the waters of Meribah?

Pause

We breathe these words out of the Silence within us, into the Silence beyond us...

O - pen our eyes that we may see
the harm we have done in the world.
O - pen our ears that we may hear
your word of warn-ing and mer - cy.
Draw us through the nar - row - est of gates
to the wide o - pen space of the pro - mise.

Pause

We did not destroy the inhabitants of the land.
Did you not command us to kill them all?
Should we have dismissed them from our hearts,
making them less than human in our sight?
But we did not even stand up for your truths,
we sought to make ourselves acceptable to them.

Pause

We followed their ways and then blamed them,
marrying them yet standing aloof.
We were seduced into worshipping idols,
and snared into deeds still more cruel.

...in the Spirit that stirs amongst us the kaleidoscope of Jesus.

Pause

With bloodlust we butchered our children,
surrendering to the demonic within us.
So the rivers were defiled with blood;
we made ourselves foul by our deeds.

Pause

Open our eyes that we may see
the harm we have done in the world.
Open our ears that we may hear
your word of warning and mercy.
Draw us through the narrowest of gates
to the wide open space of the promise.

Pause

No wonder your anger blazed,
so obtuse and wicked had we become.
It seemed that you loathed your own people,
for you let our violence recoil on our heads.

Pause

The rule of the oppressor stifled us,
stripping us of value and dignity.
Though others came to our rescue,
yet we fell once again in our waywardness.

Pause

Nevertheless you looked on our distress,
you heard the cry of our lament.
You remembered your covenant with us,
you never forgot your mercy and pity.

Pause

Before the very eyes of our enemies
your love kept working to free us.
Preserve us, O God, gather them with us,
that we may reverence and praise you for ever.

Pause

We breathe these words out of the Silence within us, into the Silence beyond us...

Open our eyes that we may see
the harm we have done in the world.
Open our ears that we may hear
your word of warning and mercy.
Draw us through the narrowest of gates
to the wide open space of the promise.

Pause

Did you command your people to destroy,
to commit even genocide? Was it your will?
Were their enemies so utterly evil
that not one of them deserved to survive?

Pause

Despite the rebellion of our ancestors
you spared them and graced them still.
Is your covenant only for a few who are favoured,
flourishing at the expense of the many?

Pause

Is not the pure race a dangerous myth,
an illusion that has never been real?
Did not your people misunderstand your call
to be special for service, not privilege?

Pause

Such old rigid thoughts are too proud,
too dangerous for our fragile earth home.
Your covenant is with all that you have made,
loving all creation through pain to its glory.

Pause

Your power, not almighty in magic,
neither capricious nor blind in its force,
will sustain and redeem your world yet,
withholding your fierce scalding fire,
refining in the heat of your love,
bringing out of evil unimaginable good.

Pause

...in the Spirit that stirs amongst us the kaleidoscope of Jesus.

**Open our eyes that we may see
the harm we have done in the world.
Open our ears that we may hear
your word of warning and mercy.
Draw us through the narrowest of gates
to the wide open space of the promise.**

Silence

May we never become so angry that we lose touch with compassion. **May we recognize divine wrath as but a projection
of our fury. May we never lose respect for other human
beings, all of us created in the image of God. May we be
empowered by the Spirit to overcome all desire to harm
and all prejudice that treats others as less than human.
O God, make us and keep us Christlike.**

107   The cry for rescue

*In solidarity with refugees, with those who have lost their way, with prisoners, with the
stormbound and bewildered, and with those trapped by their history.*

We give you thanks, O God, for you are gracious,
and your mercy endures for ever.
You bear the awful cost of a love that endures,
drawing us beyond our terror and pain.

Pause

Even as the relentless winds of the universe
raged through the silence of the ages,
your heart was stirring to bring us to life,
to gather as gifts to one another.

Pause

You are with us through all our bewilderments,
**through the impenetrable mystery of evil and pain,
redeeming our wastes and our sorrows,
hiding from us the glory to come.**

Pause

We breathe these words out of the Silence within us, into the Silence beyond us…

Sometimes we are strangers on the earth,
wanderers with no room to call our own.
We go astray in the wilderness,
lost in the trackless desert.

Pause

The mists come down in the mountains,
we wander on the featureless moors.
Aimlessly stumbling in the forests,
we find no way to a city to dwell in.

Pause

Hungry and thirsty, our spirits sink within us;
we languish and collapse, ready to die.

Then we cry to you, O God, in our trou-ble,_____

and you de - li-ver us from our dis - tress.____

Pause

You set our feet on a path we had not seen,
and you lead us to a place we can make our own.

**Let us praise you, O God, for your goodness,
your lovingkindness to the children of earth.
With nourishing food you have satisfied us,
you have slaked our aching thirst.**

Pause

We sit in darkness and the shadow of death,
shackled by misery and affliction.
We are signs of a world ill at ease,
broken and distressed, hearts torn apart,
tossing to and fro in rebellion,
spurning the word of our own deepest good.

...in the Spirit that stirs amongst us the kaleidoscope of Jesus.

Pause

Our wits are blurred by our troubles,
under their weight we stagger and fall.
Shamed by our guilt, trembling with fear,
isolated and lonely, we find no one to help.

Then we cry to you, O God, in our trouble,
and you deliver us from our distress.

Pause

You break the chains that keep us imprisoned,
you lead us gently by the hand and into the sun.

Let us praise you, O God, for your goodness,
your lovingkindness to the children of earth.
You have shattered the doors of bronze,
you have snapped in two the iron bars.

Silence

When we go down to the sea in ships
or take to the air in great birds,
we are overcome with fear and with awe
at your wonders in the deep and in the skies.

Pause

Suddenly the stormy wind arises,
lifting the waves of the sea,
stirring the turbulent clouds.
We are carried up to the heavens,
and down again to the depths:
we are tossed to and fro in peril,
we reel and stagger like drunkards,
our craftsmanship is all in vain.

Then we cry to you, O God, in our trouble,
and you deliver us from our distress.

Pause

Storms without and within cease at your word,
the waves of the sea and the air are stilled.

We breathe these words out of the Silence within us, into the Silence beyond us...

We recover our poise, panic leaves us,
we discover a presence that guides us through.
Then we are glad because we are at rest,
and you bring us to the haven where we would be.

Pause

Let us praise you, O God, for your goodness,
your lovingkindness to the children of earth.
At the gathering of the congregation your name
    be praised.
From the seat of the elders may you be glorified.

Silence

Yet again we turn to our foolishness,
caught in the cycles of disease and rebellion.
We turn away from the food that nourishes us,
even though we are brought to death's door.

Pause

We are caught in traps of poverty,
unable to move, hemmed in to despair.
We are bound by the scripts of our ancestors,
their sinewy subtleties holding us fast.

Then we cry to you, O God, in our trouble,
and you deliver us from our distress.

Pause

Your word of release sometimes heals us,
and we know we are saved from destruction.

It is hard to do more than whisper our thanks,
we lose hold of the mystery of your goodness.
Sometimes the helplessness in which we are caught
cries out in the night with no answering word.

Silence

The perplexity of your ways gives us pain;
we live between prison and freedom.   >

...in the Spirit that stirs amongst us the kaleidoscope of Jesus.

One day the doors are flung open,
only for others to close on the next.

Pause

You turn the rivers into beds of parched stones,
you dry up the springs of water.
You make the fertile land barren,
mirroring the drought of our goodness.

Pause

You fill the desert sands with water,
in the dry ground fresh springs emerge.
You bring in those who are hungry
to settle there and till the soil.

Pause

We plough fields, plant vineyards,
reap crops, graze herds.
We are blessed and our numbers increase,
yet the very next moment we seem cursed.

Pause

One day we are well content,
the next diminished again –
with plague, famine, and war,
with sorrow and stress in adversity.

Pause

Even the powerful are brought low
and wander again in the desert.
And you raise up the poor from affliction,
making them strong in the land.

Pause

Only the eye of faith can discern your ways,
and even then they mightily puzzle us.
But let us be wise and ponder these things:
wisdom still finds her way to your praise.

We breathe these words out of the Silence within us, into the Silence beyond us...

**Ever and again you protect and restrain us,
always with yet more gifts in store.
Let us therefore praise you, O God, for your goodness,
your lovingkindness to the children of earth.**

Silence

Keep us faithful, O God, **trusting in your promise and power
to rescue and redeem. In the darker places of faith's
journey help us to discern our freedom in choosing what
is difficult as if it were easy. For then we shall have faith
indeed, and even at the bleakest times we shall praise.**

108   The making of music

*In solidarity with music makers, composers, and performers; and that harsh and angry
sounds be heard and taken up into harmonies as yet unimagined.*

May the instruments of music come alive in our hands.
May the flute and the harp sing the praises of God.
May the strings of my heart make melody in the morning.
May the song of my soul be echoed by the dawn.
While oppression weighs heavy, and grief bows the heart,
let songs of consolation lighten the load.

Pause

Beloved, you embrace the universe,
reaching the depths of our darkness.
The music of your glory shimmers,
your faithfulness ever its theme.

Pause

The earth and all its inhabitants
you orchestrate into beauty.
For however discordant we sound,
you are always creating new harmonies.

Pause

...in the Spirit that stirs amongst us the kaleidoscope of Jesus.

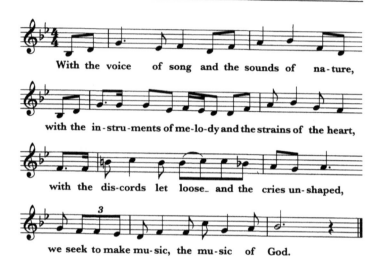

With the voice of song and the sounds of na-ture,
with the in-stru-ments of me-lo-dy and the strains of the heart,
with the dis-cords let loose_ and the cries un-shaped,
we seek to make mu-sic, the mu-sic of God.

Pause

In the music of poetry and song,
in the laughter of highland streams,
in the melody of curlew and nightingale,
we are joined in praise of your beauty.

Pause

We relish the names of the rivers,
the mountains, the lakes, and the forests,
the villages, towns, and cities,
the countries that stir our hearts.

Pause

All of them make music to you, O God,
each one of them part of your vesture,
a theme in the symphony of praise,
the sound of their name giving you glory.

Pause

We breathe these words out of the Silence within us, into the Silence beyond us...

With the voice of song and the sounds of nature,
with the instruments of melody and the strains
   of the heart,
with the discords let loose and the cries unshaped,
we seek to make music, the music of God.

Pause

The trumpet calls the army to war,
the horn gives warning to the city.
The drumbeat swells our pride,
our feet tap out in unison.

Pause

"With God on our side we will conquer."
Victory is sweet music to our ears.
The armies clash, the harmonies shatter –
can the screech of the dying sing your praise?

Pause

Where now is the music of hope?
A new sound from the heart of our God?
Can the trumpet and horn caress,
can the beat of the drum make us dance?

Pause

Will the way of the Christ bear fruit
from seeds of non-violent passion?
Can the discords of evil be transformed
in the searing flames of your love?
Can the powers that harm be disarmed?
Is our love strong enough to contain them?

Pause

Then we would hear such harmonies
as the world can barely imagine.
We would know our place in the making of music,
our very need for enemies banished for ever.

Pause

...in the Spirit that stirs amongst us the kaleidoscope of Jesus.

With the voice of song and the sounds of nature,
with the instruments of melody and the strains
**   of the heart,**
the discords let loose and the cries unshaped,
we seek to make music, the music of God.

Silence

In the music of lament and celebration, **of loyalties and**
questioning, of love and protest, of ballad and cantata, we
seek to be your partners, Creator God, in the weaving of
the patterns of glory. Inspire us, guide us, transform us.

109   An angry and fearsome cry

That we may hear the cries of rage, from within ourselves and from those around us,
neighbours on one earth; and that we may listen to one another's stories.

Let us speak out for the silenced,
giving voice to the voiceless.
Let the screams be uncorked,
and the bellows of rage resound.
The cry of the abused and violated
has far too long been unheard.

Pause

The ignorance of those uninvolved
colludes with the guilty and shamed,
all conspiring in silence,
their wounds festering unseen.

Pause

In   the   hope__   that de - fies des - pair,

when__   good - ness   it - self   is   pa - ra - lyzed,

We breathe these words out of the Silence within us, into the Silence beyond us...

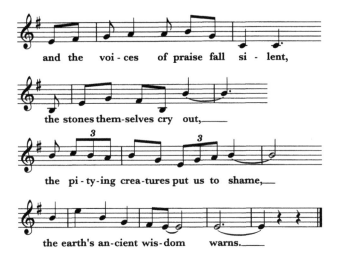

and the   voi - ces   of praise fall   si - lent,

the stones them-selves cry   out,____

the pi - ty -ing crea-tures put us to   shame,__

the earth's an-cient wis-dom   warns.____

Pause

The wealthy with bribes and corruption,
the fearful blackmailed to silence,
the lawkeepers twisting the evidence,
the advocates skilled in deceit and delay,

Pause

the ministers who can never be wrong,
establishments protecting their own,
the bullies hiding their cowardice,
the soldiers with permission to kill,
their mentors warping their minds
to think of the enemy as vermin,
the women a target for rape:

Pause

all fall under the cursing.
For the present we withhold God's blessing,
while refraining to crush in our turn.

Pause

...in the Spirit that stirs amongst us the kaleidoscope of Jesus.

In the hope that defies despair,
when goodness itself is paralyzed,
and the voices of praise fall silent,
the stones themselves cry out,
the pitying creatures put us to shame,
the earth's ancient wisdom warns.

Pause

And the women cry out in pain,
and the men and the children too.
The blood that flows cries out for revenge –
cursed be the violence of the strong.

Pause

The child howls in the lonely night –
cursed be the hand that bruised.

Pause

The woman lies sobbing on the floor –
cursed be the hard eyes and the unyielding stone.

Pause

The body that trusted lies rigid with shock –
cursed be the relishing of pain.

Pause

The weak are intimidated and afraid –
cursed be the arrogance and lust for power.

Pause

The abused shrink away in silent shame –
cursed be the evil power of secrecy.

Pause

The abusers protest their innocence –
cursed be the refusals and denials.

Pause

We breathe these words out of the Silence within us, into the Silence beyond us...

The comfortable turn away, refusing to see –
cursed be the collusion and cowardice.

Pause

In the hope that defies despair,
when goodness itself is paralyzed,
and the voices of praise fall silent,
the stones themselves cry out,
the pitying creatures put us to shame,
the earth's ancient wisdom warns.

Pause

What is the voice of the dead-strewn streets?
Of the infants buried by rubble?

Pause

"Woe to you who work evil in the land,
inventors and makers of weapons,
automatic in the spattering of blood,
of semtex packed in a purse."

Pause

"Woe to the fanatics who icily plan,
who have erased what is human from their hearts.
Woe to the launderers of money,
sleek in their cars and their treacherous prestige."

Pause

"Woe to the detonators of car bombs and missiles,
the buttons and triggers of a control so remote
from the travellers on wheels or blown from the skies."

Pause

"Woe to the traders in arms,
woe to the traffickers in drugs,
woe to the poisoners of minds,
woe to the serial killers,
woe to the men of cold eyes,   >

...in the Spirit that stirs amongst us the kaleidoscope of Jesus.

woe to the remorseless hearts,
woe to those with no pity."

Pause

In the hope that defies despair,
when goodness itself is paralyzed,
and the voices of praise fall silent,
the stones themselves cry out,
the pitying creatures put us to shame,
the earth's ancient wisdom warns.

Pause

O Christ of angry compassion,
sweeping away the exploiters,
moved to speak out for the little ones,
drawing the sting of oppression,
lift up the crushed in spirit,
empower them to find their own voice,

Pause

to shame the violators to penitence,
to hope for the time of forgiveness,
to strengthen the rule of law,
to heap coals of fire on their heads,
the fire of love's wrath and desire
for justice and truth to be shared
in reconciliation and peace for ever.

Silence

Holy and just God, **receive the feelings of our outraged and**
wounded hearts. Console our grief, melt our fear, lift the
burden of our shame. Restrain our desire for revenge, and
channel the fierce energies of our anger in the service of
justice and truth.

We breathe these words out of the Silence within us, into the Silence beyond us...

110   Power with service

In solidarity with those who exercise power; and that we may have a change of heart and mind on how conflicts can be resolved.

The oracles of old exalted the king
to stand at the right hand of God.
As priest and prince he was to rule
not by descent but by God's call.

Pause

The sceptre of power was placed in his hand,
to shatter the heads of his enemies.
Through him God routed the armies,
striding across corpses strewn in the way.

To those with power give wis-dom,
the spi-rit of true un-der-stand-ing.

Pause

A strange world to us, faded from view,
kings riding out on horseback to conquer.
The wars of our time have tarnished the glory,
the rhetoric of God masking our pride.

Pause

Arrogance and greed are the gods that we follow,
and even the wars we name holy or just
degrade those who wage them, reminding us all
how cruel and cold the world can become.

**To those with power give wisdom,
the spirit of true understanding.**

...in the Spirit that stirs amongst us the kaleidoscope of Jesus.

Pause

Yet as we dig deep in these words from the past,
we see a vision of those who would lead:
they lay on themselves the robe of the priestly,
willingly weighed down by the burden of service,
sacrificing self for the good of their land,
growing in discernment and wisdom.

Pause

They bring greater good from the conflicts around them,
and they heal the wounds of the people.

**To those with power give wisdom,
the spirit of true understanding.**

Silence

God of wisdom, **guide those in power with your Spirit of
true counsel, that they may discern the course that is just,
sacrificing themselves for the common good, not only of
their own country but of the whole earth, laying aside all
pride of wealth and status. And may we all find the
courage to use well whatever power we have.**

III   The heartbeat of God

*That we may draw deep from the wells of our faith; that we may receive one another
as companions on a journey; and that we may give true worship.*

My gratitude, O God, flows on,
like the deep and silent river,
I join in the stream of praise,
with your people gathered for worship.

Pause

We take our place in the Story,
re-kindled in the seasons' round.
We celebrate your mercies of old,
and your deeds among us today.

We breathe these words out of the Silence within us, into the Silence beyond us...

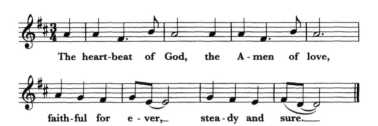

The heart-beat of God, the A-men of love,
faith-ful for e-ver,_ stea-dy and sure._

Pause

The great words resound in our ears,
we delight in the God who embodies them:
your glory and splendour and justice,
your beauty and grace and compassion,

Pause

your truth and faithfulness for ever,
your covenant of promise and life,
your creative and redeeming power,
your holiness, wisdom, and love.

**The heartbeat of God, the Amen of love,
faithful for ever, steady and sure.**

Pause

Day by day you nourish us,
feeding us with sacrament and word,
quenching our thirst from the wellspring,
the waters that never run dry.

Pause

You renew your covenant each morning,
loyal to your promise for ever.
Awesome is your love for us,
steady over aeons of time.

**The heartbeat of God, the Amen of love,
faithful for ever, steady and sure.**

Silence

...in the Spirit that stirs amongst us the kaleidoscope of Jesus.

In the doubtings of our minds, **in the fickleness of our wills, in the betrayals of our hearts, we can scarcely believe in your steady presence through the years. Startle us afresh. Take our breath away. Renew our trust.**

112   Our hatred of goodness

That we may simplify our lives and prune our possessions; and that hatreds among humankind may dissolve.

The spirit of hatred eats us alive,
gnawing away, draining our energy.
With what twisted and mocking delight
the innocent are corrupted, the gentle are scarred.

Pause

We accumulate the goods of this world,
our wealth a so-called reward for our virtue.
Yet we look down from a superior height,
despising the poor, increasing their burdens.

Pause

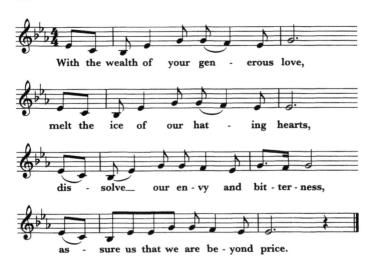

With the wealth of your gen - erous love,

melt the ice of our hat - ing hearts,

dis - solve__ our en - vy and bit - ter - ness,

as - sure us that we are be - yond price.

We breathe these words out of the Silence within us, into the Silence beyond us...

Pause

Never content with the possessions we have,
greedy for more, we harden our hearts.
Restless envy peers from our eyes,
so cold, suspicious, and harsh.

Pause

Some of us turn our hatred within,
believing we have no worth of our own.
Cold disapproval drives us to despair,
and we kill ourselves by degrees.

Pause

**With the wealth of your generous love,
melt the ice of our hating hearts,
dissolve our envy and bitterness,
assure us that we are beyond price.**

Pause

Goodness incarnate was too much to bear,
showing us how crabbed and bitter we are.
The rage to kill rose in our throats,
a satisfaction hollow and bleak.

Pause

You took to yourself, compassionate God,
all our hatred and spite.
You endured with a passion unbroken,
you left us with nothing but love.

Pause

**With the wealth of your generous love,
melt the ice of our hating hearts,
dissolve our envy and bitterness,
assure us that we are beyond price.**

Pause

...in the Spirit that stirs amongst us the kaleidoscope of Jesus.

So you impel us to justice,
generous in giving, caring for others,
no longer grudging and grim,
able to share with no need to control.

Silence

Help us, just and generous God, **not to project perfection on
to those who lead us, nor give others the illusion that we
ourselves are perfect. May we leave no room for envy and
hatred, and no longer howl with glee when the good let us
down.**

113   The energy of compassion

*That we may be compassionate; that we may do our daily tasks well; in solidarity
with the young, the destitute, the elderly, and the migrants; and that everyone may find
dignity and worth.*

As the light of dawn struggles through the gloom,
as the sun filters through the morning haze,
as the weary stretch into another day,

Pause

As the noonday sun burns and does not relent,
as the pressure mounts on the brain,
as the elderly nod through the afternoon,

Alleluia! We dare to give thanks to God.

Pause

We breathe these words out of the Silence within us, into the Silence beyond us...

As the shadows lengthen and the day declines,
as the air cools around the homeless,
as a night of grieving looms,

Alleluia! We dare to give thanks to God.

Pause

As we grow angry at senseless violence,
as we cradle the wounded in our arms,
as we patiently repair the damage,

Alleluia! We dare to give thanks to God.

Pause

As the sloucher straightens his back,
as the poor rise up from the scrapheap,
as the barren at last conceive,

Alleluia! We dare to give thanks to God.

Pause

As Sarah, Rebekah, and Rachel give birth,
as Ruth follows Naomi to a new home,
as Rahab and Tamar find their place in the story,

Alleluia! We dare to give thanks to God.

Pause

As we seek to deepen our trust,
as we glimpse the power of compassion,
as we see the divine in the outcast,

Alleluia! We dare to give thanks to God.

Pause

As we remember the tales of our ancestors,
as we recall the moments of freedom,
as we renew our strength at its source,

Alleluia! We dare to give thanks to God.

Pause

…in the Spirit that stirs amongst us the kaleidoscope of Jesus.

As the Spirit of awe overtakes us,
as the depths of compassion overwhelm us,
as the glory and splendour overshadow us,

Alleluia! We dare to give thanks to God.

Pause

As we worship at all times, in all places,
as we lovingly relish the name,
as the people sing with one voice,

Alleluia! We dare to give thanks to God.

Silence

As we seek to discern how to bless you, **O God of power and compassion, in all the circumstances and through all the events of our lives, keep our anger within bounds so that it does not destroy, and keep our caring truthful so that we do not allow ourselves to be destroyed.**

114   The God of exodus

That we and others may be rescued when we have no power of ourselves to help ourselves; in gratitude for moments of deliverance; in solidarity with those taken hostage; and with those who believe they are trapped for ever.

So often we are slaves of the cruel,
bowed down by words that sting.
Like our ancestors we cry out in distress,
in the hope of rescue and freedom.

We breathe these words out of the Silence within us, into the Silence beyond us...

Pause

Here and there in our past have been people of courage,
hearing your call to face down the powerful.
Here and there have been moments of freedom,
lives newly charged by release from constriction.

Alleluia! We give thanks to the God of rescue.

Pause

Human beings become your sanctuary,
people with whom you dwell.
You call us to live in your image,
even as the One who shows us your face.

Alleluia! We give thanks to the God of rescue.

Pause

We are creation evolved into consciousness,
giving a voice to its calm and its chaos.
Does nature itself come to our aid,
when storms are stilled, when waters part?

Alleluia! We give thanks to the God of rescue.

Pause

The mountains quake and the rocks splinter,
the sheep and lambs quiver with fear.
Amazement grips us as the scene unfolds,
this theatre which resounds with your presence.

Alleluia! We give thanks to the God of rescue.

Pause

Dance, O earth, at the appearance of God,
turning your anguish to a paean of praise.
Your rocks are turned into pools of water,
solid flint into a flowing fountain.

Alleluia! We give thanks to the God of rescue.

Pause

…in the Spirit that stirs amongst us the kaleidoscope of Jesus.

Nothing is fixed, nothing secure,
when you lead us into freedom.
The gods of nature crumble,
the noise of the powers is stilled.

Alleluia! We give thanks to the God of rescue.

Pause

O God, your greatness is awesome,
your incomprehensible grace in our rescue.
Our voices combine with those of the earth,
we give you the glory for ever.

Alleluia! We give thanks to the God of rescue.

Pause

The very earth herself is our home,
a secret not known to the powerful.
For our God was born in a cave,
and was killed cast out of the city.

Alleluia! We give thanks to the God of rescue.

Pause

You owned not a single possession,
and yet the whole world is yours.
Only the one who can never be exiled
is free at the last and always at home.

Alleluia! We give thanks to the God of rescue.

Silence

With exuberant delight and a touch of fear **we remember the
stories of our ancestors, and we rejoice in you, O God, for
you are still the God behind all the powers, with infinite
compassion and grace yearning to rescue us from all that
enslaves us. Call us out of our imprisonments. Lead us to
freedom.**

We breathe these words out of the Silence within us, into the Silence beyond us...

115   Idols and the living God

That we may become aware of our idolatries, our addictions and compulsions; that we may no longer be dominated by them; and in solidarity with those who are fatally gripped and are dying.

It is not to our name that praise is due,
but to yours, eternal God of love,
for you are faithful and kind and merciful,
surpassing us all in wisdom and care.

Al - le - lu - ia!___

We a-dore the Be-lo-ved, God_ be-yond_ gods.___

Pause

Our idols are silver and gold,
the gods of money rule in our land.
They have mouths and utter platitudes.
They have eyes and see not the poor.
They have ears but hear no cries of pain,
they have noses and keep themselves clean.

Pause

Their hands touch no one with love,
their feet never walk the streets.
Keep us from growing to be like them,
may we put no trust in possessions.

Pause

Renew our trust in you, O God:
give us courage to face our enemies.
You remember us and you bless us,
you bless all who hold you in honour.

...in the Spirit that stirs amongst us the kaleidoscope of Jesus.

Alleluia! We adore the Beloved, God beyond gods.

Pause

Creator of the universe, God beyond gods,
you give us the earth to care for.
You are far beyond our imagining,
yet you bless each one of your little ones.

Alleluia! We adore the Beloved, God beyond gods.

Pause

Those who are dead to your love do not praise you,
nor those who are gripped by one of the powers.
Keep our love and our freedom alive,
that we may praise you with joy and delight.

Alleluia! We adore the Beloved, God beyond gods.

Silence

Liberate us, redeeming God, **from all that would hold us
fast, from all the addictions to which we fall prey. Keep
us compassionate and firm with others and ourselves,
that together we may inhabit a land of true freedom.**

116   Death loses its stranglehold

In solidarity with those whose lungs are failing; and with children who are dying.

You have heard, O God, the strains of my distress,
even the silent crying of my heart.
I love you because your ear inclined to me,
I know you were there for me in the day of my trouble.

Pause

The cords of death entangled me:
the snares of the grave held me fast.
Tentacles wrapped themselves round me,
crushing me to anguish and pain.

Pause

We breathe these words out of the Silence within us, into the Silence beyond us…

Desperate for air I called out:
Help me. Deliver me. Rescue me.
My strength is sapped, my energy draining away.
With my last breath I cried out in panic.

Pause

In your healing compassion you came to me,
with the kiss of life reviving me.
At my very last gasp you held me,
you snatched me from the jaws of the grave.

Pause

You delivered me from the stronghold of death,
you wiped the tears from my eyes,
you saved my feet from stumbling,
and I walked free in the land of the living.

Alleluia! Praise to the God in whom death is no more.

Pause

How can I ever repay you, O God,
for all the gifts of your gracious love?
I shall lift high the cup of salvation,
and give thanks for your holy name.

Alleluia! Praise to the God in whom death is no more.

Pause

From time to time you rescue me, O God,
by the skills of your people, by means unknown.   >

...in the Spirit that stirs amongst us the kaleidoscope of Jesus.

You come to me in the guise of strangers,
I am humbled by their willingness to care.

Alleluia! Praise to the God in whom death is no more.

Pause

But what of the people who perish?
What of the children who are wasting away?
Can you save us through the days of our dying,
through the river of no return?

Pause

Yet you are the God not of death but of life,
no power can withstand the power of your love.
All that frightens us shrivels in your path,
the trail that was blazed by the Pioneer.

Alleluia! Praise to the God in whom death is no more.

Silence

Living Christ, **decisive clue to the love that has no end,
renew in us the steady hope that even the power of death
cannot keep us from your presence.**

117   A quiet moment of gratitude

*In solidarity with those who draw close to God in contemplation and find there all
humanity; for more silence in corporate prayer, conversations, and councils.*

A fragment of prayer from the psalmist of old:
Let all the people praise the name of our God.
In a quiet moment of praise
our gratitude whispers on the gentlest of breaths.

Al-le - lu - ia!__   We whi - sper our thanks.

Pause

We breathe these words out of the Silence within us, into the Silence beyond us...

Not always with jubilant shouts
do we sound our thanksgiving and joy.
From the depths of a silent heart
comes a word but softly spoken.

Alleluia! We whisper our thanks.

Pause

Secure in the lovingkindness of God,
knowing the love that always endures,
transforming the evils we face into good,
we waft the breeze and adore.

Alleluia! We whisper our thanks.

Silence

O God of silent loving, **keep us from the trap of believing
that the louder we shout the more genuine is our faith and
the more fulsome is our praise. Keep us aware that love is
fragile and vulnerable, and that we know it best in the
silence of the heart.**

118   The mercies of God endure

*That we may dance with one another, enemies and friends; and that gratitude may
dwell in every human being's heart.*

Let us give thanks for the goodness of God,
let the people of old shout their joy.
Let the children yet unborn hear its sound,
the harmony of a people of praise.

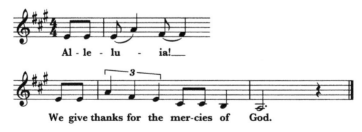

...in the Spirit that stirs amongst us the kaleidoscope of Jesus.

Pause

In the dangers we face you are with us,
you came as one of us and set us free.
We need you no longer on our side,
for your love has spread over our enemies.

Alleluia! We give thanks for the mercies of God.

Pause

Yes, I long for the downfall of those who oppress me:
with the ache of sorrow I remember their harm.
But my bitterness has warmed to compassion,
my anger channelled for justice.

Alleluia! We give thanks for the mercies of God.

Pause

I take my refuge in your presence, O God,
putting no trust in rebellious powers.
The mighty of the earth are not worthy:
humble them to a place of repentance and trust.

Alleluia! We give thanks for the mercies of God.

Pause

When all the powers surrounded me,
in your name I stood my ground.
When they swarmed around me like bees,
in your name I stood my ground.

Alleluia! We give thanks for the mercies of God.

Pause

I was pressed so hard that I almost fell,
but your power surged through my arms.
For you are my strength and my song,
and have become my salvation and rescue.

Alleluia! We give thanks for the mercies of God.

Pause

We breathe these words out of the Silence within us, into the Silence beyond us...

So we bound up the rebellious powers,
and gave them into your care.
Take from them their desire for revenge,
and heal their deepest hurts.

Alleluia! We give thanks for the mercies of God.

Pause

No one shall die and be forgotten,
not one of the little ones is lost.
If the hairs of our heads are numbered,
who can doubt the compassion of God?

Alleluia! We give thanks for the mercies of God.

Pause

We shall not die but we shall live,
and rejoice in the deeds of our God.
Even though you test us to the limit,
you do not abandon us to death.

Alleluia! We give thanks for the mercies of God.

Pause

Open for us the gates of the city,
the city of harmony and peace.
Together, restored, we enter them,
singing our songs of thanksgiving.

Alleluia! We give thanks for the mercies of God.

Pause

The stone which the builder rejected
has become the head of the corner.
The very ones we despised
are known as your specially beloved.

Alleluia! We give thanks for the mercies of God.

Pause

...in the Spirit that stirs amongst us the kaleidoscope of Jesus.

This is the festival day,
the day you have made for our joy.
We shall be glad and rejoice,
feasting with laughter and song.

Alleluia! We give thanks for the mercies of God.

Pause

Blessed are those who have journeyed in your name:
the light of our God has guided them.
They join the throng in the places of praise.
Indeed you are God: we adore you.

Silence

May we not be stingy in our gratitude **or grudging in our praise.
Loosen our stiff bodies to be exuberant and joyful. Let us
dance with delight and see the sparkle in the eyes of God.**

> *In the refrains for Psalm 119, one suggestion is that the first line be either
> said or sung by a cantor and then repeated by everybody else.*

119 i   Walking in God's path

*God's invitation to us is to follow Christ. It is a journey into love, along a path that
is rarely smooth. The way is rough, the truth is costly, the life is sacrificial. The gate
through which we are drawn by love is always narrow.*

Follow the way, the truth, the life.

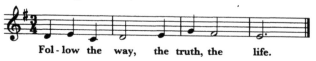

Fol - low the   way,   the truth, the   life.

Pause

Blessed are those who are honest in their ways,
who walk in the paths of God's law.
**Blessed are those who treasure God's wisdom,
who seek God with all their heart.**

We breathe these words out of the Silence within us, into the Silence beyond us…

Pause

Those who do no evil deeds
are those who tread the way of justice.
**Dear God, you have given command
that we diligently hold to your word.**

Pause

May my ways be kept steadfast
on the narrow road of your love.
**So I shall not be confounded
while I respect the whole of your counsel.**

Pause

I shall thank you with unfeigned heart
as I learn to be guided by your Spirit.
**I shall hold fast to your truths:
do not utterly abandon me.**

Silence

Enter by the narrow gate.

En - ter   by   the   nar - row   gate.

119 ii   Delighting in God's wisdom

*The path is tough, and, despite boundary marks, we wander from it. We become self-
centred; we ignore others. We are constantly invited to love others as Christ has loved
us: that degree of love is not easy, for it challenges us to bless, pray for, and help those
who are hostile to us.*

Love one another as I have loved you.

Love one   a - no - ther   as   I have loved   you.

...in the Spirit that stirs amongst us the kaleidoscope of Jesus.

Pause

How can the young find their way?
By guarding the boundary of your word.
With my whole heart I have looked for you:
let me not wander from your commandment.

Pause

I have hidden your truth within my heart,
so that I should not fail to love you.
You are blessed indeed, dear God:
teach me your wisdom.

Pause

With my lips I have been telling
of all the judgments of your mouth.
I have had greater delight in the ways of your loving
than in all manner of riches.

Pause

I shall dare to contemplate your countenance,
and I shall deeply respect your ways.
My delight will be in your counsel,
and I shall not forget your justice.

Silence

Do good to those who hate you.

Do good to those who hate___ you.

119 iii   Longing for God's justice

As travellers into God, we need guideposts which can be discerned from within the
words of the Gospels. For example, we are blessed when we hunger and thirst for the
right relationships longed for by a just God. Only by being faithful to such wisdom will
our lives be built on rock.

We breathe these words out of the Silence within us, into the Silence beyond us...

Be faithful to what I have said.

Be faith-ful to what I have said.

Pause

Deal bountifully with your servant,
that I may live, and keep your word.
Open my eyes that I may see
the wondrous things of your law.

Pause

I am a traveller upon earth:
hide not your guideposts from me.
I am consumed with a very fervent desire,
a longing that I have for your justice.

Pause

You have rebuked the pride that lurks in me,
you rescue me when I am lost and astray.
Take away from me the spirit of scorn,
hold me fast to the rock of your truth.

Pause

Keep me from suspicion and hatred:
rather may I meditate on your counsel.
For your sayings are my delight,
and they are my counsellors.

Silence

Build not on sand but on rock.

Build not on sand____ but on rock.

...in the Spirit that stirs amongst us the kaleidoscope of Jesus.

119 iv   Enduring in God's way

When the way is dusty and hot, it is easy to feel weighed down and oppressed. We have to stop and dig deep in the desert until we discover springs of refreshing water. We also need to learn to receive nourishment from other travellers, as much as in our turn give to them.

Let living water flow in you.

Let liv - ing wa - ter flow in you.

Pause

My soul is weighed down like lead:
revive me according to your word.
When I told you of my ways, you heard me.
Teach me your wisdom.

Pause

Help me understand the way of your love,
and meditate on the wonders of your deeds.
My soul droops for very heaviness:
refresh me according to your promise.

Pause

Take from me the way of lying,
and graciously teach me your truth.
I have chosen the way of faithfulness,
and your justice is before my eyes.

Pause

I cleave to your law:
let me not be put to shame.
I shall run the way of your commandment
when you have set my heart at liberty.

Silence

We breathe these words out of the Silence within us, into the Silence beyond us…

Feed the hungry; give water to the thirsty.

Feed__ the hun-gry; give wa-ter to the thir-sty.

119 V   Desiring life in God's spirit

We are called simply to follow, but with deep desire and not with reluctance. It is not a path of human cleverness, but of the Spirit of wisdom. So we are to turn our eyes from envy of others' success, and turn them towards those who are needy.

Receive the Holy Spirit.

Re-ceive the Ho - ly Spi - rit.

Pause

Teach me, dear God, the way of your truth,
and I shall follow it to the end.
**Give me understanding, and I shall keep your law,
I shall keep it with my whole heart.**

Pause

Lead me in the path of wisdom;
to do your will is my deepest desire.
**Incline my heart to your love,
and not to envious greed.**

Pause

Turn away my eyes from vanity,
and give me life in your Spirit.
**Establish me in your promise,
be faithful to those who are in awe of you.**

Pause

…in the Spirit that stirs amongst us the kaleidoscope of Jesus.

Take away from me the rejection that I fear,
for your justice is good.
See, my delight is in your commandment:
quicken me in the power of your word.

Silence

Give to everyone who asks you.

Give__ to   e - very - one who   asks you.

119 vi   Keeping God's word

To be steadfast in God's truth even when afraid of the powerful – this is to walk in a
sacred manner. It is possible only if we dwell in God's love. We shall be so delighted
in God that we shall not even want to condemn those who would harm us.

Abide in my love.

A - bide   in   my   love.

Pause

Let your steadfast love spread over me, dear God,
even your salvation, according to your promise.
So I shall have an answer for those who taunt me,
for my trust is in your word.

Pause

Take not the word of your truth utterly out of my mouth,
for my hope is in your justice.
So I shall always keep your law,
for ever and ever the ways of your love.

Pause

We breathe these words out of the Silence within us, into the Silence beyond us...

And I shall walk at liberty,
glad to fulfil your commands.
**I shall speak of your wisdom and not be ashamed,
even among the powerful of the earth.**

Pause

My delight shall be in your counsel,
which I cherish with joy.
**I shall lift up my hands in your presence,
and listen deep within for your word.**

Silence

Judge not and you will not be judged.
Condemn not and you will not be condemned.
Forgive and you will be forgiven.

119 vii   Remembering God's promise

We go astray from the path: we pursue worldly wealth at others' expense, we despise the weak, we even betray friends. To remember God's promise to be with us always, to ask that we may embody the Spirit of Christ, to contemplate and treasure wisdom: only so do we renew our pilgrimage.

…in the Spirit that stirs amongst us the kaleidoscope of Jesus.

Ask in my name.

Ask   in   my   name.

Pause

Remember your promise to your servant,
in which you have caused me to put my trust.
It is my comfort in time of trouble,
for your word has given me life.

Pause

In pride we despise one another:
may we not shrink from your law.
Let us remember your justice, O God,
and we shall be strengthened.

Pause

May my anger be cleansed by your truth,
as I confront betrayal and wrong.
Your sayings have been my songs
in the house of my pilgrimage.

Pause

I have thought upon your name in the watches of the night,
and I have treasured your wisdom.
It has been for my blessing,
when I have lived by your commandment of love.

Silence

Do not lay up for yourselves treasure on earth.

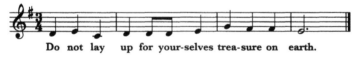

Do   not   lay   up   for   your-selves   trea-sure   on   earth.

✤

We breathe these words out of the Silence within us, into the Silence beyond us...

119 viii   Enjoying God's presence

We are enlivened and encouraged on the journey by companions – literally, those with whom we eat bread. And the stranger is to be welcomed as one who also belongs to God. We are to taste and see the goodness of the One who gives us living bread.

Eat of the living bread.

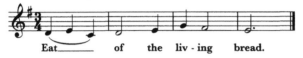

Eat_____   of   the   liv - ing   bread.

Pause

Dear God, you are my portion for ever:
I have promised to live by your Spirit.
With heart and longing I become aware of your presence:
show me your steadfast love, according to your word.

Pause

I call your truth to remembrance,
and turn my feet to your way.
I make haste, and prolong not the time,
that I might keep your commandments.

Pause

The cords of the ungodly ensnare me:
may I not forget your law.
At midnight I shall rise to give you thanks,
because the Judge of all the world acts well.

Pause

I am the companion of all who are in awe of you,
who are guided by your counsel.
The earth, O God, is full of your steadfast love:
O teach me your wisdom.

Silence

…in the Spirit that stirs amongst us the kaleidoscope of Jesus.

Welcome the stranger.

Wel - come   the   stran - ger.

119 ix   Receiving God's grace

Fortified by God and by one another we journey on. Knowing that we are accepted as
we are, we can the more readily accept and forgive others. We have received the gracious
and truthful presence of God, far more enriching than all the world's wealth.

Forgive the sins of others.

For-give the sins____   of____   o - thers.

Pause

Dear God, you have given me grace,
and so fulfilled your promise.
Teach me true understanding and knowledge,
for I have trusted your word.

Pause

Before I was afflicted I went astray,
but now I keep your counsel.
You are good and gracious:
O teach me your wisdom.

Pause

Through pride I tell lies against my neighbour:
keep me to your truth with my whole heart.
My heart grows fat and gross:
let my delight be in your love.

Pause

We breathe these words out of the Silence within us, into the Silence beyond us...

It is good for me that I have been afflicted,
that I may learn your wisdom.
**The sayings of your mouth are dearer to me
than thousands of gold and silver pieces.**

Silence

Forgive to seventy times seven.

119 X   Letting be in God's hands

*We are misled if we think our hard travelling earns us anything as of right. We have
to take time to stand still and do nothing, to let go of our concerns, and to let be in
God's hands, simply to trust and be thankful.*

Believe in the One whom God has sent.

Pause

Your hands have made me and fashioned me:
give me understanding that I may know your mind.
**Those who fear you will be glad when they see me,
because I have put my trust in your word.**

Pause

I know that your judgments are right,
that in your faithfulness you have caused me to be troubled.
**Let your merciful kindness be my comfort,
according to your promise to your servant.**

Pause

…in the Spirit that stirs amongst us the kaleidoscope of Jesus.

Let your loving mercies come to me, that I may live,
for your love is my delight.
Let my pride be confounded, with its twists of deceit,
and I will meditate on your wisdom.

Pause

Let those who fear you turn to you,
that they may know your truth.
Let my heart be found in your counsel,
that I may not be ashamed.

Silence

Hold on to your life and you will lose it.
Let go of your life and you will find it.

119 xi   Clinging to God's faithfulness

The vision with which we started out seems to shrivel. Eyesight and insight grow dim.
We harm rather than help one another. At best we doggedly endure, clinging to the
faithfulness of God who encourages us with Christ's victory over all that would drag
us down. Feeling stripped to the bone, we are yet called to clothe one another.

Be of good courage: I have overcome the world.

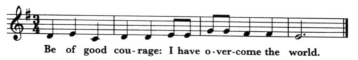

We breathe these words out of the Silence within us, into the Silence beyond us...

Pause

I faint with longing for your salvation:
with hope I still cleave to your word.
**My eyes grow dim with watching for your promise,
saying, When will you comfort me?**

Pause

For I am like a wineskin shrivelled in the smoke,
yet I do not forget your wisdom.
**How long must your servant endure?
When will you judge those who oppress me?**

Pause

Yet I too have laid traps for others,
and I have not obeyed your law.
**All your commandments are true:
they challenge our falsehoods and deceit.**

Pause

We have almost made an end of ourselves upon earth:
draw us back who have forsaken your way.
**Quicken me in your loving kindness:
and I shall keep the counsel of your Spirit.**

Silence

Clothe the naked.

119 xii   Trusting in God's purpose

In the very midst of constriction the vision is renewed. Sustained by the eternity and reliability and promised fulfilment of the purpose of God's love, nourished by the blood-red wine of the very life of God, we continue to walk with our burdens, simply following the way.

...in the Spirit that stirs amongst us the kaleidoscope of Jesus.

Live in the true vine.

Pause

Dear God, your eternal word of love
endures for ever in the universe.
Your truth stands fast from one generation to another:
you have laid the foundations of the earth, and it abides.

Pause

In fulfilment of your purpose it continues to this very day,
for all things serve you.
If my delight had not been in your ways,
I should have perished in my trouble.

Pause

I shall never forget your truths,
for with them you have given me life.
I belong to you; heal me and save me,
for I have sought your counsel.

Pause

Many are the traps that could destroy me,
but I shall meditate on your law.
I see all things have their limits,
but your wisdom can never be contained.

Silence

Take up your cross and follow me.

We breathe these words out of the Silence within us, into the Silence beyond us...

119 xiii   Loving God's truth

We miss our way if we do not become childlike in our trust and delight in the tastiness of God's gifts. Even the commandment to love in a tough, enduring, non-possessive way is as honey to our deepest selves. We come to relish the wisdom, counsel, and truths of God.

If you love me keep my commandment.

Pause

Dear God, how I love your wisdom:
all day long is my study in it.
Your counsel makes me wiser than my adversaries,
for it is always in my heart.

Pause

I have more understanding than my teachers,
for I meditate on your word.
I am wiser than the aged
because I keep your truths in my heart.

Pause

I hold back my feet from evil ways,
that I may obey your will.
When I do not turn aside from your way,
I know that you are my guide.

Pause

How tasty are your sayings to my mouth,
sweeter than honey to my tongue.
Through your guidance I learn understanding:
therefore I hate all evil ways.

Silence

…in the Spirit that stirs amongst us the kaleidoscope of Jesus.

Become like children.

119 xiv   Being guided by God's light

The way becomes obscure, but there is sufficient light once our eyes are accustomed to the dark. We may not realize that we are being guided in a particular direction, but the shepherd's crook is kindly prompting. We may be troubled, but an imperceptible inclination of the heart in prayer is all that is needed for our calming.

Let the good shepherd guide.

Pause

Your word is a lantern to my feet,
a light searching out all my ways.
**I have sworn, and am steadfastly purposed
to keep the way of your justice.**

Pause

I am troubled beyond measure:
give me life dear God according to your promise.
**Accept my offerings of praise,
and teach me your truths.**

Pause

My life is always in your hands,
and I do not forget your law.
**The ungodly have laid a snare for me:
may I not swerve from your commandment.**

Pause

We breathe these words out of the Silence within us, into the Silence beyond us…

I have claimed your wisdom as my heritage for ever,
it is the very joy of my heart.
**I incline my heart to your counsel,
always, even to the end.**

Silence

Pray simply.

119 XV   Bringing evil to God's judgment

We try to avoid being refined by God's truth. We resist the pruning of our self-centredness. We are unfaithful to our promises, we are cunning in our self-deceits, we become weighed down with our vain pursuits of earthly security. Even while hating hypocrisy, we practise it. Only through the astringent love of God will our greedy and inordinate desires cease, our lust for possessions fade.

Be pruned, and so be fruitful.

Pause

I hate all doublemindedness and hypocrisy,
but your law do I love.
**You are my defence and my shield,
and my trust is in your word.**

Pause

Away from me, all desire to do evil:
I will keep the commandments of my God.
**Uphold me according to your promise, and I shall live:
let me not be disappointed of my hope.**

...in the Spirit that stirs amongst us the kaleidoscope of Jesus.

Pause

Support me, and I shall be safe:
my delight shall ever be in your wisdom.
Relentlessly expose my unfaithfulness;
may my cunning be in vain.

Pause

Rake out ungodliness from me like dross,
for I desire your refining truths.
My flesh trembles in awe of you,
and I am afraid of your judgments.

Silence

Do not look lustfully, possessively.

Do not look lust - ful - ly, poss - ess - ive - ly.

119 xvi   Serving God's will

*As servants of the will of God, called to love God's wisdom as a precious jewel, we
begin to discover that indeed possessions are of no account. We appreciate the wealth
that comes to us through enjoying the smallest acts of kindness, the simplest acts of
generosity, given and received. No earthly greatness could ever compensate for such true
treasure.*

Wash one another's feet.

Wash____ one an - oth - er's feet.

Pause

There is much that I have done that is not right:
the air that I breathe is heavy with oppression.

We breathe these words out of the Silence within us, into the Silence beyond us...

Give me delight in all that is good,
that pride and arrogance may not defeat me.

Pause

My eyes waste away with looking for your salvation,
for the fulfilment of your promise to be just.
Embrace me in your steadfast love,
and teach me your wisdom.

Pause

I seek to serve you in friendship:
give me understanding that I may walk in your path.
It is high time that you acted, O God,
for your law which holds us together is being destroyed.

Pause

How I desire truly to love your counsel
beyond all gold and precious stones.
Therefore I direct my feet in your way,
and all false steps I shall utterly abhor.

Silence

Whoever would be great among you must be your servant.

Who - e - ver would be great a-mong you must be your ser - vant.

119 xvii   Rejoicing in God's love

God's love is reliable, steadfast, constant. In that knowledge we can walk firmly, freed
from the weight of oppression, with a light step. Even in frightening places, it is as if
we are already in the safety of the sheepfold. Living in the spirit of that freedom, we
are more able, simply by our presence, to give courage to those who are constricted by
illness or imprisonment.

…in the Spirit that stirs amongst us the kaleidoscope of Jesus.

Come in by the door of the sheepfold.

Pause

Your steadfast love is wonderful:
therefore I treasure your wisdom.
When your word goes forth
it gives me light and inner understanding.

Pause

I opened my mouth and drew in my breath,
for my desire was for your counsel.
Look upon me and show me kindness,
for such is your delight towards those who love
      your name.

Pause

Keep my steps steady in your word,
and no wickedness will get dominion over me.
Relieve me from the weight of oppression,
and I shall keep your commandments.

Pause

Show the light of your face upon your servant,
and teach me your way.
My eyes shed streams of sorrow
because of those who do not heed your promise.

Silence

Visit the sick and those in prison.

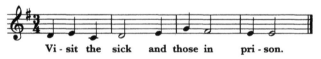

We breathe these words out of the Silence within us, into the Silence beyond us...

119 xviii   Thirsting for God's justice

*Freed from the weight of worldly expectations and possessions, humbled and poor, even,
like a grain of wheat, dying unnoticed, the followers of the way are the only ones who
can know what it would be like to see God's justice, God's commonwealth, established
on earth. They cry with yearning to see right prevail. They strive to make it so.*

Let the grain of wheat fall into the earth and die.

Let the grain of wheat fall in-to the earth and   die.

Pause

You are righteous, O God,
and your judgments are true.
**The ways that you have commanded
are just and true.**

Pause

My zeal has consumed me
because my enemies have forgotten your words.
**Your promise has been well tested,
and your servant loves and delights in it.**

Pause

I am small, and of no reputation,
yet I do not forget your wisdom.
**Your righteousness is an everlasting righteousness,
and your law is the truth.**

Pause

Trouble and heaviness have taken hold of me,
yet my delight is in your justice.
**The righteousness of your will is eternal:
give me understanding, and I shall live.**

Silence

…in the Spirit that stirs amongst us the kaleidoscope of Jesus.

Yearn and strive to see right prevail.

119 xix   Urgently needing God's guidance

Nevertheless, it is not easy to keep our sense of spiritual direction. We are easily misled and we have to face the malice of the frightened. We shall lie awake at night, seeking to settle our hearts and wills on God. We shall urgently pray for guidance in the day. We may be given the gift of God's peace, but we shall do well to strive with our enemies sooner rather than later.

Receive my gift of peace.

Pause

I call with my whole heart:
hear me, O God, I shall keep your commandments.
Urgently do I cry to you:
help me, and I shall follow your way.

Pause

Early in the morning I cry out to you,
for in your word is my trust.
My eyes are awake in the watches of the night,
that I might meditate on your promise.

Pause

Hear my voice according to your steadfast love,
quicken me, in fulfilment of your will.
They draw near who persecute me with malice:
they are far from your law.

We breathe these words out of the Silence within us, into the Silence beyond us...

Pause

But you, O God, are near at hand:
for all your counsel is true.
Long since I have known of your wisdom,
that you have grounded it for ever.

Silence

Make friends quickly with your adversary.

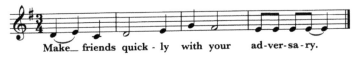

119 XX   Cherishing God's command

*Not one of us can plead innocence or perfection. There is great contrast between our
unfaithfulness and the steadfast love of God. This is painful truth. Only by immers-
ing ourselves in God's love, only by sharing the cup of affliction which was drained to
the full by the only One who was indeed whole, can we be given the life that we desire.
On the way we have to deny ourselves much of what we now hold dear.*

Drink the cup.

Pause

Look on my affliction and deliver me;
may I not forget your law.
Plead my cause and redeem me:
give me life according to your word.

Pause

Salvation is far from my wickedness,
when I have no regard for your commandments.

…in the Spirit that stirs amongst us the kaleidoscope of Jesus.

Great is your loving kindness, dear God:
give me life, for such is your joy and delight.

Pause

There are many who trouble me, my adversaries:
may I not swerve from your way.
It grieves me to see our unfaithfulness
when we ignore all that you promise.

Pause

Consider how I cherish your wisdom:
give me life, according to your steadfast love.
Your word is eternally true,
and your justice stands fast for ever.

Silence

Deny your self-centred desire.

119 xxi   Standing firm in God's counsel

If we keep to the way shown to us, we shall discover the treasures of the wisdom of God – love, truth, peace, saving health, justice. We are invited to trust and not be faithless, to open the devices of our locked hearts to God. Then, at peace, we shall absorb and reconcile conflicts, and so be makers of peace.

Be not faithless but believing.

Pause

We breathe these words out of the Silence within us, into the Silence beyond us…

The powerful oppress me without cause,
but my heart stands firm in awe of your word.
**I rejoice in your love
more than one who finds great spoils.**

Pause

As for lies, I hate and abhor them,
but your law do I love.
**Seven times a day do I praise you
because of the justice of your way.**

Pause

Great is the peace of those who treasure your wisdom:
nothing can make them stumble.
**I have looked for your saving health,
and followed your counsel.**

Pause

My whole being holds fast to your justice,
which I love and long for exceedingly.
**Guide me in the path of your truth,
all the ways of my heart are open before you.**

Silence

Be a maker of peace.

119 xxii   Praising God's salvation

In the maze we find our way by the thinnest of threads. We often go astray in cul-de-sacs. Found there by the 'angels' of God, we in turn can at times be a 'presence' of God to others. In dark, hidden places we can still give, and pray, and fast. In the end we shall be brought home rejoicing in the God who saves, in and through and beyond our hopes and fears.

…in the Spirit that stirs amongst us the kaleidoscope of Jesus.

Feed my sheep.

Feed____ my sheep.

Pause

Let my cry come to your ears, dear God:
give me understanding, according to your word.
See the confusion of my ways:
guide me through this maze, according to your promise.

Pause

My lips will tell of your praise,
for you show me the path of wisdom.
My tongue will sing of your love
and praise your justice to the skies.

Pause

Let your hand guide me,
steady me with the counsel of your Spirit.
I have longed for your saving health, O God,
and in your truth is my delight.

Pause

Let me live, that I may praise you:
let your love and your justice help me.
I have gone astray like a sheep that is lost:
seek your servant, and bring me home rejoicing.

Silence

Give secretly; pray secretly; fast secretly.

Give se-cret-ly;   pray se-cret-ly;   fast se-cret-ly.

✛

We breathe these words out of the Silence within us, into the Silence beyond us...

120

The pilgrim psalms: 1

Help and harm: Will I ever be free?

In solidarity with neglected and wounded infants.

From the days before I knew there were days,
in the darkness of continuing night,
I was caught in an alien country,
my enemies the source of my life.

Trapped and be-sieged, un-a-ble to move,—
I— cry from my pri-son, Let my jour-ney be-gin.

Pause

Bewildered by the smiles of welcome and peace,
nourished, it seemed, for my good,
I lay close to pretence and deceit,
seen only in the light of another's esteem.

**Trapped and besieged, unable to move,
I cry from my prison, Let my journey begin.**

Pause

I breathed the air of whispered betrayal,
entangled as I was in the voice of the lie.
Infected by words that were bitter and sharp,
I found it hard to resist the desire for revenge.

**Trapped and besieged, unable to move,
I cry from my prison, Let my journey begin.**

Pause

...in the Spirit that stirs amongst us the kaleidoscope of Jesus.

Like a fledgling my whole being trembled,
shaken by my first faltering steps.
At last I could leave the place of my peril,
glimpsing your love which is true and assured.

Pause

So you gave me the beginnings of freedom:
the arrows will turn back on those who pursue me,
the burning of the broom tree will shrivel the lie,
my betrayer's heart seared to life by the truth.

Silence

Give me courage, pillar of flame, **as I begin to follow you on
the pilgrim way. Create a calm and glowing centre within
me that I may resist the cruelties of those who seem
to love me. May I be firm in refusing all collusion. May
I be harmed no more. Keep me steady when I arouse
unresolved conflicts in others, for you love them as much
as you love me. Loose my chains in the dungeons, and free
them from their prisons too.**

121   The pilgrim psalms: 2

Refreshment and rigour: Have I the courage to trust?

*In solidarity with those travelling through dangerous places; and with those who live
in the mountains.*

I look towards the mountain ranges,
and fear their lurking terrors.
The pilgrim path takes me through them,
by rocks and ravines, ambush and vultures.

Pause

Stormy winds swirl round the summits,
avalanches threaten across trackless screes.
The hills themselves give no courage or strength,
and I turn once again to my God.

We breathe these words out of the Silence within us, into the Silence beyond us…

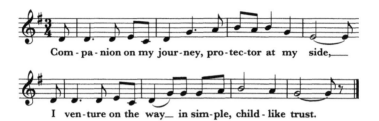

Com - pa - nion on my jour-ney, pro-tec-tor at my side,___

I ven-ture on the way__ in sim-ple, child-like trust.

Pause

Tempted to slide back into mud,
down to the bliss of oblivion,
yet I hear the lure of my lover,
whispering through my story's confusion.

Pause

The God who draws me is urging me on,
and I discover my faltering Yes.
I stumble along the rough pathways,
surprised by a hand that is grasping my own.

**Companion on my journey, protector at my side,
I venture on the way in simple, childlike trust.**

Pause

To and fro, back and forth,
on the twists of the journey,
courage moves me onwards,
faith trusts in the future;
wisdom makes me pause,
I rest by the stream;
taking time to delve deep,
I listen for a voice.

Silence

I reach for the unknown mountain,
to the summit where God speaks anew,
on the boundary of earth and heaven,
the frontier of time and eternity,   >

...in the Spirit that stirs amongst us the kaleidoscope of Jesus.

the place of a special revealing,
marked by the stones of a cairn.
As I ponder the codes of my dreaming,
I am surprised by the mystery of God.

**Companion on my journey, protector at my side,
I venture on the way in simple, childlike trust.**

Pause

The hills themselves slowly change,
never as firm as they seem;
shrouded, brooding, and dark,
their rocks splintered by frost,
worn away by the lashing of storms,
no strength in themselves to support me,
only from God comes my help.

**Companion on my journey, protector at my side,
I venture on the way in simple, childlike trust.**

Pause

With the wind of the Spirit empower me,
stirring the substance of earth,
moving my innermost being,
yet keeping me from all lasting harm.

Pause

Keep watch, do not slumber, guardian of your people,
shade from the heat, healer and guide.
Nourish the life of my truest self,
from this moment on and for ever.

Silence

Deepen my trust in your presence, my God, **for you seem often
absent and hidden, and I am afraid of what the way will
bring. Deepen my trust.**

We breathe these words out of the Silence within us, into the Silence beyond us…

122   The pilgrim psalms: 3

Peace and perplexity: What will become of the city?

In solidarity with all the peoples of Jerusalem, Jewish, Christian, and Muslim.

I was glad when my companions of faith
ventured with me to the house of our God.
Weary and tired, yet our feet will stand
within the gates of the city of peace,
Jerusalem the goal of our longing,
where the pilgrims gather in unity.

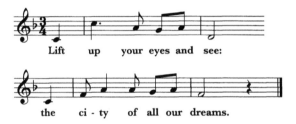

Lift up your eyes and see:
the ci-ty of all our dreams.

Pause

Drawn ever closer to the city,
to the place of prayer and of presence,
to faith renewed and hope restored,
to the healing and peace of the promise,
we your people climb to the gates,
to the seat of your judgment and mercy.

**Lift up your eyes and see:
the city of all our dreams.**

Pause

We pray for the peace of Jerusalem.
May those who love you prosper.
Peace be within your walls,
prosperity in all your households.
For the sake of my kindred and friends,
I will pray from my heart for your peace.   >

...in the Spirit that stirs amongst us the kaleidoscope of Jesus.

For the sake of the house of our God,
I will do all that I can for your good.

**Lift up your eyes and see:
the city of all our dreams.**

Silence

Bless the people of Jerusalem, **all who look to Abraham as
their ancestor in faith. Take the energy of our prayers and
deeds, and transform both place and people into a city
of pilgrimage and peace for the whole world. Bring all of
us there, so that we may taste and see your generous and
gracious love.**

123   The pilgrim psalms: 4

Delight and devastation: Will I survive the piercing eye?

*In solidarity with those who are pursued by the eyes of others; with those whose task
it is to watch and look; and with the makers and workers of satellites; and that we may
be aware of the look in our own eyes.*

The haughty look of the powerful,
the contemptuous stare of the wealthy,
the cutting glance of the clever,
the mocking glint of the cowardly:

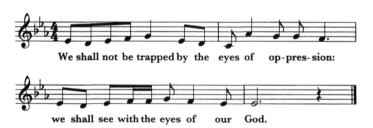

We shall not be trapped by the eyes of op-pres-sion:
we shall see with the eyes of our God.

Pause

We breathe these words out of the Silence within us, into the Silence beyond us...

Burdened by eyes that enslave us,
cast down by eyes of derision,
oppressed by eyes that pursue us,
held fast by eyes that never relent:

**We shall not be trapped by the eyes of oppression:
we shall see with the eyes of our God.**

Pause

The eyes of cameras following us,
the shadow of spies in the dark,
the screen displaying the data,
the silent satellite unseen:

**We shall not be trapped by the eyes of oppression:
we shall see with the eyes of our God.**

Pause

Fiery eyes, angry for justice,
compassionate eyes, warming the poor,
courteous eyes, attentive and waiting,
steady eyes, calm and courageous:

**We shall not be trapped by the eyes of oppression:
we shall see with the eyes of our God.**

Pause

A reverent look awed and still,
a ready glance, willing to obey,
a look of hope, expectant of good,
a look of trust, as between friends.

Silence

Fill us with the Spirit of love, **all-seeing and all-compassionate
God, that we may look with fierce yet kindly eyes on those
who oppress us, and shame them to a change of heart and
deed.**

…in the Spirit that stirs amongst us the kaleidoscope of Jesus.

124   The pilgrim psalms: 5

Deliverance and destruction: Will we weather the storm?

For steadiness when faced with fury; and for the transformation of all the powers that be.

If you had not been our strength and our wisdom
when destructive powers rose up and barred our path,
if you had not been committed to our good,
like monsters they would have swallowed us alive.

Pause

Their anger was kindled against us,
like the sweep of the forest fire.
Their fury bore down upon us,
like the raging torrent in flood,
the waters of chaos that know no limits,
trespassers that are hard to forgive.

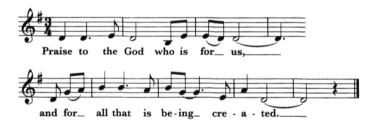

Praise to the God who is for us, and for all that is being created.

Pause

Thanks be to you, our deliverer,
you have not given us as prey to their teeth.
We escaped like a bird from the snare of the fowler:
the frame snapped and we have flown free.

Pause

In the joy of deliverance we praise you, O God.
Our hearts expand in a new generosity:
we embody the love with which you create.

We breathe these words out of the Silence within us, into the Silence beyond us...

Pause

Even the powers you do not destroy:
you redeem all our failures to live,
you are strong to bring good out of evil.

Praise to the God who is for us,
and for all that is being created.

Silence

In the dangers and risks of the pilgrim way **you are with us, our**
companion God. Strengthen us to face the perils of storm
and hunter that would overwhelm us, and show us again
that your creative love is stronger than anything else in the
universe.

125   The pilgrim psalms: 6

Trustworthiness and treachery: Are we dependable?

That we may be aware of the subtleties of deceit, in ourselves and in others; and that
trust may spread among us in public life.

Those who put their trust in you, O God,
shall be as if they were Mount Zion itself,
rooted in the depths of the earth,
never to be shaken, enduring for ever.

We trust the love that ne-ver fails,

the God who stands se - cure.

Pause

...in the Spirit that stirs amongst us the kaleidoscope of Jesus.

The mountains stand protecting Jerusalem,
city of ramparts and walls that are solid.
So stands our God around the people,
moment by moment, now and for ever.

**We trust the love that never fails,
the God who stands secure.** .

Pause

So may we be constant and true,
giving no sway to the sceptre of wickedness,
establishing the rule of justice in the land,
lest even the righteous be tempted to evil.

**We trust the love that never fails,
the God who stands secure.**

Pause

Yet our hidden deceits sap the foundations,
masked by the buildings of goodness and courage.
We are wheat and tares indeed for the sifting,
at the place of judgment and mercy.

**We trust the love that never fails,
the God who stands secure.**

Silence

O God of truth, **give us the spirit of resistance to the
subtleties of evil, insinuating themselves as we grow
stronger on the journey. May we be honest pilgrims,
steadfast, trustworthy, and true of heart, rooted only in
your love.**

We breathe these words out of the Silence within us, into the Silence beyond us…

126   *The pilgrim psalms:* 7

Exile and exultation: Will we come home?

In solidarity with those in exile; and with refugees and asylum seekers.

When God takes us home from our exile,
we shall wake from this nightmare and live again.
Bars of iron will be shattered: we shall walk free
from gulag and ghetto, from dungeon and tower.

Home   at   last,   con - ten-ted   and   grate-ful.

Pause

We shall sing and laugh for joy,
echoed by birdsong and breeze of the spring.
The land itself will rejoice in God,
the whole world give praise for the wonders we have seen.

Home at last, contented and grateful.

Pause

Lead us home, renew our hope, bring us to life,
like impossible rivers in the cursed and barren desert.
We go on our way sadly, with tears sowing seeds that will die,
we shall return with joy, with gladness bearing our sheaves.

Home at last, contented and grateful.

Silence

Restore the years, O God, **that we have lost, that the locusts
have eaten. Give to us the future that we thought we
should never see. Make of the present moment a firstfruit
of true liberation. Even when we feel exiled, locked in,
despairing, move secretly within us and among us, and
without our realizing it, keep us moving on our journey to
your city.**

...in the Spirit that stirs amongst us the kaleidoscope of Jesus.

127   The pilgrim psalms: 8

Care and consumption: How well are we building?

In solidarity with those who build and those who guard; and with those responsible for the nurture of children; and that we may be at ease and laugh together.

Eternal God, our rock and our foundation,
without you all that we build is but rubble.
Blindly and cheaply we construct on sand,
and the buildings subside and crumble.

Fru-strate our schemes and de-signs,

yet bless us in ci-ty and home.

Pause

Those who guard the city do so in vain;
the watchman cannot see the corruption within.
The lights in the towers shine on through the night:
Is it all for vain profit? Will they soon turn to dust?

**Frustrate our schemes and designs,
yet bless us in city and home.**

Pause

Foolish we are to rise up so early,
drawn to the work that consumes us.
The bread of anxiety sours and gnaws at us,
we forget you give gifts while we sleep.

**Frustrate our schemes and designs,
yet bless us in city and home.**

Pause

We breathe these words out of the Silence within us, into the Silence beyond us...

Let us turn to our children and play with them,
a glorious waste of mechanical time!
They are our heritage, a gift only from you:
content are those who build steady around them.

**Frustrate our schemes and designs,
yet bless us in city and home.**

Pause

Of such buildings is the lasting city made:
blessed are those who delight in such priceless gifts.
They will stand assured when facing their adversaries,
they and their children will grow in stature and wisdom.

Silence

Keep us building slowly, steadily, truly. **Keep us from being
Babel-like, top-heavy and empty. Keep us building one
another up in wisdom and love. And let us take no anxious
thought for tomorrow.**

128   The pilgrim psalms: 9

Embrace and exclusion: Do I belong?

*In solidarity with families and small communities; and with partners, children, and
friends; and for generous and simple hospitality.*

From our ancestors to our children's children
let us be grateful for the blessings of home.

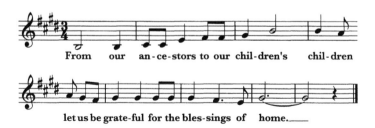

From our an-ce-stors to our chil-dren's chil-dren

let us be grate-ful for the bles-sings of home.___

…in the Spirit that stirs amongst us the kaleidoscope of Jesus.

Pause

We are blessed if we hold God in awe,
if we walk in the paths of our Creator.
The labour of our hands will bear fruit:
all will be well, we shall rest content.

Pause

Husband and wife will be happy together,
partners and friends will sustain one another:
in intimacy and trust they will embrace,
and gather to tell tales by the fire.

Pause

Children will be a blessing round the table,
guests will bring grace to festival times.
As branches of vine and of olive,
each will be God's presence to the other.

**From our ancestors to our children's children
let us be grateful for the blessings of home.**

Pause

We are blessed if we keep the counsels of God,
who dwells in the secret places of our hearts,
who comes to life between us in love,
who shares bread and wine round our hearth.

Pause

God will bless us indeed:
we shall have known Jerusalem –
an outpost of the city of peace,
a sign of shalom on the earth.

**From our ancestors to our children's children
let us be grateful for the blessings of home.**

Silence

We breathe these words out of the Silence within us, into the Silence beyond us...

Let even the outcast and exile, **within us or beyond our gate,
not begrudge the contentment of simple blessings. Let the
fortunate open wide their gates to welcome the outcast
and the exile home. In quiet ways may sorrows be eased
and envy dispelled.**

129   The pilgrim psalms: 10

Golgotha and genocide: Can faith survive?

*That everyone may resist the temptation to act from cold conviction and hatred; that
guns may always point upwards; and that no one people may see another as ripe only
for slaughter.*

The litany of lament grows loud and long:
the pulse of faith grows weak.

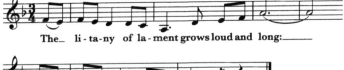

The— li-ta-ny of la-ment grows loud and long:____

the— pulse of faith grows weak.

Pause

Does the power of the wicked have no limit?
Why do you not restrain them, O God?
Your people of old knew a measure of affliction,
but they praised you for deeds of deliverance.

Pause

Their enemies scored their backs with ploughshares,
opening long furrows of crimson.
But you would not let the adversary prevail,
you cut your people free from the chafing bonds.

...in the Spirit that stirs amongst us the kaleidoscope of Jesus.

**The litany of lament grows loud and long:
the pulse of faith grows weak.**

Pause

Their anger welled up within them,
cursing the enemy with withering scorn:
"May they be as grass that shrivels in the heat,
may they never come to the ripeness of harvest."

Pause

An easy exchange it seems to us now,
faced as we are with cruelty unleashed –
exquisite refinements of torture's black arts,
children knifed and dumped in the gutters.

**The litany of lament grows loud and long:
the pulse of faith grows weak.**

Pause

Woe to us when to cleanse means to slaughter,
when genocide seems the simple solution,
when bullets explode into a thousand splinters,
when young and old are abused and discarded.

Pause

Why do you not act, mute God, in your justice?
How dare we name you as good any more?
We have entered deep darkness in the midst of the journey,
and the pilgrims are paralyzed, unable to move.

**The litany of lament grows loud and long:
the pulse of faith grows weak.**

Silence

We receive no answers to our prayers, silent God, **and yet still
we pray to you lest we despair. Justify your ways to us,
and do not silence us, like Job, with power and grandeur.
Convince us again of the invincible strength of vulnerable
and crucified love, even when Golgotha and genocide
seem worlds apart. Do not fail us in our extremity.**

We breathe these words out of the Silence within us, into the Silence beyond us...

130   The pilgrim psalms: 11

Watching and waiting: Dare I enter the dark?

In solidarity wih the exhausted and despairing; and for courage to say Yes to the unknown future.

Empty, exhausted, and ravaged,
in the depths of despair I writhe.
Anguished and afflicted, terribly alone,
I trudge a bleak wasteland, devoid of all love.

Pause

In the echoing abyss I call out:
no God of compassion hears my voice.
Yet still I pray, Open your heart,
for my tears well up within me.

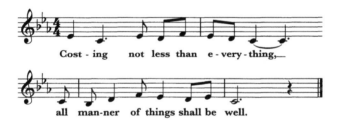

Cost - ing   not less than   e - very - thing,___

all   man-ner   of things shall be   well.

Pause

If you keep account of all that drags me down,
there is no way I can stand firm.
Paralyzed and powerless, I topple over,
bound by the evil I hate.

Pause

But with you is forgiveness and grace,
there is nothing I can give – it seems like a death.
The power of your love is so awesome:
I am terrified by your freeing embrace.

…in the Spirit that stirs amongst us the kaleidoscope of Jesus.

**Costing not less than everything,
all manner of things shall be well.**

Pause

Drawn from the murky depths by a fish hook,
I shout to the air that will kill me:
Must I leave behind all that I cherish
before I can truly breathe free?

Pause

Suspended between one world and the next,
I waited for you, my God.
Apprehension and hope struggled within me,
I waited, I longed for your word.

**Costing not less than everything,
all manner of things shall be well.**

Pause

As a watchman waits for the morning,
through the darkest and coldest of nights,
more even than the watchman who peers through the gloom,
I hope for the dawn, I yearn for the light.

Pause

You will fulfil your promise to bring me alive,
overflowing with generous love.
You will free me from the grip of evil,
O God of mercy and compassion.

Pause

Touching and healing the whole of my being,
you are a God whose reach has no limit.
All that has been lost will one day be found:
the communion of the rescued will rejoice in your name.

**Costing not less than everything,
all manner of things shall be well.**

Silence

We breathe these words out of the Silence within us, into the Silence beyond us...

Through the dark despairing depths, **through the drought of the desert, through the abyss opened up by our failings and folly, we dare to risk our cry to the living God. For you will not let us escape from our greatest good. In our struggle with you, fierce, fiery lover, let some new glory be wrought, and new and unexpected life come to birth.**

131   The pilgrim psalms: 12

Calm and contentment: I shall praise

That we may find deep contentment in everyday routines; that we may be fully present in the moment; and that we may learn to be silent and still.

In quietness and confidence is our strength,
in utter trust our contentment and joy.

In   quiet-ness   and   con-fi-dence   is   our   strength,

in   ut-ter   trust   our   con-tent-ment   and   joy.

Pause

Dear God, my heart is not proud,
nor are my eyes haughty.
I do not busy myself in great matters,
or in what is beyond me.

Pause

I am glad I depend on my neighbour,
I make no great claims of my own.
Sealed off by myself I would never know gifts,
never know the bonding of trust.

...in the Spirit that stirs amongst us the kaleidoscope of Jesus.

**In quietness and confidence is our strength,
in utter trust our contentment and joy.**

Pause

I have calmed and quietened my whole being,
I am like a child contented at the mother's breast.
In the stillness I look into the eyes of my lover,
I am absorbed in the task of the moment.

Pause

It is like the silence of an evening in spring,
made intense by the bleat of a lamb.
It is like the waves of the sea come to rest,
no more than a whisper in the caress of the shore.

**In quietness and confidence is our strength,
in utter trust our contentment and joy.**

Pause

The silence and stillness lift the woodsmoke of prayer,
a song of quiet gratitude wafting it high.
Aware of descendants and ancestors with us,
we join the soft chorus of praise.

Silence

May we cherish the silence and not be afraid. **May we know
it not empty but full of presence. May the love at its
heart calm our fears. May we know the gentle touch of a
trusting hand.**

❖

We breathe these words out of the Silence within us, into the Silence beyond us...

132   The pilgrim psalms: 13

Beauty and bliss: I shall wonder

*In solidarity with poets, playwrights, artists, composers, and sculptors; and with those
who are beginning to discover their creative ability with material stuff; and in gratitude
for beauty crafted and shared.*

The splendour of the ark of the covenant,
housed in the glory of the Temple,
crowning the city of peace –
the pilgrims were drawn by the beauty of God.

Pause

No wonder that David of old
vowed not to enter his house,
to sleep in the comfort of his bed,
till the ark of the presence found rest.

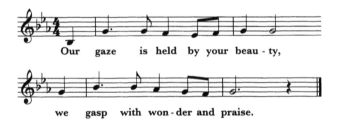

Our   gaze   is held by your beau - ty,

we   gasp   with won - der and praise.

Pause

We are stirred by the festival day,
the ark in triumphal procession,
the people decked out in splendour,
the faithful shouting for joy.

Pause

Your covenant with your people is strengthened,
your beauty attracting and leading us on,
to the goodness at the heart of your law,
to the truth brought to life in our deeds.

...in the Spirit that stirs amongst us the kaleidoscope of Jesus.

Pause

The beauty of carvings in wood and in stone,
of people transformed in their presence,
the beauty of words and of music,
bring us close to the heart of our God.

**Our gaze is held by your beauty,
we gasp with wonder and praise.**

Pause

Yet more was promised to David that day:
a descendant would inherit the covenant.
Would we be shown a more lasting beauty,
gloriously embodying the divine and the human?

Pause

And yet – most wonderful paradox –
the beauty of God touched the outcast:
nothing in the crucified to delight us,
only to faith's eye is God's glory revealed.

Pause

If the ugliest of scars can shine with new light,
if you can fashion new forms from our chaos,
if poets can bring hope from genocide's ashes,
we can rejoice once again in the beauty of God.

**Our gaze is held by your beauty,
we gasp with wonder and praise.**

Silence

Keep alive in us, Spirit of God, **even in desperate days, a
vision of a true and godly beauty, shaped from the least
likely matter of your creation, that graced and cheered,
we may not perish but be encouraged to glory.**

We breathe these words out of the Silence within us, into the Silence beyond us...

133   The pilgrim psalms: 14

Loving and loved: I shall love

For the sharing of stories, of griefs, angers, and fears, and of joys and laughter.

At oases on the pilgrim way we rest together,
sharing the stories and meals that refresh us.
O God, you do not judge us by success or by failure:
you call us to be faithful and true,
to do your will, to delight in your blessing.

May we be   one   in the ex-chan-ges of   love,

in the look of the   eyes   be-tween   lo-ver and   loved.

Pause

Brothers and sisters, friends of God,
how joyful and pleasant a thing it is –
like the gathering of a mountain range –
when we dwell together in unity.

Pause

It is like a precious and fragrant oil,
like the dew of early morning,
or the scent of summer in the forest –
gifts beyond all expectation.

Pause

It is like the very beauty of holiness itself,
a sense of presence in the places of prayer,
the Godward eyes of faithful people,
the times we are surprised by new blessings.

...in the Spirit that stirs amongst us the kaleidoscope of Jesus.

May we be one in the exchanges of love,
in the look of the eyes between lover and loved.

Pause

So we give you heartfelt thanks, O God,
that we can glimpse the harmony of humanity,
that we can trust that all creation will be restored,
that all things will be suffused with the light of your glory.

May we be one in the exchanges of love,
in the look of the eyes between lover and loved.

Silence

God of communion, **may we hear your gracious invitation to**
share the hospitality of your table and the dance of your
love. So may we take delight in everything that you have
created for us to enjoy.

134 The pilgrim psalms: 15

Blessing and beginning: I shall be blessed

For special places and the making special of ordinary places; and that we may not
linger and find that joy has turned to dust.

Lead us on, pillar of flame,
always moving ahead of us.

Lead us on, pil-lar of flame,

al-ways mov-ing a-head of___ us.

Pause

We breathe these words out of the Silence within us, into the Silence beyond us...

We your friends and servants bless you, O God,
as we stand night and day in your presence.
We lift up our hands to the holiest of places,
whose walls pray the prayers of the pilgrims.

Pause

To the city of peace we have come at the last,
and give you, our God, our heartfelt praise.
Bless us and all you have given us,
Creator of heaven and earth.

**Lead us on, pillar of flame,
always moving ahead of us.**

Pause

Bless us as we turn away from the shrines,
lest by lingering we become pillars of salt.
Even the stones will decay into dust:
the presence will depart from among them.

Pause

Absorbing the gifts our ancestors left to us,
we set out once more on our journey.
What we thought was our goal was but a stage on the way,
and the Spirit is urging us on.

**Lead us on, pillar of flame,
always moving ahead of us.**

Silence

Drawn as we may be by Enlli and Lindisfarne, **by Iona and
Durham, by Canterbury and Jerusalem, by Santiago and
Rome, let us take courage from our ancestors of faith,
but let us now seek to make holy the places where we
live, and to be made holy ourselves by the God who goes
on before us.**

...in the Spirit that stirs amongst us the kaleidoscope of Jesus.

135   Small and great, exile and settler, poor and wealthy

In solidarity with the first peoples of the world; with migrant workers and their families back home; with farmers and gardeners; and with the powerful and wealthy.

We praise you, Beloved, we give thanks to your name;
in the loyalty of friendship we give you praise.
In the house where we heard your promises
we give thanks for the blessings of your covenant.

Pause

We praise you for your grace and your courtesy,
we sing praise to your name for it is good.
You have chosen us for particular service,
a priestly people whose love is not narrow.

Praise to the God___ who cre-ates us and calls us,

and pro-mi-ses___ an a-bun-dance of bless-ing.

Pause

You are indeed the glorious Creator,
awesome in your freedom and power.
Your will stretches round the great globe,
echoing to the ocean depths.

Pause

You shine through the fierce heat of the sun,
tempered by the tenderness of clouds and rain.
You howl through the winds of the desert,
whilst giving oases of sheltering green.

We breathe these words out of the Silence within us, into the Silence beyond us...

Praise to the God who creates us and calls us,
and promises an abundance of blessing.

Pause

You yearn for each of us to have a home,
a piece of the earth to cherish and care for.
Your heart goes out to the wandering exile,
in Egypt, in Babylon, in migrants today.

Pause

You lived among us a vulnerable child,
fleeing from the wiles of the powers that be.
You know what it means to be cast out of the walls,
yet you prepare a city beyond our imagining.

Praise to the God who creates us and calls us,
and promises an abundance of blessing.

Pause

Fortunate they are who have houses to dwell in,
whose roots reach far in the ground of the past.
Blessed are those with a language of their own,
through which they can hear your marvellous works.

Pause

Inheritors as we are of an ancient story,
we find our place in the greater world.
Through art and music we are consoled and inspired,
through the touch of our neighbours we know we belong.

Praise to the God who creates us and calls us,
and promises an abundance of blessing.

Pause

Let us not fall into the grip of idols,
dazzled by displays of silver and gold.
Let not our wealth feed a monstrous addiction,
growing tall and slowly destroying us.

Pause

...in the Spirit that stirs amongst us the kaleidoscope of Jesus.

Let us live from the point of our need,
of the poor, the outcast, the friendless,
the hurt child who lives in us all,
the needy who bring us the gift of your presence.

**Praise to the God who creates us and calls us,
and promises an abundance of blessing.**

Pause

Let all the first peoples bless you, O God,
aboriginal, in touch with earth's wisdom.
Let the migrant workers bless you, O God,
nomadic in spirit, with no earthly resting place.

Pause

Let the settlers on the land bless you, O God,
who husband the earth for its harvest.
Let the powerful bless you, O God,
who hold the earth in their hands.

Silence

Creator of the universe, **yet friend to each one of us, giving
us our homes, yet planting in us a yearning for a true
and lasting city, disturbing the settled and comforting
the restless wanderer, may we all come together in your
praise.**

136   Love without end

*In solidarity with research scientists; and with those who help others handle change and
resolve conflicts; and in gratitude for a marvellous universe.*

We give you thanks, O God, for your goodness,
for your mercies endure for ever.
By solemn promise you are bound to us,
source of grace for ever and ever.

We breathe these words out of the Silence within us, into the Silence beyond us…

Al - le - lu - ia!

We sing of your love, now and for e - ver.

Pause

You are the God beyond gods,
a mystery too profound for our thoughts.
In the shadows of the light we discern you,
we are struck by your dazzling darkness.

Alleluia! We sing of your love, now and for ever.

Pause

You reveal the marvels of the universe
to those who listen and patiently look –
from atoms and genes hidden from our eyes
to the shafts of light from long dead stars.

Alleluia! We sing of your love, now and for ever.

Pause

For the beauty of forms ever-changing,
for the slow turning of the sun and the seasons,
for the miracle of the newly born child,
for the rising of our daily bread:

Alleluia! We sing of your love, now and for ever.

Pause

At the turning points of our lives you are with us,
through times of bewildering change.
At the crossing of the boundaries of the known
by strangers and dreams you encourage us.

Alleluia! We sing of your love, now and for ever.

...in the Spirit that stirs amongst us the kaleidoscope of Jesus.

Pause

You rescue us from slavery and exile,
you are with us on our desert journey,
you give us a place we can cherish,
where the vulnerable find their protection.

Alleluia! We sing of your love, now and for ever.

Pause

You have given us our parts in the story,
from our ancestors whose names are forgotten
to our descendants whose names are not known,
to each a new name in your presence.

Alleluia! We sing of your love, now and for ever.

Pause

You gave of yourself in the one called Yeshua,
showing us the way of dying to live;
you renewed the gifts of your Spirit,
your glory has shone through your saints.

Alleluia! We sing of your love, now and for ever.

Pause

In you we are bound to one another,
linked by threads seen and unseen,
destined for love in eternity,
when all that has decayed is restored.

Alleluia! We sing of your love, now and for ever.

Silence

As we contemplate, discern, and endure through the years, **may
we hold in the presence of God all that is intractable and
unresolved in the life of this planet and its peoples – and
in our own lives also – until the time comes when the
Spirit of gratitude spreads over all things, and for all that
has been, we shall in truth give our thanks, and to all that
is coming to be, we shall indeed sing our Yes.**

We breathe these words out of the Silence within us, into the Silence beyond us...

137   By the waters of Babylon

In solidarity with those whose cities and towns, villages and homes have been devastated by natural disaster or human conflict; and with those who rebuild, across the boundaries of creed or race.

By the waters of Babylon we sat down and wept
when we remembered the smouldering city.
We hid our harps in the thickets of the willow;
silently and bitterly we grieved.

Pause

They who drove us captive from our homeland
demanded of us a song of our joy.
Goaded by their torment we cried out,
"How can we sing of our God in this strangest of lands?"

Pause

"How can we throw our pearls before swine?
You trample on our name, you rob us of hope,
we cannot betray what is holy and precious.
To proclaim what is intimate is to lose it for ever."

Pause

"It is hard to be faithful and firm,
as despair overwhelms us in torrents.
Troubled we are and uncertain,
no longer assured of God's presence."

Pause

"O God, do you hear the cries of our hearts,
now that we are so far from your city?
On foreign soil can we worship you still?
Have you withdrawn from us for ever?"

Pause

"Yet if I forget you, Jerusalem,
may the hand that plucks the harp wither.
May my tongue cleave to the roof of my mouth
if I do not give Jerusalem my heart's desire."

...in the Spirit that stirs amongst us the kaleidoscope of Jesus.

Pause

"Great anger rises within me, a thirst for revenge
against those who have destroyed the city.
Even our kin wanted Jerusalem ruined,
stripped bare to its very foundations."

Pause

"Colonial power and neighbouring tribe
laid us waste with their scorn and their greed.
'May your cities be burnt to a cinder,
your children dashed to pieces on the rocks.'"

Pause

O God, hear the honesty in my rage,
the sharp pain in my heart.
To you alone I can yield the hatred I feel,
trusting you will somehow use it for good.
But how? What to do with my anger?
For its power I need: it must not be taken from me.

Bless - ed are those who hun - ger and strive
for all that is just and good.

Pause

We who have lost so much, hear us.
We who have been so much abused, hear us.
We who now live on the margins, hear us.
We who are denied our own language, hear us.

**Blessed are those who hunger and strive
for all that is just and good.**

Pause

We breathe these words out of the Silence within us, into the Silence beyond us...

Yet truly their life has no meaning,
their hearts as hollow as their mockery.
They destroy themselves by their cruelty,
they become as the dust of the city they destroyed.
No, do not let them vanish for ever,
but shame them to repentance and justice.

**Blessed are those who hunger and strive
for all that is just and good.**

Pause

Work in us the deeds of your grace.
May we restrain our furious desires,
refusing to be dragged down to their mire.
But keep us from too easy a kindness.
With patient tenacity may we endure;
keep alive the power of our anger.

**Blessed are those who hunger and strive
for all that is just and good.**

Pause

Create a new heart in all who oppress,
break down the structures that bind them.
So you will give us the sign that we need
for the grace at the last to forgive.

Pause

For now let us mightily strive with our enemies,
until all of us, limping, are blessed.
Together may we sing a new song
as we build a more glorious city.

Silence

As cracks split the walls of the houses of prayer, as the faiths are
compromised by collusion with oppression, as we betray you by
killing one another in your name, as the Spirit of the ages moves
on, challenge us again, mysterious God, in homeland or in exile –
in delving within, expecting to be changed – in anger and truth
changing the world – that we may see beyond the convictions with

...in the Spirit that stirs amongst us the kaleidoscope of Jesus.

which we bind and cage both you and one another, and having
seen, may act. As no stone was left standing on another in
Jerusalem, so it will be in Canterbury and Rome. They will fall
because their vision is too narrow. May we not rebuild them as of
old, but keep them as empty silent spaces that they may speak to us
eloquently of what is beyond us.

**Empower us to build the city of peace wherever we are.
May we discern your call to protect and shape city and
home, farm and wilderness, body and community, all in
harmony with your will. May they alone become temples
of your presence, the places of our prayer, and the new
Jerusalem for which we dream and long.**

138   God's gentle touch

In solidarity with the homeless; and for courage to cross invisible boundaries.

Homeless and restless, I sleep on the streets,
huddled in the doorway of the jeweller's store.
Why are they afraid of me who can do them no harm?
Why do they all pass hurriedly by?

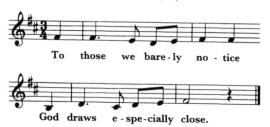

Pause

A woman stops, eyes steady and clear:
her hand clasps mine, enclosing a coin.
She speaks a few words, spends a few seconds,
risking the laughter of those who pass by.

**To those we barely notice
God draws especially close.**

We breathe these words out of the Silence within us, into the Silence beyond us...

Pause

A man draws close with hesitant step,
embarrassed and awkward when faced with the strange.
yet he stays long enough to give me some broth,
a waste in the thoughts of those who pass by.

To those we barely notice
God draws especially close.

Pause

The crypt of a church lies dusty, unused,
till a few catch a vision of a haven of care.
There are some who give food with a listening ear,
a hope unknown to those who pass by.

To those we barely notice
God draws especially close.

Pause

A few with pure hearts among those who are wealthy
keep stirring the conscience of people with power,
pressing for the changes that justice requires,
sword in the path of those who pass by.

To those we barely notice
God draws especially close.

Pause

Do they give me a glimpse of an unusual God?
Is there glory in the costly giving of self?
Is it through them that I know I am loved?
Is God far from those who pass by?

To those we barely notice
God draws especially close.

Pause

The skilled and the powerful think they are favoured,
they call on their God to buttress their pride.   >

...in the Spirit that stirs amongst us the kaleidoscope of Jesus.

They miss the gentleness of a touch that is loving,
fearful hands push away and of course they pass by.

Silence

We give you thanks, surprising God, with all our hearts. **Through
the poor man of Nazareth who embodied your love, and
whose Spirit inspires us still, you keep alive the hope that
the true strength of the gentle and merciful will overcome
the brittle force of the fearful and powerful, that at the last
the unrecognized will indeed inherit the earth.**

139   Light of light

That all the faiths may acknowledge the divine presence in every human being.

Light of light, you have searched me out and known me.
You know where I am and where I go,
you see my thoughts from afar.
You discern my paths and my resting places,
you are acquainted with all my ways.

Pause

Yes, and not a word comes from my lips
but you, O God, have heard it already.
You are in front of me and you are behind me,
you have laid your hand on my shoulder.
Such knowledge is too wonderful for me,
so great that I cannot fathom it.

Pause

Al - ways   a - ware of   us,

e - ver - pre - sent   with   us,

We breathe these words out of the Silence within us, into the Silence beyond us…

cease - less - ly cre - at - ing us,

we   re - spond in   love,_____

we   trem - ble and a - dore,

our___ God, my - ste - ri - ous and faith - ful.

Pause

Where shall I go from your Spirit,
where shall I flee from your presence?
If I climb to the heavens you are there:
if I descend to the depths of the earth you are there also.

Pause

If I spread my wings towards the morning,
and fly to the uttermost shores of the sea,
even there your hand will lead me,
and your right hand will hold me.

Pause

If I should cry to the darkness to cover me,
and the night to enclose me,
the darkness is no darkness to you,
and the night is as clear as the day.

Pause

...in the Spirit that stirs amongst us the kaleidoscope of Jesus.

Always aware of us,
ever-present with us,
ceaselessly creating us –
we respond in love,
we tremble and adore,
our God, mysterious and faithful.

Pause

For you have created every part of my being,
cell and tissue, blood and bone.
You have woven me in the womb of my mother;
I will praise you, so wonderfully am I made.
Awesome are your deeds:
and marvellous are your works.

Pause

You know me to the very core of my being;
nothing in me was hidden from your eyes
when I was formed in silence and secrecy,
in intricate splendour in the depths of the earth.
Even as they were forming you saw my limbs,
each part of my body shaped by your finger.

Pause

Always aware of us,
ever-present with us,
ceaselessly creating us –
we respond in love,
we tremble and adore,
our God, mysterious and faithful.

Pause

How deep are your thoughts to me, O God,
how great is the sum of them.
Were I to count them they are more in number
than the grains of sand upon the sea-shore –
and still I would know nothing about you –
yet still would you hold me in the palm of your hand.

We breathe these words out of the Silence within us, into the Silence beyond us...

Silence

Yet my trust falters. **I see all that is wrong in the world and in my heart, all the mutual loathing and hatreds, all the betrayals and lies. Scour our hearts, refine our thoughts, strengthen our wills, guide us in your way.**

140   Against evildoers

For the restraining and confining of those who commit evil deeds; and for the liberation of those who are confined and constrained.

Those who defraud the poor of their pensions,
those who deprive the poor of their land,
those who grow wealthy on the backs of the poor:

God of jus-tice and power,____ ____

re - strain them,   con - fine__ them,

bring them to their knees.__

Pause

Those who have no coins for the meter,
those who walk far for their fuel,
those whose backs are bent low:

>

God of com-pas-sion and power,____

res-cue them,   li-ber-ate them,

lift____ up their hearts._____

Pause

Those who fly flags of convenience,
those who pollute the rivers and streams,
those who release acid to clouds:

**God of justice and power,
restrain them, confine them, bring them to their knees.**

Pause

Those who sweat in the engine rooms,
those whose health is damaged by their work,
dwellers in forests where the leaves shrivel:

**God of compassion and power,
rescue them, liberate them, lift up their hearts.**

Pause

Those who trade in drugs that destroy,
those who smuggle arms that recoil on their makers,
governments who cynically collude:

**God of justice and power,
restrain them, confine them, bring them to their knees.**

Pause

We breathe these words out of the Silence within us, into the Silence beyond us...

Those with poison in their veins,
those who will never walk again,
people deprived of their rights:

**God of compassion and power,
rescue them, liberate them, lift up their hearts.**

Pause

Those who with malice slander their neighbours,
those who twist words for the sake of a scandal,
those who use words to boost their esteem:

**God of justice and power,
restrain them, confine them, bring them to their knees.**

Pause

Those who are deprived of their name,
those without value or worth,
those who know not their own language:

**God of compassion and power,
rescue them, liberate them, lift up their hearts.**

Pause

Those who beat the young to submission,
those who torture and rape,
those who violate their children:

**God of justice and power,
restrain them, confine them, bring them to their knees.**

Pause

Children who cower in fear,
all who are wounded and scarred,
survivors who twist in the darkness:

**God of compassion and power,
rescue them, liberate them, lift up their hearts.**

Silence

...in the Spirit that stirs amongst us the kaleidoscope of Jesus.

With the psalmist our anger rises at the harm we human beings cause one another. **We cry out for the oppressed and defenceless. Let the arrogant and mighty crumble under the weight of their own evil. Let them be plunged into the quaking mire. Let burning coals rain down on their heads. Let them be hunted to an exhausted and terror-struck end. Temper our fury but channel the energy of our anger to bring them to their knees at the last, restrained, confined, powerless to harm, at the mercy of those they have wronged.**

141   Impossible dream?

In solidarity with those in prison, lawfully or unlawfully.

My whole being reaches towards you, my God:
my heart yearns for your welcoming love.
I would run to embrace you as to a friend,
my voice leaping and singing for joy.

Pause

Like incense my prayer rises to meet you,
carried on the breath from my lungs.
My arms stretch out, lifting me high,
seeking the hand that is eager to touch.

Pause

To the unheard music my feet start dancing;
embodied in movement I become as my joy.
From the depths of my belly arises a cry,
a glorious Yes to the whole of my life.

Pause

O that it were so! It is only a dream,
far from the walls of this imprisoning cell.
Exhausted and limp, I stagger and fall,
my prayer no more than a flickering thought.

We breathe these words out of the Silence within us, into the Silence beyond us...

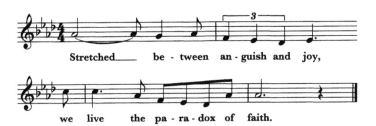

Stretched_____ be - tween an - guish and joy,

we live the pa - ra - dox of faith.

Pause

Silenced by the greedy and scared,
I have no one to utter a passionate cry,
the heartfelt anguish of the unjustly imprisoned,
from the narrow cells underground.

**Stretched between anguish and joy,
we live the paradox of faith.**

Pause

I scratch my name on the prison wall,
frightened I am losing all sense of my being.
Will no one speak on behalf of the mute,
will not the Judge of the earth do right?

**Stretched between anguish and joy,
we live the paradox of faith.**

Pause

Is the hope of my heart an impossible dream?
Will I ever dance in the rays of the sun?
Will I know the warmth of a welcoming hand?
Will a voice of love ever call me by name?

**Stretched between anguish and joy,
we live the paradox of faith.**

Silence

May the fitful tremblings of our prayer **move through the world
with compassion to give to someone in prison, neglected
and forgotten, at least a moment's respite from despair.**

...in the Spirit that stirs amongst us the kaleidoscope of Jesus.

142   Trust though rejected

In solidarity with those in solitary confinement; and with those isolated because of their physical or mental illness; and for the dissolving of stigmas.

I call to you, my God, with heartfelt cry:
insistent in my need, I seek your presence.
Barely do I believe, yet still do I pray,
and make no secret of all my troubles.

A - lone___ and re-jec-ted   dare I trust,

hear-ing   on-ly   the si-lence   of God?

Pause

When my voice croaks and is faint,
when weariness overtakes me on the way,
do you hear my whisper and know where I walk?
Do you know there is much that makes me stumble?

**Alone and rejected dare I trust,
hearing only the silence of God?**

Pause

I am left in the silence with no one to help me,
not even a hand draws close to touch me.
I can no longer speak, I drift in a vacuum,
thick glass hems me in: no one can see me.

**Alone and rejected dare I trust,
hearing only the silence of God?**

Pause

We breathe these words out of the Silence within us, into the Silence beyond us...

With a cry without words or sounds,
I search for your presence, O God.
Do you still have the power to rescue me?
Do you care enough for my plight?

**Alone and rejected dare I trust,
hearing only the silence of God?**

Pause

Save me from all that oppresses me,
from the powers that are too strong for me.
Lift me from the dungeon that confines me,
that I may laugh and sing again.

Pause

With generous heart beyond measure,
will you come to my healing and rescue?
Then I shall rejoice in the voices of praise,
and give you the glory for ever.

Silence

Rejected and isolated, **we seek warmth and affirmation,
nourishment and good company. Come, living Spirit, with
the wind and the bread, the touch, the water, and the
word, the fire and the balm.**

143   Afraid of death

In solidarity with those who are desperate and with those who are dying.

My heart is open, I come without guile,
I dare to pray to a God who is faithful.
I cannot justify myself in your presence;
with trembling I bring my desperate need.
I make no plea for justice,
I depend on your mercy and grace.

Pause

...in the Spirit that stirs amongst us the kaleidoscope of Jesus.

Dis - solv - ing   in - to   the   void,

dis - in - te - grat - ing   to____   dust,

I   cry   out   in   de - sper - ate   need.__

De - li - ver   me   from   the   fear   of   death.

Pause

The devourer is crushing my bones,
the ravenous hounds knock me to the ground,
the unconscious dark overshadows me;
dumped in the ditch I am given up for dead.

Pause

My will to live grows faint within me,
my heart is appalled and terrified.
No longer does the stream flow through me:
my taste is of death, acrid and dry.

Pause

**Dissolving into the void,
disintegrating to dust,
I cry out in desperate need.
Deliver me from the fear of death.**

Pause

I cling to the memories of faith,
my heart once lifted in gratitude.

We breathe these words out of the Silence within us, into the Silence beyond us...

When I least expected your presence,
with the deepest joy you surprised me.
Let me be calm and reflect on your goodness,
on the innumerable gifts you have given me.

Pause

Trembling I stretch out my hands,
hungry for the food that sustains.
Without you I cannot but perish,
starved in the depths of my being.

Pause

Long have I believed you are with me,
however unaware I become.
Do not sever the threads that connect us,
lest I drift into space for ever.

Pause

Dissolving into the void,
disintegrating to dust,
I cry out in desperate need.
Deliver me from the fear of death.

Pause

Let me hear of your compassion and mercy,
rising with the warmth of the sun.
Show me the way I should travel,
your kindly Spirit giving me courage.
Deliver me from the shades of death;
for the sake of your name calm me.

Pause

Dissolving into the void,
disintegrating to dust,
I cry out in desperate need.
Deliver me from the fear of death.

Pause

...in the Spirit that stirs amongst us the kaleidoscope of Jesus.

Release the grip of the power of death,
disarm all those who oppress me.
May death and death-dealers have no meaning:
shrivel us to dust and transfigure us to glory.

Silence

Like the disciples of old, **we are afraid of the power of the
storm that destroys and terrified of the power of the love
that transfigures. May we hear again the accents of
encouragement: Do not be afraid. Be of good courage.
I am with you.**

144   The creator lover

*For the flourishing of sexual love; for the discipline of giving attention; and for the
courage of passionate engagement.*

Blessed be you, O God our Creator:
you are the source of our power and skill,
you teach our hands to shape chaos,
our fingers to mould intractable clay.
You swive with us in a dance of delight,
creating what is new with your partners.

Pause

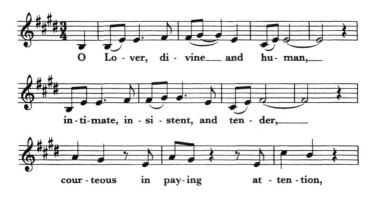

O Lo - ver, di - vine____ and hu - man,____

in - ti - mate, in - si - stent, and ten - der,____

cour - teous   in   pay-ing   at - ten - tion,

We breathe these words out of the Silence within us, into the Silence beyond us...

pas - sion-ate in whole-hearted em - brace,_____

bring__ us a - live__ and a - light,_____

each__ a sin-gu-lar cre - a - tion._____

Pause

We seem to ourselves to be but a breath,
our days a shadow that soon passes by,
insignificant in the vastness of space.
But O the wonder and marvel of your touch –
awesome that you should draw so near,
embracing, empowering the children of earth.

Pause

O Lover, divine and human,
intimate, insistent, and tender,
courteous in paying attention,
passionate in wholehearted embrace,
bring us alive and alight,
each a singular creation.

Pause

You bring us alive with electrifying power,
you touch us with the fork of lightning.
Flesh and blood can hardly contain you,
yet your power does not destroy us.

Pause

...in the Spirit that stirs amongst us the kaleidoscope of Jesus.

At the heart of the flame is a tender calm,
in courtesy you never intrude.
Little by little you warm us to life,
and we take part in the work of creation.

Pause

O Lover, divine and human,
intimate, insistent, and tender,
courteous in paying attention,
passionate in wholehearted embrace,
bring us alive and alight,
each a singular creation.

Pause

You strive with evil, with destructive powers,
not with the matching of force,
but absorbing their harm in your dying,
in the expending of love and of life.

Pause

Hold us steady when we are faced with chaos and fear,
when the waters foam and rage through the night,
that we may pierce to the eye of the storm,
and know the love that sustains.

Pause

So we shall sing a new song,
on flute and trumpet singing your praise.
We and our children shall be people of beauty,
burgeoning with life, maturing to vintage.

Pause

The earth will produce in abundance,
the sheep will lamb in their thousands,
there will be no distress of miscarriage,
no loud lamentation in our streets.

Silence

We breathe these words out of the Silence within us, into the Silence beyond us...

Creator Spirit, **surge through us with the thunder of the pounding waves, breathe through us with the whisper of the evening breeze, dance through us with the leaping flames of the sun, ripple through us with the merriment of the mountain stream.**

145   Regular blessings

In gratitude…

For the dawning of the light,
for the sun at midday,
for the shade of the evening,
we give thanks to our God.

The beat of your heart,
re - li - a - ble and stea - dy,
the voice of your faith - ful - ness.

Pause

For the rising of the moon,
for the guiding stars,
for the comets on cue,
we give thanks to our God.

**The beat of your heart,
reliable and steady,
the voice of your faithfulness.**

Pause

…in the Spirit that stirs amongst us the kaleidoscope of Jesus.

For the breaking of the fast,
for noontide's refreshment,
for the meal round the table,
we give thanks to our God.

**The beat of your heart,
reliable and steady,
the voice of your faithfulness.**

Pause

For the greening of the woodland,
for the grains of the harvest,
for the fruits in their season,
we give thanks to our God.

**The beat of your heart,
reliable and steady,
the voice of your faithfulness.**

Pause

For the cry of the baby,
for the flowering of youth,
for the strength of maturity,
we give thanks to our God.

**The beat of your heart,
reliable and steady,
the voice of your faithfulness.**

Pause

For laws that protect us,
for those on alert,
for the routines of safety,
we give thanks to our God.

**The beat of your heart,
reliable and steady,
the voice of your faithfulness.**

Pause

We breathe these words out of the Silence within us, into the Silence beyond us...

For the hidden who serve us,
for the water and power,
for work taken for granted,
we give thanks to our God.

**The beat of your heart,
reliable and steady,
the voice of your faithfulness.**

Pause

For the fall of the autumn,
for the quiet of winter,
for the boundary of death,
we give thanks to our God.

**The beat of your heart,
reliable and steady,
the voice of your faithfulness.**

Pause

For the trust of friends,
for the blessings of home,
for the covenants of love,
we give thanks to our God.

**The beat of your heart,
reliable and steady,
the voice of your faithfulness.**

Pause

For the unfailingly generous,
for the wisdom of years,
for constant compassion,
we give thanks to our God.

**The beat of your heart,
reliable and steady,
the voice of your faithfulness.**

Silence

...in the Spirit that stirs amongst us the kaleidoscope of Jesus.

God of good gifts, **surprise us again with how reliable you are. Thank you for the trustworthiness of so many people in their repeated tasks for the common good. We touch a mystery unsearchable and wonderful, the marvel of the everyday. And you, O God, are constant and faithful, abundant in steadfast love, passionate and limitless in the giving of yourself to us and all the world, partners as we are in your covenant of creation.**

146   Concluding psalms of praise: 1

Society restored: Justice and Jerusalem

In gratitude to the God of justice; and in hope for the rule of justice.

We praise you, God beyond gods;
with a world restored we praise you.
In faith we anticipate that day,
and praise you for the firstfruits of its coming.

Pause

We do not put our trust in passing fashions,
or in the promises of powerful people.
They are powerless to save, their ashes are scattered,
their words soon crumbling to dust.

Pause

To the Creator of the infinite heavens,
of the earth and the seas and their creatures,
who works unceasingly for justice,
we give our heartfelt praise.

Praise   to   the God   of   jus - tice and peace:

We breathe these words out of the Silence within us, into the Silence beyond us...

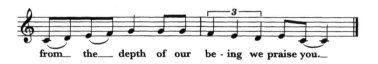

from_ the_ depth of our be - ing we praise you._

Pause

You keep faith with your promises for ever,
you put right the wrongs of the oppressed;
you give food to the hungry and thirsty,
you set the captives free.

**Praise to the God of justice and peace:
from the depth of our being we praise you.**

Pause

You give sight to the blind,
your arms lift up those who are bowed down,
you love those who live simply,
you care for the strangers, the widowed, the orphans.

**Praise to the God of justice and peace:
from the depth of our being we praise you.**

Pause

At times we do these things with you,
surprising ourselves by our courage,
giving voice to those who are not heard,
troubling and pressing those who make laws.

**Praise to the God of justice and peace:
from the depth of our being we praise you.**

Pause

The cities we know are a patchwork,
a jostling of places of hope and despair.
Yet still we give thanks for the vision
of the city of harmony and peace.

Silence

...in the Spirit that stirs amongst us the kaleidoscope of Jesus.

In the justice of relationships made right, **in the peace that is well-being for all, we worship the God of justice and peace. We add our voice to the music of God; we fall silent in the presence of mystery, in wonder and awe and love, the mystery that is the source of our being and the goal of our longing, beautiful, utterly holy, glorious light, unbounded love: Alleluia! Alleluia!**

147 Concluding psalms of praise: 2

Promises fulfilled: City and countryside

In gratitude for repair and recovery; and in hope for a people at ease, in city and in countryside.

The earth itself is transformed,
the cities of peace are established.
Creatures in their thousands leap for joy,
and the people dance in the streets.

Pause

The scattered outcasts greet one another,
kings and clowns tumble together,
the hobbling teach the dancers new steps,
the scars of the wounded shine.

Pause

We breathe these words out of the Silence within us, into the Silence beyond us...

The torn hills heal over with grass,
the gnarled trees put forth new shoots.
Ramblers and farmers take care of the land,
the scattered homesteads dwell in safety.

Pause

Protesters and politicians sit down together,
the clever sit at the feet of the wise.
The frantic are calmed by those in wheelchairs,
the sexually diverse are welcomed in love.

Praise God whose promise is fulfilled:
it gives us great joy to give thanks.

Pause

The cattle are released from their pens,
the hens run free from their sheds.
The walls of the camps are demolished,
numbers are forgotten and names are restored.

Pause

No longer do we glory in the might of our arms,
taking pride in the weapons we polish.
No more is the tallest and biggest the best;
no one even thinks of trampling the weak.

Praise God whose promise is fulfilled:
it gives us great joy to give thanks.

Pause

Women and men bring their gifts to each other;
no longer are they driven to harm and abuse.
In eyes that speak truth they see each other,
and know how to touch in the sparkling of love.

Pause

Marvellous rarities are tasted by all,
bread that is wholesome is baked once again.
The water we drink springs clear from the hills,
the finest wines grace every table.

...in the Spirit that stirs amongst us the kaleidoscope of Jesus.

Praise God whose promise is fulfilled:
it gives us great joy to give thanks.

Pause

The skaters spiral on the frozen lakes,
the skiers exult on the mountain slopes,
the gliders swoop and soar through the skies,
the surfers ride the thunder of the waves.

Pause

Through the artists a world of bliss is unveiled,
through the poets fresh images of truth are revealed,
through the scientists what is hidden comes to the light,
through the lovers unfolds the joy of new life.

Praise God whose promise is fulfilled:
it gives us great joy to give thanks.

Pause

Restored, fulfilled, gathered together,
we know we belong to the universe.
In songs of harmony we embrace one another,
transfigured in the presence of the One who is All.

Silence

In the celebration that embraces the exile and outcast, **in the**
joy that sings of freedom at last, we praise the God of
freedom and joy. We add our voice to the music of God;
we fall silent in the presence of mystery, in wonder and
awe and love, the mystery that is the source of our being
and the goal of our longing, beautiful, utterly holy,
glorious light, unbounded love. Alleluia! Alleluia!

✤

We breathe these words out of the Silence within us, into the Silence beyond us...

148   Concluding psalms of praise: 3
                                       Creation renewed: Touched and transfigured

In gratitude for the love that can transfigure us and everything around us.

Let the alleluias ring out in the dark,
the darkness that dazzles with unfathomable light.
Let the people of the way sing their praise,
alive in the communion and mystery of love:

Pause

the Lover, the Beloved, the Spirit Between,
the love that cannot but be outpoured,
pulsing, cherishing, urging new life,
astonishing, wonderful, marvellous to see.

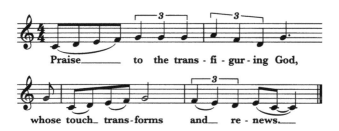

Praise____ to the trans-fi-gur-ing God,
whose touch_ trans-forms and_ re-news._

Pause

The threads binding together this extraordinary love
are gossamer and golden, invisible and strong,
reaching out to connect all creation for ever,
from amoeba to human, from atom to brain.

Pause

So diverse and complex is this web that we share,
so many forms to name and delight in,
we needs must choose to focus our praise,
our voices finding words for those who are silent.

**Praise to the transfiguring God,
whose touch transforms and renews.**

...in the Spirit that stirs amongst us the kaleidoscope of Jesus.

Pause

Let the sun and the moon and the stars
and the earth and the ocean give praise.
We are bound with them; they belong with us:
all change – must it be to decay?

Pause

The mountains levelled to plains are changed;
the ocean's bed buckles to rise from the sea;
the rivers carry silt and make the vales fertile,
the snows melt to release the spring.

Praise to the transfiguring God,
whose touch transforms and renews.

Pause

Seeds yield their life in the darkness of earth,
the flowers, the fruits, and the grains all grow.
Some change in the earth to be seen only at harvest,
their abundance deepening our sense of well-being.

Pause

The worms and the parasites, hidden from view,
all work their mysterious ways,
puzzling destruction a prelude to life,
a transformation that stuns us to silence.

Praise to the transfiguring God,
whose touch transforms and renews.

Pause

All is changed and may seem to be lost,
and we too know death and decline.
Yet working within us, unnoticed, unseen,
is the thread that binds and transforms.

Pause

And we touch one another to pain and to pleasure,
our skin so vulnerable, so finely tuned.

We breathe these words out of the Silence within us, into the Silence beyond us...

Can we reach out and create life with our God?
Can we lose yet discover ourselves?

**Praise to the transfiguring God,
whose touch transforms and renews.**

Pause

What once was a curse can become a wise wound,
the hand that abused can caress and be kind,
violation can change to the sharing of passion,
we can be warmed to life by an intimate fire.

Pause

Praise, praise above all,
all that is No is transformed into Yes,
Yes to the One in whom we belong,
belong together in the dance of delight.

**Praise to the transfiguring God,
whose touch transforms and renews.**

Silence

In the love that has taken and shaped every power, **in the new
creation that rises from the totally dead, we adore the God
of love and new life. We add our voice to the music of
God; we fall silent in the presence of mystery, in wonder
and awe and love, the mystery that is the source of our
being and the goal of our longing, beautiful, utterly holy,
glorious light, unbounded love. Alleluia! Alleluia!**

149   Concluding psalms of praise: 4

Reconciliation embraced: Held and healed

In gratitude for forgiveness and reconciliation; and in hope of peace.

Blessed are those who refuse to take vengeance,
blessed are those who cause no harm,
blessed are those who break the cycles of slaughter,
blessed are those who bless and do not curse.

Pause

Blessed are those who resist the temptations of power,
who refuse to gather it to themselves.
Blessed are the little ones who find new courage
to claim and inhabit their own.

Praise to the God who o-ver-comes all di-vi-sions, who bears the pain of our heal-ing.

Pause

Blessed are those who seek to reconcile,
who themselves form a bridge for strange meetings.
Blessed are those who repent their oppression,
blessed are the harmed who show them mercy.

Pause

Blessed are those who absorb others' hurts,
who refuse to give back in like manner.
Blessed are those who keep in touch with their enemies,
who refuse to let them go.

We breathe these words out of the Silence within us, into the Silence beyond us...

**Praise to the God who overcomes all divisions,
who bears the pain of our healing.**

Pause

Blessed are the judges who wisely discern,
who help to put right what is wrong,
who bring together those who are estranged,
at no little cost to themselves.

Pause

Blessed are those who use the sword as a scalpel,
to be accurate and clear in their scouring of wrong,
who protect and probe but do not destroy,
whose wounds serve only to purify and prune.

**Praise to the God who overcomes all divisions,
who bears the pain of our healing.**

Pause

Blessed is the One who bears the world's pain,
who loves and endures to the end,
who holds to the heart a wincing world,
who surprises us with healing and hope.

Silence

In the reconciliation that is based on repentance and mercy, **in
the healing that has held and enfolded the pain, we bless
the God of reconciliation and healing. We add our voice to
the music of God; we fall silent in the presence of mystery,
in wonder and awe and love, the mystery that is the source
of our being and the goal of our longing, beautiful, utterly
holy, glorious light, unbounded love. Alleluia! Alleluia!**

...in the Spirit that stirs amongst us the kaleidoscope of Jesus.

150   Concluding psalms of praise: 5

Harmony celebrated: Sound and silence

In gratitude for music and beauty and celebration; and in hope of universal harmony.

We praise you, O God, holy and beloved.
We praise you for your glory and wisdom.
We praise you for your creative power.
We praise you for your deeds of deliverance.

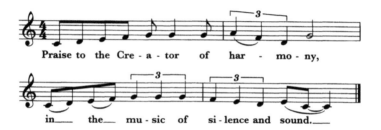

Praise to the Cre - a - tor of har - mo - ny,
in___ the___ mu - sic of si - lence and sound.___

Pause

We praise you in a glorious symphony.
We praise you on the flute and harp.
We praise you with the caress of the trumpet.
We praise you with the solace of the cello.

Praise to the Creator of harmony,
in the music of silence and sound.

Pause

We praise you on the quickening horn.
We praise you on the strumming guitar.
We praise you with the pipes of the clans.
We praise you on the deep resounding drums.

Praise to the Creator of harmony,
in the music of silence and sound.

Pause

We breathe these words out of the Silence within us, into the Silence beyond us...

We praise you in the unnoticed pauses
that make music of disordered sounds.
We praise you in the depths of the silence,
in the music of the dance between eyes that love.

**Praise to the Creator of harmony,
in the music of silence and sound.**

Pause

We praise you for all your gifts.
We praise you for your mysterious being.
We praise you for weaving us together.
We praise you that we belong to the universe.

**Praise to the Creator of harmony,
in the music of silence and sound.**

Pause

Let everything that breathes under the sun,
let the voices of our ancestors of old,
let worlds unknown, within and beyond,
all on this glad day give you praise.

**Praise to the Creator of harmony,
in the music of silence and sound.**

Silence

In the music that is wrought from the silence, **in the silence
where we hear the quietest of echoes, we glorify the God
of harmony and bliss. We add our voice to the music of
God; we fall silent in the presence of mystery, in wonder
and awe and love, the mystery that is the source of our
being and the goal of our longing, beautiful, utterly holy,
glorious light, unbounded love. Alleluia! Alleluia!**

...in the Spirit that stirs amongst us the kaleidoscope of Jesus.

LISTENING

For suggested readings from the Gospels,
please look at the Calendar
on pages 1–18.

DELIGHTING

I   An unfolding of the Te Deum, part 1

Men and women: praise the God of love!
Earth and sky: worship the Creator!
Angelic powers of light eternal,
penetrating the ancient dark:
lift your voices with the song:
**Holy, holy, holy, strange mysterious power,
the whole creation is full of your glory.**

Saints and holy fools of every generation,
sing alleluia, alleluia.
Prophets crying out for justice,
sing alleluia, alleluia.
Martyrs who carried you in their wounds,
scars embodied in their glory,
sing alleluia, alleluia.
Your holy and stumbling people
in all times and places,
sing alleluia, alleluia.

Giver of life, of splendour and wonder,
tender, of infinite patience!
Bearer of pain, graceful and true,
with wounds bringing salve!
Maker of love, flaming and passionate,
guiding us into the truth!

2   An unfolding of the Te Deum, part 2

Universal Christ,
we greet you in your glory,
hidden deep in the being of God,
**Word made flesh to deliver us,
brought to life by human touch,**

glad to be born of Mary,
embodying the divine,
**withdrawing the sting of death,
terrifying us with love unbounded,**   >

…in the Spirit that stirs amongst us the kaleidoscope of Jesus.

offering to fulfil all we could desire,
opening the road to God's presence for ever,
guarding the freedom of the creation,
yearning for the gathering of the harvest.

Come, then, judge and deliver us,
who are freed at the cost of your life;
give us integrity to refuse what is evil,
give us your Spirit to discern what is true,
and lead us with all your saints
to lands of eternal glory.

3   An unfolding of the Benedictus

We praise you, God of freedom,
releasing all who are imprisoned,
raising up for us a powerful deliverer,
a descendant of your servant David.

Such was your promise, long, long ago,
by the lips of your holy prophets,
that you would free us from the grip of evil,
from the powers that ensnare us.

This was your covenant of old,
that you would treat us with justice and compassion,
that we might serve you without fear,
truthful and courageous our whole life long.

John, forerunner, from the womb you were called
to be a prophet to prepare God's way,
going before the Liberator who will lead us
   to our freedom,
disarming the powers of evil and opening
   the prison doors.

For in the tender mercies of our God
the rising sun has burst upon our lives,
giving light to those who dwell in darkness
   and in the shadow of death,
and guiding our feet into ways of peace.

We breathe these words out of the Silence within us, into the Silence beyond us...

4   An unfolding of the Magnificat

My soul-body swells with love of my Creator,
joy fires my heart for my lover, my God.
**My beloved has noticed me and loved me,
a nobody from among the powerless poor.**

From this time to the end of days,
all generations will call me blessed.
**For Love has drawn me from the shadows:
wonderful indeed is the name of our God.**

Your lovingkindness embraces those
who are awestruck with wonder and love,
held in eternity's moment in time.
**Your gentleness has shown great strength:
the proud have been scattered
in the fantasies and deceits of their minds.**

Those drunk with imperial power
have fallen from their arrogant thrones.
**The dispossessed on the scrapheap
have been empowered one with another.**

The homeless and the hungry
have been fed with their share of the harvest.
**The greedy who hold on to their wealth
have seen it all crumble and vanish.**

Just and compassionate God,
giving a new name to the deprived and invisible,
you fulfil your covenants of promise.
**Long ago you gave Abraham your blessing,
and to Sarah, both faithful and true.**

Your love reaches to every generation,
to the earth's little people, for ever.
**Now is the blessing renewed:
I give you my heartfelt thanks
with eyes that are shining with love,
with the Presence gestating within me.**

…in the Spirit that stirs amongst us the kaleidoscope of Jesus.

5   An unfolding of the Nunc Dimittis

Thanks be to God, I have lived to see this day.
God's promise is fulfilled, and my duty done.
At last you have given me peace,
for I have seen with my own eyes
the revelation you have prepared for all peoples,
a light to the world in its darkness,
the glory of all who serve your love.

6   An unfolding of the Cantate Domino

We praise you O God with a new song,
for you have done marvellous things.
With the strength of endurance and the folly of weakness,
with the wisdom of justice and the power of gentleness,
you have won the greatest of victories,
bringing triumph from the midst of defeat.
The rebellious powers lay down their arms,
the people of the earth rejoice in your will.

So you have declared your salvation,
wide-ranging freedom for your people.
You have fulfilled your promise to be faithful
towards the house of Israel.
Your healing and peace have shone forth,
even to the far-flung islands of the world.

Show yourselves joyful in God, all you peoples,
sing, rejoice, and give thanks.
We praise you, O God, upon the harp,
singing a song of thanksgiving.
With trumpets and echoing horns
we show ourselves joyful in your presence.

Let the sea roar, and all its creatures,
the round earth, and those who dwell upon it.
Let the hills clap their hands,
and the streams sing merrily in your presence.

We breathe these words out of the Silence within us, into the Silence beyond us...

For you have come to judge the earth,
at last making all things well.
You restore the people with justice,
with a wisdom and mercy beyond our comparing.
You are holy and loving,
endless in compassion, gentle and true.

7   An unfolding of the Deus Misereatur

God, be gracious to us and bless us:
show us the light of your countenance
and be merciful to us,
that your way may be known upon earth,
your saving health among all nations.
Let the people praise you, O God,
let all the people praise you.

Let the nations rejoice and be glad,
for you judge the people with wisdom,
and you guide the nations upon earth.
Let the people praise you, O God,
let all the people praise you.

Then shall the earth bring forth the harvest,
and God, even our own God, shall give us great blessing.
Dear God, you will bless us indeed,
and all the ends of the earth shall praise your holy name.

8   An unfolding of the Benedicite

Let all created beings bless you, great God,
praise your name and adore you for ever.
May the heavens bless you, Beloved,
praise your name and glorify you for ever.

Let the angels bless you, great God,
the archangels sing your praise.
May the cherubim and seraphim bless you, Beloved,
praise your name and glorify you for ever.   >

...in the Spirit that stirs amongst us the kaleidoscope of Jesus.

Let the sun and the moon bless you, great God,
the stars of night sing your praise.
May rain and dew bless you, Beloved,
praise your name and glorify you for ever.

Let the winds that blow bless you, great God,
fire and heat sing your praise.
May scorching wind and bitter cold bless you, Beloved,
praise your name and glorify you for ever.

Let sunset and dawn bless you, great God,
the nights and days sing your praise.
May light and darkness bless you, Beloved,
praise your name and glorify you for ever.

Let frost and cold bless you, great God,
ice and snow sing your praise.
May lightning and thunder bless you, Beloved,
praise your name and glorify you for ever.

Let the earth bless you, great God,
mountains and valleys sing your praise.
May all that grows in the ground bless you, Beloved,
praise your name and glorify you for ever.

Let springs of water bless you, great God,   .
seas and rivers sing your praise.
May whales and all that swim in the waters bless you, Beloved,
praise your name and glorify you for ever.

Let the birds of the air bless you, great God,
animals wild and domestic sing your praise.
May all who dwell on the face of the earth bless you, Beloved,
praise your name and glorify you for ever.

Let your people bless you, great God,
your ministers sing your praise.
May your friends bless you, Beloved,
praise your name and glorify you for ever.

We breathe these words out of the Silence within us, into the Silence beyond us...

Let those of upright spirit bless you, great God,
the holy and humble of heart sing your praise.
May we bless you, Lover, Beloved, and Mutual Friend,
praise your name and glorify you for ever.

9   A Benedicite for creation

Let the chuckling brooks bless you, great God,
the quiet tarns sing your praise.
May the breaking waves and waterfalls bless you, Beloved,
praise your name and glorify you for ever.

Let the roaring forties bless you, great God,
the blue-green ocean sing your praise.
May the fjords and straits bless you, Beloved,
praise your name and glorify you for ever.

Let the mighty rivers bless you, great God,
the great lakes sing your praise.
May the placid canals bless you, Beloved,
praise your name and glorify you for ever.

Let the limestone and chalk bless you, great God,
the sands and clays sing your praise.
May the slates and granites bless you, Beloved,
praise your name and glorify you for ever.

Let the cairns of the mountains bless you, great God,
the meadows and crops sing your praise.
May the marshes and forests bless you, Beloved,
praise your name and glorify you for ever.

Let the oaks and the elms bless you, great God,
the silver birches sing your praise.
May the chestnuts and beeches bless you, Beloved,
praise your name and glorify you for ever.

Let the albatrosses bless you, great God,
the penguins and dolphins sing your praise.
May the whales and the plankton bless you, Beloved,
praise your name and glorify you for ever.   >

...in the Spirit that stirs amongst us the kaleidoscope of Jesus.

Let the migrating swallows bless you, great God,
parrots and finches sing your praise.
May the soaring and weaving flocks bless you, Beloved,
praise your name and glorify you for ever.

Let the wolves of the tundra bless you, great God,
the dogs and the cats sing your praise.
May the gazelles and the snow leopards bless you, Beloved,
praise your name and glorify you for ever.

Let the world of the atom bless you, great God,
the genes and molecules sing your praise.
May the ceaseless dance of life bless you, Beloved,
praise your name and glorify you for ever.

Let the breathing and pulsing planet bless you, great God,
this blue and white sphere sing your praise.
May the inhabitants of earth bless you, Beloved,
praise your name and glorify you for ever.

Let the sun and the moon bless you, great God,
the Milky Way sing your praise.
May the far-flung reaches of space bless you, Beloved,
praise your name and glorify you for ever.

10   A Benedicite for the city

Let the sounds of the city bless you, great God,
the quiet hum of engines sing your praise.
May the laughter of children bless you, Beloved,
praise your name and glorify you for ever.

Let the people next door bless you, great God,
the passers-by sing your praise.
May strangers and friends bless you, Beloved,
praise your name and glorify you for ever.

Let the wheely-bin collectors bless you, great God,
the meter readers sing your praise.
May the deliverers of letters and parcels bless you, Beloved,
praise your name and glorify you for ever.

We breathe these words out of the Silence within us, into the Silence beyond us...

Let the city council bless you, great God,
those who care for the streets sing your praise.
May the park keepers and tree surgeons bless you, Beloved,
praise your name and glorify you for ever.

Let the health authority bless you, great God,
the local surgeries sing your praise.
May the hospitals and hospices bless you, Beloved,
praise your name and glorify you for ever.

Let those who work with computers bless you, great God,
those who sweep offices sing your praise.
May those who keep guard and those in charge bless you, Beloved,
praise your name and glorify you for ever.

Let the shopping malls and leisure centres bless you, great God,
the swimming pools sing your praise.
May the sports grounds and stadiums bless you, Beloved,
praise your name and glorify you for ever.

Let the cinemas and theatres bless you, great God,
the concert halls sing your praise.
May the pubs and cafés bless you, Beloved,
praise your name and glorify you for ever.

Let the police and the courts bless you, great God,
the firefighters sing your praise.
May the ambulance drivers bless you, Beloved,
praise your name and glorify you for ever.

Let the taxis and buses, the trains and trams bless you, great God,
the drivers and conductors sing your praise.
May the mechanics and engineers bless you, Beloved,
praise your name and glorify you for ever.

Let the places of prayer bless you, great God.
the cathedrals and churches sing your praise.
May the synagogues, mosques, and temples bless you, Beloved,
praise your name and glorify you for ever.

...in the Spirit that stirs amongst us the kaleidoscope of Jesus.

11   A Benedicite for human work

Let the sowers of seeds bless you, great God,
the gardeners and farmers sing your praise.
May the fishers and foresters bless you, Beloved,
praise your name and glorify you for ever.

Let the bread from the grain bless you, great God,
the wine from the grape sing your praise.
May the transformations of cooks bless you, Beloved,
praise your name and glorify you for ever.

Let the spinners and weavers bless you, great God,
the designers of clothes sing your praise.
May the potters and silversmiths bless you, Beloved,
praise your name and glorify you for ever.

Let the sounds and silences of music bless you, great God,
the great composers sing your praise.
May the improvisers of jazz bless you, Beloved,
praise your name and glorify you for ever.

Let the cellos and trumpets bless you, great God,
the echoing horns sing your praise.
May the clarinets and pianos bless you, Beloved,
praise your name and glorify you for ever.

Let the actors and mime artists bless you, great God,
the singers and musicians sing your praise.
May the dancers and clowns bless you, Beloved,
praise your name and glorify you for ever.

Let the novelists bless you, great God,
the poets and critics sing your praise.
May the essayists and playwrights bless you, Beloved,
praise your name and glorify you for ever.

Let the sculptors and scientists bless you, great God,
the portrait painters and photographers sing your praise.
May the artists and architects bless you, Beloved,
praise your name and glorify you for ever.

We breathe these words out of the Silence within us, into the Silence beyond us...

A hymn to Wisdom: 1

My soul yearns for wisdom:
beyond all else my heart longs for her.
She has walked through the abyss,
she has measured its boundaries.

She was there from the beginning:
apart from her not one thing came to be.
She played before the world was made,
and in her hands all things hold together.

She has danced upon the face of the deep,
and all that has breath is infused with her life.
The mystery of creation is in her grasp,
yet she delights to expound her ways.

In the streets of the city she is calling,
on the roads she encounters those who pass by.
At the gates of the camp she sings in triumph,
and in the law courts she lifts up her voice.

With the timid and fearful she takes her stand,
in the mouths of children she is heard to speak.
She cries out to the foolish to listen,
and the wise take heed to her words.

But among her own she is not recognized,
those who need her have thrust her out.
She has been pushed aside like the poor,
and broken like those of no account.

So she abandons those who are wise in their own conceits,
but with those who are ready to receive her she makes her home.
For her delight is in the truth,
she takes no pleasure in deceitful ways.

Her integrity is more to be desired than comfort,
her discernment is more precious than security.
In her alone is the life of humanity:
therefore while I live I shall search her out.
Whoever is fed by her will never hunger,
all who drink from her will never thirst again.

…in the Spirit that stirs amongst us the kaleidoscope of Jesus.

13   A hymn to Wisdom: 2

Mother God, wise and healing woman,
carrying us in the womb of being,
bringing us forth in great labour,
caring for us, bearing our pain,
letting us go to discover our life and truth,
sharing with us our deepest joy,
we rest in your presence,
in contentment and gratitude.

14   A hymn to Wisdom: 3

Living God, like a mother you gather your people to you,
as a mother hen gathers her brood to protect them.
Gentle with us, you weep over our pride,
tenderly you draw the sting of our hatreds.
You comfort us in sorrow and bind up our wounds:
in sickness you nurse us, with milk you nourish us.
Despair turns to hope through your goodness:
through your courage we face all our fears.
Your warmth gives life to the gloomy and deadened,
your touch calms our throbbing pain.
In your compassion you heal us,
in your love you restore us.
In your grace you forgive us,
to your beauty you draw us.
We yearn with gratitude and awe,
made strong in your presence for ever.

15   A hymn to Wisdom: 4

Holy Wisdom, **delight of our God,**
you open our ears, we hear your word.
You enter deep into the being of humanity;
foolish to the world, you unmask our follies.

We breathe these words out of the Silence within us, into the Silence beyond us...

You are a shelter to us by day,
and a steady flame through the night.
You lead us through turbulent waters,
and bring us safe to dry ground.
Holy Wisdom, **delight of our God,**
you open our ears, we hear your word.
You open the mouths of those who are mute,
you loosen the tongues of infants in their cries.
A little child takes us by the hand,
and leads us to freedom and truth.
Holy Wisdom, **delight of our God,**
you open our ears, we hear your word.

16   A song of blessing and gladness: 1

Blessed be God,
holy and most glorious Trinity.
Blessed be God,
Creator of the universe.
Blessed be God,
Father and Mother.
Blessed be God,
Companion and Lover.
Blessed be God, in Jesus, the Christ,
the same yesterday, today, and for ever.
Blessed be Christ in us,
the hope of glory.
Blessed be God,
Holy and life-giving Spirit.
Blessed be God,
Spirit of wisdom.
Blessed be God,
Spirit of fire.
Blessed be God,
moving deep within us.
Blessed be God,
spinning the thread of attention among us.   >

...in the Spirit that stirs amongst us the kaleidoscope of Jesus.

Blessed be God,
whose glory is a human being fully alive.
Blessed be God,
shining through the saints.
Blessed be God,
shining through the creation.
Blessed be God.

17   A song of blessing and gladness: 2

God of our ancestors' faith, we bless you,
sing of your love, now and for ever.
We bless your holy and glorious name,
sing of your love, now and for ever.
We bless you on the heights of the mountains,
sing of your love, now and for ever.
We bless you in deep and secret places,
sing of your love, now and for ever.
We bless you in songs of animals and birds,
sing of your love, now and for ever.
We bless you in the sounds of the city,
sing of your love, now and for ever.
We bless you even in the midst of distress,
sing of your love, now and for ever.
We bless you on the lips of courageous people,
sing of your love, now and for ever.
We bless you in places where justice glows,
sing of your love, now and for ever.
We bless you in the crucified and risen,
sing of your love, now and for ever.
We bless you, great Trinity of love,
sing of your love, now and for ever.

We breathe these words out of the Silence within us, into the Silence beyond us...

18   A song of blessing and gladness: 3

Great and wonderful are your deeds,
O God of love and glory.
Just and true are your ways,
O ruler of the peoples.
Who shall not revere your name?
For you alone are holy.
All peoples shall come and worship in your presence,
for your redeeming love has shone in all its glory.
Praise and honour, glory and love,
be given to the One who reigns,
whose way of love is sustained,
at a cost we can barely imagine,
a way that wins through in the end,
through the worst of evil, of pain, and of death.

19   A song of blessing and gladness: 4

You have called us to live your good life,
you have anointed us for your service.
Your Spirit wells up within us, among us,
gladdening our hearts, empowering our wills.

You send us to bring good news to the oppressed,
and to bind the wounds of those broken in heart,
to proclaim liberty to the captives,
and the opening of prisons to those who are bound,
to announce the year of your grace,
to comfort all who mourn,
to give them a garland of consolation,
instead of the ashes of mourning,
the oil of gladness and healing,
and the rolling tears that wash away sorrow.   >

So may we be called oaks of righteousness,
trees that you plant to shade and sustain.
As the earth puts forth its blossom,
and as seeds in the garden spring up,
so you make justice flower,
and bear its fruit of peace among the peoples.

You have called humanity to be priestly,
you have anointed us to serve your creation.

20   A song of love: 1

Many waters cannot quench love,
nor can the floods drown it.
You set me as a seal upon your heart,
as a signet ring upon your finger.
For love is stronger than death,
its passion fiercer than the grave.
Its flashes of fire rage and sear,
no water can quench its desire.
If we offered all our wealth for love,
it would be utterly scorned.
Many waters cannot quench love,
nor can the floods drown it.

21   A song of love: 2

Living God, you invite us to love one another,
for love is the heart of your being.
Everyone who follows you in the ways of your love
is born of you and knows you well.
Everyone who does not love
does not know you, for you are love.
You risked your life in love for us,
embodying that love in a human being,
vulnerable, unconditional, persistent to the end,
our gateway to your presence.

We breathe these words out of the Silence within us, into the Silence beyond us...

In this is love shown true,
not that we loved you,
but that you loved us to the end,
and bore the cost of our release from evil's grip.
Since you love us so much,
you empower us to love one another.
And if we love one another,
you abide in us, and we in you.
Your love will bear fruit through us,
complete and perfect at the harvest.

22   For everything a season

For everything there is a season
and a time for every matter under heaven:
a time to be born, and a time to die;
a time to plant, and a time to pluck up what is planted;
a time to kill, and a time to heal;
a time to break down, and a time to build up;
a time to weep, and a time to laugh;
a time to mourn, and a time to dance;
a time to cast away stones, and a time to gather stones together;
a time to embrace, and a time to refrain from embracing;
a time to seek, and a time to lose;
a time to keep, and a time to cast away;
a time to rend, and a time to sew;
a time to keep silence, and a time to speak;
a time to love, and a time to hate;
a time for war, and a time for peace.

…in the Spirit that stirs amongst us the kaleidoscope of Jesus.

23   Canticle of the sun: 1

The One beyond all names, yet our good Lord,
praise, glory, and honour be given to you with one accord.

**To you alone, dear God, does praise belong,
yet none is worthy to make of you her song.**

Be praised my God with all your works whate'er they be,
our noble brother sun especially,
whose brightness makes the light by which we see,
and he is so fair and radiant, so splendid and so free,
a likeness of your glory that we have yet to see.

**Be praised my God for sister moon and every star
that you have formed to shine so clear from heaven afar.**

Be praised my God for brother wind and air,
breezes and clouds and weather foul or fair –
to everyone that breathes you give a share.

**Be praised my God for sister water, sure,
none is so useful, humble, or so pure.**

Be praised my God for brother fire, whose light
you have given to illuminate the night,
and he is fair and merry and strong and bright.

**Be praised my God for sister earth our mother,
who nourishes and gives us food and fodder,
and the green grass and flowers of every colour.**

Be praised my God for those who for your love forgive,
contented unavenged in quiet to live.
Blessed those who in the way of peace are found –
by you O most beloved they shall be crowned.

**Be praised my God for sister bodily death,
from whom none can escape that has drawn breath.
Woe to those who life and love do kill,
blessed those who find that in your holy will
the second death to them will bring no ill.**

Praise and bless our God, and give your service due,
with humblest thanks for all that God has given you.

We breathe these words out of the Silence within us, into the Silence beyond us…

24   Canticle of the sun: 2

We give praise and thanks
to our glorious father the sun,
and the hosts of ancestor-stars,
for they are our energy and mass.

**We give praise and thanks
to our mother the holy earth,
for without her neither life nor breath,
nor any home in the cosmic cold.**

We give praise and thanks
to our gentle guardian the air,
nourishing us with breath,
sheltering us from burning rays.

**We give praise and thanks
to our mother the ocean,
source of earth-life,
and her sister clouds, rain, and storms.**

We give praise and thanks
to our sisters the plants,
holders of earth,
builders with the sun,
base of the food chain,
fountains of living air.

**We give praise and thanks
to our brothers the animals,
insects, reptiles, fish, and birds,
inheritors with us of the evolving earth.**

We give praise and thanks
to the father and mother who gave us birth,
to children of our flesh and spirit,
and all the holy family that surrounds us.

**We give praise and thanks
to the ground and being
that sustains these kinships,
father, mother,**   >

…in the Spirit that stirs amongst us the kaleidoscope of Jesus.

that we seek and need not seek,
for our sisters and brothers,
fathers and mothers,
are all around us.
We praise them.

25 A song for the spring

Thanks, thanks above all:
thanks for the shy clothing of green,
for the hazy sun,
for the chorus of dawn,
for the scurrying of little creatures,
for the surging of hope,
for the sharp showers,
for the sudden shafts of sunlight,
for the smell of earth after rain,
for the bursting of the buds,
for the rushing of the sap,
for the opening of desire,
for the pilgrim setting forth again.
Thanks, thanks above all.

26 A song for the summer

Thanks, thanks above all:
thanks for the cosseting of the sun,
for the play and sparkle of water,
for the gentle rain,
for the ripening of the grain,
for the shade of the woodland,
for the quiet sunsets,
for the long and lingering twilight,
for the nectar of night.
Thanks, thanks above all.

We breathe these words out of the Silence within us, into the Silence beyond us...

27   A song for the autumn

Thanks, thanks above all:
thanks for the bright slanting sun,
for the quiet warmth of the afternoon,
for the long clear horizons,
for the crisp curl of the leaves,
for the stretched and luminous flesh,
for the astringent mornings,
for the gathering of the fruits,
for the misty drizzle,
for the disintegration into dust,
for the letting go in trust,
for the pyres of the dead,
for the time of remembrance.
Thanks, thanks above all.

28   A song for the winter

Thanks, thanks above all:
thanks for the quiet earth,
for the uncompromising rocks,
for the great rains,
for the mantle of snow,
for the tracery of the trees,
for the restful fog,
for the invigorating cold,
for the sharpness of the stars,
for the fullest of moons,
for the wise boundary of death.
Thanks, thanks above all.

…in the Spirit that stirs amongst us the kaleidoscope of Jesus.

29   A canticle for Advent: 1

Let the wilderness and the thirsty land be glad,
let the desert rejoice and burst into flower.
Let the crocus bloom in abundance,
let it rejoice and sing for joy.

The glory, the splendour, of Lebanon, of Carmel,
of canopied forest and soaring mountain,
these too will see the glory of God.

Strengthen the weary arms, steady the trembling knees,
say to the anxious, Be strong, take courage, be not afraid.
See, your God comes with true justice:
with doom and mercy God comes to save you.

Then the eyes of the blind will be opened,
and the ears of the deaf unstopped;
then will the lame leap like a deer,
and the tongue of the dumb sing for joy.

For water will spring up in the desert,
and streams flow in parched land.
The scorched earth will become a lake,
the waste land bubbling springs.

A causeway will be there, the holy way:
nothing unwholesome will travel on it.
It will be a pilgrims' way: no robber will prowl there,
no lion will devour there, nor any ravenous beast.

But the redeemed will walk there,
those whom God has rescued will return.
Joy and gladness will be their escort,
sorrow and sighing will flee away.
They will enter the city with shouts of triumph,
crowned with everlasting joy.

We breathe these words out of the Silence within us, into the Silence beyond us…

30   A canticle for Advent: 2

From the stump of an old gnarled tree,
a new shoot will yet spring forth.
From roots hidden deep in the ground,
a sapling will grow again.

The Spirit of God will rest upon you,
the spirit of wisdom and understanding,
the spirit of counsel and might,
the spirit of knowledge and godly fear.

You will not judge by what your ears hear,
nor decide by what your eyes see.
You will judge the poor with justice,
and defend the humble of the land with equity.

Your mouth will be a rod to strike down the ruthless,
and with a word you will devastate the wicked.
Round your waist you will wear the belt of justice,
and good faith will be the girdle round your body.

Then the wolf will dwell with the sheep,
and the leopard will lie down with the kid;
the calf and the young lion will grow up together,
and a little child will lead them.

The cow and the bear will feed
and their young will lie down together.
The lion will eat straw like cattle;
the infant will play over the hole of the cobra,
and the young child dance over the viper's nest.

They will not hurt or destroy in all your holy mountain,
for the earth will be full of the knowledge of God
as the waters cover the sea.

...in the Spirit that stirs amongst us the kaleidoscope of Jesus.

31   A canticle for Advent: 3

Give comfort to my people, says your God.
Speak tenderly to the city, to Jerusalem.
Announce this news to them all:

**Your rebellion is ended, your iniquity is pardoned,
your slavery is abolished, your imprisonment is over.**

A voice cries:
In the wilderness prepare the way of the Living One:
make straight in the desert a highway for our God.
Every valley will be lifted up,
and every mountain and hill be made low;
the uneven ground will become level,
and the rough places a plain.
And the glory of the living God will be revealed.

So have I heard from the mouth of the great I AM,
and so do I announce to all who will listen.

A voice said to me,
Cry!

And I said,
What shall I cry?

All flesh is grass,
and its beauty is like the flower of the field.
The grass withers and the flower fades,
when the wind of our God blows upon it.
Surely you are like grass.
**The grass withers, the flower fades,
but the word of our God will stand for ever.**

A voice said to me,
Get you up to a high mountain,
herald of good tidings to Zion;
**lift up your voice with strength,
herald of good news to Jerusalem:**
Lift it up, fear not:
say to the cities of Judah,
Behold your God!

We breathe these words out of the Silence within us, into the Silence beyond us...

32   A canticle for Christmas: 1

Living, loving God,
embracing flesh and blood, delighting in humanity,
delivering us from the dominion of evil, pain, and death,
and bringing us into the domain of goodness, joy, and life,
you have rescued us from the bands of slavery,
you have forgiven all our failure to love,
you have bound the powers that rebel.

For Christ is the image of your invisible being,
the first-born of all creation,
in whom the universe is being made,
the earth and the sun and the other stars,
things visible and things invisible,
through whom and for whom all things were formed,
who is before all things,
and in whom all things hold together.

Christ is the head of the body, the Church,
the beginning, the first-born from the dead.
For it pleased you, O God,
that in Christ all fulness should dwell,
and through Christ all things be reconciled to yourself.

33   A canticle for Christmas: 2

The people who walked in darkness
have seen a great light;
those who dwelt in a land of deep darkness,
upon them has the light dawned.

As a child you have been born to us,
as a son you have been given to us:
Wonderful counsellor, Creator God,
Beloved Abba, harbinger of peace.   >

...in the Spirit that stirs amongst us the kaleidoscope of Jesus.

From the days of our ancestors of faith
in fulfilment of the covenants of promise,
your word of love has struggled to be born,
and at last is made clear in the word made flesh.

34   A canticle for Christmas: 3

Eternal Word of the living God,
dream from before the beginning,
in whom and through whom everything has come to be,
in you is life, the life that is our light,
the light that shines on in the darkness,
which the darkness has never overcome,
the true light, enlightening humanity,
shining in the world.

Yet we did not recognize you.
You came to your own people –
and we did not know you.
You came to your own home –
and we did not receive you.

But to those who heard a whisper of the Word,
who were stirred to life by the dream,
to those who believed in your mysterious name,
you gave power to become your children,
to be known as your servants and your friends,
who were born, not of the desire and will of our flesh,
but of the desire and will of your love.

Living Word of light and love,
you became a human being,
and lived the fulness of our humanity,
full of grace and truth.

We saw your glory,
divine glory shining through a human face,
as a mother's eyes live through her daughter's,
as a son reflects his father's image,
your glory in a human being fully alive.

We breathe these words out of the Silence within us, into the Silence beyond us...

35   A canticle for Christmas: 4

From the days of our ancestors of faith,
in fulfilment of the covenants of promise,
your dream of love, dear God, is born,
alive for us in a baby's cry.

Gratitude that we belong to you for ever!
Gratitude for the power of love,
loosening the grip of evil,
transforming pain to joy,
swallowing death for ever.

Gratitude for the vulnerable baby.
Gratitude for the weakness stronger than our strength,
bringer of solid joys and lasting treasure.
Gratitude for the gifts of one another,
given that we may learn to bear the beams of love.

From the days of our ancestors of faith,
in fulfilment of the covenants of promise,
your dream of love, dear God, is born,
alive for us in a baby's cry.

36   A canticle for Epiphany: 1

The lights of the city shine in the darkness,
extending the day into winter's night.
The lamps in the streets guide the traveller,
the lights in the houses bid welcome.

Let the cities of God's commonwealth rejoice,
the light of the world reflected in their window panes.
Let the people gather at festival times,
to give thanks in the cities of peace.

For the light and glory of God have come,
illuminating the darkest of alleyways,
enlightening the darkest of hearts and minds,
giving wisdom to those in authority.   >

...in the Spirit that stirs amongst us the kaleidoscope of Jesus.

In the light of Christ all strife will shrivel away,
the sounds of violence no longer heard in their streets.
The doors of hospitality will be open,
the stranger given welcome and lodging.

The sun will no longer be their light by day,
nor will the moon give light to them by night.
For God will be their everlasting light,
and their God will be their glory.

37   A canticle for Epiphany: 2

The grace of God has appeared
for the salvation of all people.
Lift up your eyes, cities of God, and see:
people of all lands coming together,
greeting one another from all over the world.

So you will know and be glad,
your heart will thrill and rejoice.
Arise, shine, Jerusalem, for your light has come,
and the glory of God has risen upon you.

Glory to God in the highest, **alleluia!**
On earth peace to people of goodwill, **alleluia!**
All the ends of the earth have seen
the salvation of our God: **alleluia!**

38   A canticle for Epiphany: 3

Arise, shine, for your light has come,
and the glory of God is shining upon you,
even though darkest night still covers the earth,
and thick darkness the peoples.
The city has no need of sun or moon to shine upon it,
for the glory of God is its light,
and its lamp is the human one, shining and transfigured.

We breathe these words out of the Silence within us, into the Silence beyond us...

God will arise upon you like the dawn,
and God's glory will be seen in your midst.
Nations shall come to your light,
rulers to the brightness of your rising.
The city has no need of sun or moon to shine upon it,
for the glory of God is its light,
and its lamp is the human one, shining and transfigured.

The sun will no more be your light by day,
nor will the moon give light to you by night,
for God will be your everlasting light,
and your God will be your glory.
The city has no need of sun or moon to shine upon it,
for the glory of God is its light,
and its lamp is the human one, shining and transfigured.

39   A canticle for Lent and Passiontide: 1

Gratitude for the love that accepts us whatever!
Gratitude for the love that floods our inmost hearts!

Gratitude for the love that brings peace out of strife!
Gratitude for the love that floods our inmost hearts!

Gratitude for the love that loosens the grip of evil!
Gratitude for the love that floods our inmost hearts!

Gratitude for the love that binds us together for ever!
Gratitude for the love that floods our inmost hearts!

Gratitude for the love that never ceases to forgive!
Gratitude for the love that floods our inmost hearts!

Gratitude for the love that enfolds with gentleness!
Gratitude for the love that floods our inmost hearts!

Gratitude for the love that endures the suffering!
Gratitude for the love that floods our inmost hearts!

Gratitude for the love that trusts that Nothing shall be All!

…in the Spirit that stirs amongst us the kaleidoscope of Jesus.

40   A canticle for Lent and Passiontide: 2

When we were children you loved us:
yearning for us to grow in freedom,
rescuing us from captivity,
calling us home from exile.

But the more you called us,
the more we resisted you.
We bowed down to false gods,
we put our trust in idols.

Our stony hearts provoked you,
but what purpose would our destruction serve?
You grew warm in your anger,
near neighbour to compassion in your care for us.

You cannot let loose with your wrath,
your love cannot desert us.
Our human failings are not yours,
for you are God and not mortal,
supreme in the power of your lovingkindness.

Wash us with the tears of compunction,
heal us with the touch that is true,
speak to us the word that endures,
embrace us round the table of joy.

41   A canticle for Lent and Passiontide: 3

You reach out to the rejected and lost:
you touch those who have been pushed out of sight.
Your heart yearns with compassion and justice.

You utter a word in due season,
its truth changes our lives for ever.
We are healed by your touch, set free by your word.

By your touch the banished belong once again,
their healing goes deeper than cure.
Your heart yearns with compassion and justice.

We breathe these words out of the Silence within us, into the Silence beyond us...

Your words pierce our hearts,
puncturing our pride and our pomp.
We are healed by your touch, set free by your word.

You embrace without condition the guests round your table,
the powers set over us are brought in from their cold.
Your heart yearns with compassion and justice.

Your word of forgiveness loosens our bonds,
setting us free from the traps that ensnare us.
We are healed by your touch, set free by your word.

42   A canticle for Lent and Passiontide: 4

Praise be to God,
calling us to the strangest of ways,
turning us inside out, upside down,
revealing a new world to eyes that are open.

Fools to the world, we know the wisdom of God.
Unknown, we cannot be ignored.
Dying, we still live on.
Disciplined by suffering, we are not beaten down.
Knowing sorrow, we have always cause for joy.
Poor ourselves, we make many rich.
Penniless, we own the world.

Praise be to God,
calling us to the strangest of ways,
turning us inside out, upside down,
revealing a new world to eyes that are open.

Steadfastly we turn our wills towards God,
to meet hardships and afflictions,
hunger and weariness, illness and failure,
with sincerity, insight, patience, kindness,
speaking the truth in love,
resilient in the power of the Spirit.   >

...in the Spirit that stirs amongst us the kaleidoscope of Jesus.

Praise be to God,
calling us to the strangest of ways,
turning us inside out, upside down,
revealing a new world to eyes that are open.

43   A canticle for Lent and Passiontide: 5

We wander far away:
we return once again.
We have become dry and withered:
we come back to the living source.

You have torn us:
you will heal us.
You have struck us down:
you will bind up our wounds.

We thought we knew you:
but your ways puzzle us.
Our hearts protest at the pain:
are you bearing the suffering with us?

We press on to know you,
trusting your appearing,
sure as the dawn,
lifegiving as the rain.

Our love is like the morning mist,
vanishing like the dew on the grass.
The words of the prophets hammer us,
you judge us like the searing sun.

You desire our steadfast love,
not the rituals and habits we build out of fear.
You yearn for us to offer our hearts and our lives,
that we might act justly, love kindness,
and walk humbly with you, our God.

We breathe these words out of the Silence within us, into the Silence beyond us…

44   A canticle for Lent and Passiontide: 6

Praise to God whose love has embraced us in Christ.
Praise to the One who quells the power of evil.
Praise to the One whose heart transforms our suffering into joy.
Praise to the One whose abundant life swallows up death.

You grew up in our sight like a young plant,
whose roots in arid ground we did not water.
We made sure you had no grace or beauty,
nothing that would delight our eyes.
We disfigured and rejected you,
you were sorrowful, acquainted with grief.
With cold and mocking eyes
we turned our faces from you.
You became as one who is refuse,
never of use to our systems of power,
squeezed out from the bottom of the pile,
expendable in the schemes of the wealthy.

Yet you took our burden upon yourself,
all our sickness and grief, enduring our sorrow and pain,
refusing to throw our projections back in our faces,
the scapegoat to end all scapegoating.
Our bitter hearts rang with hollow laughter,
"Those we push away deserve to be punished."
So easily we repeat the old falsehood –
the diseased and the stricken are to blame.

The fire of your love is unbearable,
searing us with terrifying truth.
We can never escape you: you refuse to let us go,
your wounds and your scars our doom and deliverance.
You endure in the midst of our pain,
scourged and bruised, but with no cry of revenge.
You have broken the vicious circle of harm,
you have neutered the powers that rebel at your love.   >

...in the Spirit that stirs amongst us the kaleidoscope of Jesus.

Praise to God whose love has embraced us in Christ.
Praise to the One who quells the power of evil.
Praise to the One whose heart transforms our suffering into joy.
Praise to the One whose abundant life swallows up death.

45   A canticle for Lent and Passiontide: 7

Praise to the mysterious God,
whose heart bears the pain of creating,
pressing through the points of anguish and death.

Praise to the pioneer who showed us the way,
calling us to join in the greatest of stories,
to follow and embrace the path of true love.

God-revealing Christ, no guile was found on your lips.
When you were reviled you did not give back in due measure.
When you suffered, you did not threaten revenge.
In the justice of God you put all your trust.

You carried our disease in your body to the tree,
that in your wounds our sin might shrivel and die.
We contemplate you in awe and wonder,
we ponder the cost of the burden of glory.

We have erred and strayed from your ways:
call us again to the place of our healing,
to the solid strength of the vulnerable,
to the guardian of our truest selves.

46   A canticle for Lent and Passiontide: 8

God of intimacy and justice,
drawing close to warm us to life,
restoring relationships battered and torn,
we praise and thank you that you call us –
to open our hearts in compassion,
to bear the cost of the righting of wrongs.

We breathe these words out of the Silence within us, into the Silence beyond us...

You have chosen us and we delight in you.
**You embrace us with joy and we respond in deep
pleasure.**

You bring your Spirit to life in us,
, the fountain of water from wells deep within.
**You open our eyes to a vision of justice,
our ears to the word that will never let go.**

May we not call out like demagogues and zealots,
or harangue in the streets and at rallies.
**May we be too courteous to break a bruised reed,
too gentle to snuff out a flickering flame.**

Never wavering, never giving up,
let us make justice shine in every land,
planting it throughout the whole world,
as far as the islands that wait and yearn.

**You have called us to serve the cause of justice,
you have grasped us by the hand,
sealing your covenant, giving us courage and strength,
enlightening us to be beacons of hope.**

You have called us to open eyes that are blind,
to bring prisoners out of their dungeons,
**to set free the oppressed from the tyrants,
to heal the stigmatized by the common touch.**

O the terrifying cost of a morsel of justice!
O the rage of the powerful that beats upon the flesh!
**Praise to the Judge of all the world,
restoring and reconciling, embracing the pain.
We have seen a new thing in our midst,
the glory that shines through the darkness of a cross.**

…in the Spirit that stirs amongst us the kaleidoscope of Jesus.

47   A canticle for Easter: 1

We praise you, O Christ,
risen from the dead,
breaking death's dominion,
rising from the grave.

Absorbing in yourself
the force of evil's ways,
you destroyed death's age-old sting
and are alive for evermore.

Let us find our life in you,
breaking through our fear of everlasting void.
For you are risen from the dead,
the firstfruits of those who sleep.

From the days of first awareness
we betrayed the call of life,
yet yearned for that communion
which still we dimly sense.

Pain and evil, malice and cruel greed,
these deepened the sorrow of our hearts.
Yet they are done away in light of glorious dawn,
the victory of resurrection day.

At one with all who've lived,
so all of us have died;
at one with your humanity
all shall be made alive.

48   A canticle for Easter: 2

The One who walked as one of us,
in the Spirit obedient to the call,
in the sight of all created powers:
Risen Christ, we greet you! Alleluia!

We breathe these words out of the Silence within us, into the Silence beyond us...

You have been proclaimed among the nations,
believed in throughout the world,
transfigured into glory:
Risen Christ, we greet you! Alleluia!

We have set our hope on you,
the human face of God,
the Liberator of all the world:
Risen Christ, we greet you! Alleluia!

49   A canticle for Easter: 3

God of unbounded love and mysterious joy,
drawing and guiding us to unimaginable glory,
giving us the firstfruits of that fulfilment in Jesus,
we give you thanks for our hope in the last great day.

We shall sing for joy, full of gratitude,
on that last great day.
We shall trust you and have nothing to fear,
on that last great day.
We shall praise you for the sternness and kindness of love,
on that last great day.
We shall praise you for your wisdom and discernment,
on that last great day.
We shall join our song to that of the stars,
on that last great day.
Everything and everyone will shine with glory,
on that last great day.

God of unbounded love and mysterious joy,
drawing and guiding us to unimaginable glory,
giving us the firstfruits of that fulfilment in Jesus,
we give you thanks for our hope in the last great day.

...in the Spirit that stirs amongst us the kaleidoscope of Jesus.

50   A canticle for Easter: 4

Blessed are you, great God of the universe.
You give us of your very Self in Jesus.
Alleluia! Christ is risen! Alleluia!

In your abundant mercy we have been born anew to a living hope
by the resurrection of Jesus Christ from the dead!

In this hope we rejoice,
even in the midst of many trials,
trials which test the metal of our faith,
more precious than gold refined in the fire,
a faith that will resound with gratitude and praise
when with all creation we see Christ face to face.

Without having seen you we love you,
we believe in you and rejoice with unutterable joy.

Your power guards us, your compassion saves us, your glory fills us:
you promise an inheritance that nothing can destroy.

Blessed are you, great God of the universe.
You give us of your very Self in Jesus.
Alleluia! Christ is risen! Alleluia!

51   A canticle for Easter: 5

Blessed are you, Creator God,
who dreamed of humankind and brought us into being,
from before the foundation of the world
to the end of time and the mystery of beyond,
that we should become whole,
transfigured and made holy by your presence.

You destined us in love to be your sons and daughters in Christ,
according to the purpose of your will:
so we praise you for your cascading grace,
freely lavished upon us in the Beloved.

We breathe these words out of the Silence within us, into the Silence beyond us...

In Christ you have freed us at great cost,
that we too may dissolve great evil and live.
The Spirit of forgiveness flows through our veins,
retaliation and vengeance wither away.
The riches of your grace are a sumptuous feast:
all humankind is invited to your table.

For you have made known to us the mystery of your will,
your purpose to unite all things in Christ,
the ceaseless web of matter and energy,
through the earth and the stars of the universe,
so that all may resound in heavenly music,
from glory to glory for ever.

52   A canticle for Easter: 6

Alleluia!
Alleluia!
Praise to the living Christ!
You are the pioneer of our salvation,
you have triumphed through suffering and death,
you are the firstborn among many sisters and brothers,
you have led the way into the presence of God.

Our true bearing towards one another
flows out of our life in you.
You share the nature of God,
revealing a strange kind of power,
never overpowering, never overbearing,
power that is shared, power given up,
yet strong as the light
that shrivels the darkness
of the powers of this age.

You lived among us as a slave,
a nameless nobody in the eyes of the mighty.
You accepted all that came,
reduced to nothing in the death of the cross,
the offering of a humble obedience,
a life poured out, a sacrifice made.   >

...in the Spirit that stirs amongst us the kaleidoscope of Jesus.

You followed the way to the end,
to the new unexpected beyond,
freed of the constraints of space and of time,
a body of glory that soars in the Spirit,
greeted by the dead and the living
and given the greatest of names.

Alleluia!
Alleluia!
Praise to the living Christ!
You are the pioneer of our salvation,
you have triumphed through suffering and death,
you are the firstborn among many sisters and brothers,
you have led the way into the presence of God.

53   A canticle for Easter: 7

Saviour God, you have set us free:
we shall trust you and not be afraid.

You are our strength and our song:
you have become our salvation,
leading us to wide open spaces of freedom.

With joy we draw living water
slaking our thirst from the deep cool wells,
the hidden springs of your love that redeems.

We thank you, O God,
and we call upon your name.

We shall make your deeds known among the nations,
the mysterious and harrowing struggle,
marked by the limp and the wounds,

a face at peace, full of compassion,
alight and alive, death swallowed for ever.

So we proclaim your glorious name:
Alleluia! Alleluia! Alleluia!

We breathe these words out of the Silence within us, into the Silence beyond us...

Most marvellously have you triumphed:
let it be known all over the earth.

Let us shout and sing for joy:
Great in our midst is the beloved and holy God.

54   A canticle for Pentecost

Creating Spirit, brooding over the formless deep,
breathing life into all that is coming to be,
we open our flesh that you may breathe through us.

Pause

From the depths of our being
we praise you for the surge of life.

Holy Spirit, cleansing and cool from the mountains,
breathing into us air that is sharp and astringent,
we wait for the gift of holiness that is yours alone.

Pause

From the depths of our brokenness
we praise you for the balm of healing.

Life-giving Spirit, wind from every quarter of the earth,
breathing into our dry bones that they may live,
we lie as dead before you, silent as the grave.

Pause

From the depths of our decay
we praise you for the rise of new life.

…in the Spirit that stirs amongst us the kaleidoscope of Jesus.

55   A canticle for Trinity Sunday

We give you glory, Giver of life,
great thanksgiving, Bearer of pain,
to the Maker of love, unending praise!
Alleluia! Alleluia! Alleluia!

Voices of countless angels praise you,
myriad upon myriad, thousands upon thousands,
sing in your presence without ceasing:
Alleluia! Alleluia! Alleluia!

Holy, holy, holy is God, just, wise, and compassionate,
who was and who is and who is to come:
Alleluia! Alleluia! Alleluia!

Mysterious, unfathomable, unconditional in love,
God of the silence beyond all words,
beyond our imagining and conceiving:
Alleluia! Alleluia! Alleluia!

We look to you in awe and love,
your light transforming our faces to bliss:
Alleluia! Alleluia! Alleluia!

Our God, our faithful Creator, has fulfilled the promise:
Let us exult and shout for joy and give you glory:
Alleluia! Alleluia! Alleluia!

We give you glory, Giver of life,
great thanksgiving, Bearer of pain,
to the Maker of love, unending praise!
Alleluia! Alleluia! Alleluia!

We breathe these words out of the Silence within us, into the Silence beyond us...

56   A canticle for the feast of the Transfiguration

Estranged from the light and the glory,
we miss the many-splendoured presence.
We see through veils and mists,
we glimpse through glass but darkly.
Like the people of old we dare not look on the face
of those who have dared the presence of God.

Yet with unveiled faces we may believe
we shall behold the transfigured one,
the human being in whose destiny we share,
the light of the divine shining through us all.

The God who said, Let light shine in the darkness,
has shone in our hearts, has illuminated our minds,
to give the light of the knowledge of the divine glory
in the face of Jesus transfigured on the mountain.

Our disfigured faces know affliction now,
yet we are being prepared for a weight of glory,
as we look not to the things that are seen,
but to those that are as yet unseen,
not to that which shall change and decay,
disintegrating into dust in the wind,
but to that which is eternal,
solid joys and lasting pleasure.

57   A canticle for saints' days: 1

Living and mysterious God,
calling us to recognize our communion with your saints,
making us holy as we allow your Spirit to shape us,
empowering us to follow in the path of the Little Nazarene,
we give you thanks for their example,
we are awed by the cost they bore,
we are disarmed by their laughter and compassion,
we are drawn through their narrow gate to glory.

…in the Spirit that stirs amongst us the kaleidoscope of Jesus.

58   A canticle for saints' days: 2

Great praise and thanks be to you, Creator God!
You have brought us through our darkness
to shine in the glory of the face of Christ.
You have brought us into the communion of saints,
to share in their heritage of light.

Praise be to you, Jesus the Christ.
You are the image of the invisible and eternal One.
You are the firstborn of creation,
in whom all things in the universe came to be,
all that we see and all that remains unseen.

You dwell in the heart of the Eternal,
from eternity to eternity.
In you all things have their being,
and in you all things find their destiny.

You called into being your people,
you are the source of their life,
the firstborn from the dead,
the head of the living body.

Creator God, you delight that all things
should find their beauty, their completion, in Christ,
and that all things in the universe
should be reconciled in Christ,
who brought peace by his life
and by his death upon the cross.

Great praise and thanks be to you, Creator God!
You have brought us through our darkness
to shine in the glory of the face of Christ.
You have brought us into the communion of saints,
to share in their heritage of light.

We breathe these words out of the Silence within us, into the Silence beyond us...

59   A canticle for saints' days: 3

Beloved Jesus, embodier of God,
vulnerable, wounded, pinioned to death,
your power came to full strength in weakness,
dissolving evil, transforming pain, swallowing death.
**Your victory will be shared by your followers,
called and chosen and faithful. Alleluia!**

These are the words of the First and the Last,
who was dead and came to life again:

To the one who is victorious
I shall give the right to eat from the Tree of Life
that stands in the garden of God. Alleluia!
**Be faithful to death,
and I shall give you the crown of life. Alleluia!**

To the one who is victorious
I shall give some of the hidden manna,
and I shall give also a white stone. Alleluia!
**And on the stone will be written a new name,
known only to the one who receives it. Alleluia!**

To the one who is victorious,
who perseveres in doing my will to the end,
I shall give authority among the nations. Alleluia!
**It is the same authority that I received from the Eternal,
illuminated by the gift of the star of dawn. Alleluia!**

The one who is victorious
will be made a pillar in the temple of God
and will never leave it. Alleluia!
**Upon that pillar I shall write the name of my God
and the name of the city of my God,
and my own new name. Alleluia!**

To the one who is victorious
I shall give a place in my company,
as I myself was victorious. Alleluia!
We shall dwell in the presence of the Eternal. Alleluia!   >

...in the Spirit that stirs amongst us the kaleidoscope of Jesus.

These are the words of the Amen,
the faithful and true witness.

Beloved Jesus, embodier of God,
vulnerable, wounded, pinioned to death,
your power came to full strength in weakness,
dissolving evil, transforming pain, swallowing death.
Your victory will be shared by your followers,
called and chosen and faithful. Alleluia!

60   A canticle for All Souls and Consummation: 1

I saw in my mind's eye a vision:
a new realm, a new order, a new earth,
for the old had decayed and passed away.
Even the seas of chaos had been calmed.

And I saw the holy city, new Jerusalem,
coming out of the clouds of God's presence,
prepared as a bride and bridegroom
are adorned as gifts to each other.

And I heard the voice of the One who reigns:
Behold, I come to dwell among you, my people,
and you will live in my presence.

I shall wipe away every tear from your eyes,
and death will be no more,
neither will there be mourning,
nor crying, nor pain, any more.
The former things have passed away:
Behold, I make all things new.

We breathe these words out of the Silence within us, into the Silence beyond us...

61   A canticle for All Souls and Consummation: 2

In the midst of the city flows the water of life,
pouring forth as a river bright as crystal,
its source in the heart of the Living One,
a spring that will never fail.
On each side of the river stands a tree of life,
whose leaves are for the healing of humankind.

There is no church or temple in the city,
for every stone cries out, Holy.
There is no need for sun or moon to shine there,
for the glory of God is its light,
and its lamps are the faces of its people.

The gates of the city are never shut by day,
and there is no night there.
By the light that shines the wise govern its ways,
and justice and peace flourish there.

There we shall see the face of our God,
and our own true faces.
A new name will be written on our foreheads,
and we shall belong with God for ever.

62   A canticle for All Souls and Consummation: 3

Nothing can separate us from the love of God.

No affliction, no hardship
nothing can separate us from the love of God.
No hunger, no thirst, no cold, no fire,
nothing can separate us from the love of God.
No persecution, no danger, no sword,
nothing can separate us from the love of God.
No terror, no knife, no bomb,
nothing can separate us from the love of God.
No land mines, no guns, no disease,
nothing can separate us from the love of God.   >

...in the Spirit that stirs amongst us the kaleidoscope of Jesus.

No poison, no shock, no sudden death,
nothing can separate us from the love of God.
There is nothing in death or in life,
nothing that can separate us from the love of God.
No powers that be, no evil's grip,
nothing can separate us from the love of God.
In the world as it is or the world as it shall be,
nothing can separate us from the love of God.
There is nothing in the whole of creation,
nothing that can separate us from the love of God.

You have embodied your love for us in Jesus:
in your Spirit we stammer our thanks.
We shall trust in your presence through all that is to come.
Nothing can separate us from your love.

CONNECTING

1   In solidarity: 1

In solidarity with the body of humankind, and with the body of all creation, we bring into mind's eye and heart's care the needs of this planet and its peoples, allowing the energy of our concern to be charged with the Spirit of God and flow out from among us to their and our greater good. And we do so in silence, or whispering on our breath those needs and names that have been laid upon us...

2   In solidarity: 2

Let us will a blessing, that our energy, focused and magnified by the divine energy, attuned to the Spirit and open to that greater power, may flow towards others and to the creation, to our mutual well-being in God...

3   In solidarity: 3

We re-member our solidarity with humankind and with the whole creation, willing that we be transfigured and glorified, that we may become one with the divine. In the go-between Spirit, and after the pattern of Jesus, let us send the blessing of God...

4   In solidarity: 4

We let the Spirit well up within us.
**We let the Spirit spin the threads that connect us
   with others.**
We let the Spirit move beyond us in waves
to touch those we now bring into mind's eye and heart's care.
**We breathe out towards them the Spirit of love:
compassion, justice, mercy, wisdom, peace, joy.**

...in the Spirit that stirs amongst us the kaleidoscope of Jesus.

5   In Solidarity: 5

When aware of particular people:

NN, I greet you...
I hold you to my heart...
and to the heart of the Mystery...
with love...
I breathe towards you...
wisdom, deep wisdom...
life in abundance...

6   In Solidarity: 6

When aware of particular people who have died:

NN, God bless you richly,
grow in grace,
make love,
keep us in loving mind,
hold us close in the Presence,
guide us,
pray for us.

GATHERING

1

God bless the shire,
and keep our fists from ire,
lest we fall apart.

* God bless the state,
and keep our fists from hate,

God bless the hearth,
the kitchen and the garth,
that we may rest.

God bless the city
with justice and with pity,
lest we seek to blame.

God bless the towns,
the festivals and clowns,
that we may laugh.

God bless the village,
the grazing and the tillage,
lest we cease to care.

* God bless the farms,
the grazing and the barns,

God bless this place
with presence, silence, grace,
that we may pray.

God bless these days
of rough and narrow ways,
lest we despair.

God bless the night
and calm our trembling fright,
that we may love.

God bless this land
and guide us with your hand,
lest we be unjust.

God bless the Earth
through pangs of death and birth,
and make us whole.

* *For those parts of the English-speaking world that do not have shires or villages.*

...in the Spirit that stirs amongst us the kaleidoscope of Jesus.

2 Towards reconciliation

In mind's eye and heart's presence
come the hungry and the overfed.

Pause

May we all have enough.
May we all have enough.

In mind's eye and heart's presence
come the mourners and the mockers.

Pause

May we laugh together.
May we laugh together.

In mind's eye and heart's presence
come the victims and the oppressors.

Pause

May we share power wisely.
May we share power wisely.

In mind's eye and heart's presence
come the peacemakers and the warmongers.

Pause

May clear truth and stern love lead us to harmony.
May clear truth and stern love lead us to harmony.

In mind's eye and heart's presence
come the silenced and the propagandists.

Pause

May we speak our own words in truth.
May we speak our own words in truth.

We breathe these words out of the Silence within us, into the Silence beyond us...

In mind's eye and heart's presence
come the unemployed and the overworked.

Pause

May our impress on the earth be kindly and creative.
May our impress on the earth be kindly and creative.

In mind's eye and heart's presence
come the troubled and the sleek.

Pause

May we live together as wounded healers.
May we live together as wounded healers.

In mind's eye and heart's presence
come the homeless and the cosseted.

Pause

May our homes be simple, warm, and welcoming.
May our homes be simple, warm, and welcoming.

In mind's eye and heart's presence
come the vibrant and the dying.

Pause

May we all die to live.
May we all die to live.

3   People on the move

For people forced to travel:
refugees...the homeless...wayfarers...
Be with them on the road:
Be present to them.

For people beset by danger:
living in war zones...victims of crime...those working on front
  lines...
Be with them in their anxiety:
Be present to them.   >

...in the Spirit that stirs amongst us the kaleidoscope of Jesus.

For people lacking direction:
the confused...the listless...the despairing...
Show them the way:
Be present to them.

For people whose way is barred:
the hungry...the prisoners...the unemployed...
Set their feet on the road:
Be present to them.

For people who want to turn back:
the persecuted...the failed...the discouraged...
Encourage them and strengthen them:
Be present to them.

For people who refuse to move:
the smug...the contented...the satisfied...
Give them a hunger for justice:
Be present to them.

For people who wander in darkness:
the depressed...the bereaved...the dying...
Shed your light upon them:
Be present to them.

For people who often walk alone:
the isolated...the handicapped...the housebound...
Be their companion:
Be present to them.

For people who are travelling:
by land...by sea...by air...
Be the hidden energy that sustains them:
Be present to them.

For people on pilgrimage:
walking to the ancient places...facing the hazards of the road...
journeying deep within...
Be the cairns on their path:
Be present to them.

We breathe these words out of the Silence within us, into the Silence beyond us...

4   Praying with Mary

Rejoicing with you,
grieving with you,
Mary, graced by God –
Love's mystery did come to you –
of our race we deem you most the blessed,
save but the blessed One,
the child who came to birth in you.
Woman holy,
trembling at the presence of the angel,
willing the rare and marvellous exchange,
in the darkness holding the Unseen,
bearing forth the word made flesh for earth's redeeming,
take to your heart our world,
and pray for humankind,
that we with you be bearers of the Christ,
through this and all our days,
and at the last.

5   Praying in Christ: Sunday, Wednesday

Life-giver, Pain-bearer, Love-maker,
source of all that is and that shall be,
Father and Mother of us all,
loving God, in whom is heaven:

The hallowing of your name
  echo through the universe.
The way of your justice
  be followed by the peoples of the world.
Your heavenly will
  be done by all created beings.
Your commonwealth of peace and freedom
  sustain our hope and come on earth.   >

With the bread we need for today,
feed us.
In the hurts we absorb from one another,
forgive us.
In times of temptation and test,
strengthen us.
From trials too severe to endure,
spare us.
From the grip of all that is evil,
free us.

For you reign in the glory
of the power that is love,
now and for ever. Amen.

6   Praying in Christ: Monday, Thursday

Abba, our Father,
Amma, our Mother,
Beloved, our God,
Creator of all:
your name be held holy,
your domain spread among us,
your wisdom be our guide,
your way be our path,
your will be done well,
at all times, in all places,
on earth as in heaven.
Give us the bread
we need for today,
the manna of your promise,
the taste of your tomorrow.
As we release those
indebted to us,
so forgive us our debts,
our trespass on others.
Fill us with courage
in time of our testing.

We breathe these words out of the Silence within us, into the Silence beyond us...

Spare us from trials
too severe to endure.
Free us from the grip
of the powers that bind.
For yours is the goodness
in which evil dissolves;
yours is the joy
that sounds through the pain;
yours is the life
which swallows up death.
Yours is the glory,
the transfiguring light,
the victory of love,
for time and eternity,
for age after age.
So be it. Amen.

7   Praying in Christ: Friday

Dear God, our Creator,
beloved companion and guide upon the way,
eternal Spirit within us and beyond us.

Pause

Let us honour your name
in lives of costly, giving love.

Pause

Let us show that we and all whom we meet
deserve dignity and respect,
for they are your dwelling place and your home.

Pause

Let us share in action
your deep desire for justice and peace
among the peoples of the world.

Pause   >

...in the Spirit that stirs amongst us the kaleidoscope of Jesus.

Let us share our bread with one another,
the bread that you have shared with us.

Pause

Let us in the spirit of your forgiving us,
**make friends with those we have harmed
and failed to love.**

Pause

Let us overcome our trials and temptations,
our suffering and dying,
in the strength and courage
with which you overcame them too.

Pause

Let us in your love free the world from evil,
transforming darkness into light.

Pause

For the whole universe is yours,
and you invite us to be partners
in the work of your creating.

Amen.
So be it. So will we do it.

8   Praying in Christ: Tuesday, Saturday

*In celebration of the firstfruits
and in anticipation of the gathering*

With energy and expectancy

1   PapaMama,
2   MotherFather,
3   AbbaAmma,
All   **we love you.**

We breathe these words out of the Silence within us, into the Silence beyond us...

1	Beloved our God,
2	Source of our life,
3	Creator of all,
All	**we adore you.**

1	Giver of life,
2	Bearer of pain,
3	Maker of love,
All	**we embrace you.**

1	Your name be hallowed,
2	Your name be honoured,
3	Your name be embodied,
1,2,3	as in heaven,
All	**so on earth.**

1	Your justice rule us,
2	Your shalom unite us,
3	Your compassion enfold us,
1,2,3	as in heaven,
All	**so on earth.**

1	Your wisdom be our guide,
2	Your way be our path,
3	Your will be done well,
1,2,3	as in heaven,
All	**so on earth.**

1	The bread of our need
All	**give us today.**
2	The manna of enough
All	**give us today.**
3	The taste of your tomorrow
All	**give us today.**

1	Our debts remit
All	**as we remit.**
2	Our hurts forgive
All	**as we forgive.**
3	Your mercy show
All	**as we show mercy.**

>

…in the Spirit that stirs amongst us the kaleidoscope of Jesus.

1	In the hour of temptation
All	**keep us steadfast.**
2	In the times we are tested
All	**fill us with courage.**
3	In the worst of trials
All	**give us fortitude.**

1	From the powers that bind
All	**release us.**
2	From the coils that trap
All	**free us.**
3	From the grip of evil
All	**deliver us.**

1	For yours is the goodness
All	**in which evil dissolves.**
2	Yours is the joy
All	**which sounds through the pain.**
3	Yours is the life
All	**which swallows up death.**

1	Yours is the glory,
All	**the transfiguring light.**
2	Yours is the victory,
All	**the triumph of love.**
3	Yours is the world
All	**at last made new.**

1	For time and eternity,
All	**for ever and ever.**
2	For age after age,
All	**for ever and ever.**
3	So be it. Amen.
All	**So be it. Amen.**

We breathe these words out of the Silence within us, into the Silence beyond us…

PROCEEDING

ORDINARY TIME

Sunday

Lord of the dance,
in whom we live and move and exult for joy,
guide our steps through the complex spirals of your love,
that we may flow in the river dance of the whole creation,
in the Spirit of Yeshua, our partner and our brother.

Monday

From this lookout, this planet earth,
remote outpost of the universe,
contemplating the stars at night,
racing with our brother planets
forty thousand miles an hour through space...

on the surface of our earth,
warmed to life by mother sun,
orbiting around her six hundred million miles a year,
wakened by our day star that seems so close...

at morning turn-around of earth,
spinning on her axis at a thousand miles an hour,
fulness of day beyond the eastern horizon,
thick night way out beyond the west...

we breathe in quiet exhilaration,
we move into this new day in trust.

...in the Spirit that stirs amongst us the kaleidoscope of Jesus.

Tuesday

Living God,
may we encounter you this day
in the laughter of children,
in the skills of those who create,
in the pauses of the elderly,
in the patience of those who teach,
in the loyalty of friends,
in the dedication of those who serve,
in the exuberance of animals,
in those willing to make fools of themselves.
May we be your blessing to one another.

Wednesday

In our hearts and our homes the love of God;
in our coming and going the peace of God;
in our life and believing the strength of God;
at our end and beginning the welcome of God.

Thursday

Christ be with me, Christ within me,
Christ behind me, Christ before me,
Christ beside me, Christ to win me,
Christ to comfort and restore me.
Christ beneath me, Christ above me,
Christ in quiet, Christ in danger,
Christ in hearts of all that love me,
Christ in mouth of friend and stranger.

We breathe these words out of the Silence within us, into the Silence beyond us...

Friday

Fleshly God, bless to us our selves embodied.
Living God, bless to us our enlivened souls.
Loving God, bless to us this lifelong day.
Hidden God, bless to us our striving faith.
Future God, bless to us our striding forth.

Saturday

I clothe myself today
with shoes to protect my feet
from the cuts and bruises of the road.

I abandon myself this day
to those who will hold me
in the power of service.

I clothe myself this day
with covering for my head
from the glare of sun and heat.

I abandon myself this day
to those who need my clear thoughts,
who trust me to speak in words of truth.

I clothe myself this day
with garments to warm me
from the shivering of rain and cold.

I abandon myself this day
to the naked skin of love
which has no protection but itself.

…in the Spirit that stirs amongst us the kaleidoscope of Jesus.

SPECIAL TIME

Advent

Deepen our roots in the dark earth.
May they spread in silence,
hidden from view,
tapping the nourishment far below.

Draw our leaves towards the sun.
May they unfold in their green,
dancing in daylight,
taking their part in life's regeneration.

Steady the slowly growing trunks.
May we be sturdy as oaks,
content to be where we are,
yearning towards the skies of our destiny.

Christmas

Christ has no body now on earth but ours,
no hands but ours,
no feet but ours.

Ours are the eyes
through which Christ's compassion
cares for the people of the world.

Ours are the feet
with which Christ is to go about
doing good.

Ours are the hands
through which Christ now brings
a blessing.

So I promise this day to keep awake,
to live each moment to the full,
to look with eyes of compassion,
and to act with kindness.

We breathe these words out of the Silence within us, into the Silence beyond us...

Lent

From the fear that holds me rigid,
God of gentleness, ease me forward.
In my fear of surrender,
God of warmth, melt the ice round my heart.
From my fear of making decisions,
God of power, release me.
In my fear of losing respect,
God of courage, steady me.
From the fear of facing my fear,
God of laughter, loosen me.
But in the fear that marks your presence,
God of love, keep me in awe and wonder.

Passiontide

Tender God,
you see my affliction
and you are unbinding my eyes;
you are bereaving me of the burden
to which I cling;
you are weaving my pain
into patterns of integrity;
the wounds that I cherish
you are turning into worships,
and the scars I keep hidden
into marks of truth.
You are touching me gently;
I see your face, and I live.

...in the Spirit that stirs amongst us the kaleidoscope of Jesus.

Easter

God of resurrection,
bright morning star,
lord of the dance,
leap of faith,
stillness of joy,
bless us this day
and all who journey with us.

Pentecost and Trinity Sunday and the week following each

May God's goodness be ours.
Well, seven times well, may we spend our lives.
May each of us be an isle in the sea,
may each of us be a star in the dark,
may each of us be a staff to the weak.
May the love Christ Jesus gave fill every heart for us.
May the love Christ Jesus gave fill us for every heart.

FOR
PERSONAL USE

We breathe these words out of the Silence within us, into the Silence beyond us...

...in the Spirit that stirs amongst us the kaleidoscope of Jesus.

...in the Spirit that stirs amongst us the kaleidoscope of Jesus.

.

...in the Spirit that stirs amongst us the kaleidoscope of Jesus.

SOURCES & ACKNOWLEDGMENTS

There are many scriptural phrases and images woven in and out of these prayers, psalms, and canticles, too numerous to list. If you want to trace them, a good concordance will be indispensable. The Sunday Greeting connects with Psalm 150 in the morning and an early Christian hymn in the evening. The weekday greetings connect with Psalms 95 and 100. The greeting for Advent harks back to Isaiah, for Christmas to Luke and John, for Lent to Psalm 95, and for Passiontide to the ancient prophets.

Some specific acknowledgments are due in the Psalms: 4 & 11 to Julian of Norwich; 9b to Alan Ecclestone's *The Dark Sky of the Lord*, published by Darton Longman and Todd in 1980, extracts from which can be found in *Through the Year with Alan Ecclestone*, Cairns Publications, 1997; 53 owes much to Daniel Berrigan in his book *Uncommon Prayer*, which as far as I know is now out of print; 73 draws upon some reflections by Frank Lake in his book *Clinical Theology*, also now out of print; 86 has reference to Martin Buber's translation of 'I am who I am' in Exodus; 107 has reference to W. H. Auden's poem 'For the time being'; and 136 to Dag Hammarskjøld's *Markings*.

The Canticles: 1 & 2 traditional, unfolded; 3–5 based on Luke 1; 6 unfolded from Psalm 98, 7 from Psalm 67; 8 traditional, unfolded; 9–11 compiler; 12 by Janet Morley, adapted, and used by kind permission; 13–15 compiler; 16 traditional, adapted; 17 compiler; 18 traditional, adapted; 19 Isaiah unfolded; 20 Song of Songs, unfolded; 22 Ecclesiastes, adapted; 23 attributed to St Francis of Assisi, versified, source unknown; 24 Patrick Huddie, *Song of the Universe*, Creation Spirituality Books, used with permission; 25–28 compiler; 29–31 Isaiah, adapted; 32 Colossians, adapted; 33 Isaiah, adapted; 34 John 1, unfolded; 35 compiler; 36 compiler, with reference to Revelation; 37 Isaiah, unfolded; 38 Revelation, unfolded; 39 compiler; 40 Hosea, unfolded; 41 compiler; 42 St Paul, adapted; 43–46 Isaiah, unfolded; 47 St Paul, unfolded; 48 Easter Anthems, traditional, unfolded; 49 compiler; 50 1 Peter, adapted; 51 compiler;

52 Philippians, unfolded; 53 compiler; 54 Ezekiel, unfolded; 55 Revelation, unfolded; 56–57 compiler; 58 Colossians, unfolded; 59–61 Revelation, unfolded; 62 Romans, adapted.

The Gathering prayers: 1 & 2 compiler; 3 Anonymous, printed in Hannah Ward & Jennifer Wild, *Human Rites*, Mowbray, 1995; 4 'Hail Mary' unfolded; 5–8 the Lord's Prayer, unfolded.

Of the Proceeding prayers, Monday's is derived from information in Edward Hays' *Prayers for a Planetary Pilgrim*, Forest of Peace Publishing, Leavenworth, Kansas, USA; Thursday's is part of St Patrick's Breastplate; and Saturday's I have mislaid the reference to the source, for which my apologies.

Also apologies for any other acknowledgment not made. Corrections will be made in any future edition, and any fair copyright fee paid. I am also aware that some of the prayers have a Celtic flavour, but I am not able to be more specific than that.

INDEX OF THEMES IN PSALMS & CANTICLES

*The numbers refer to the psalm unless followed by the letter c:
this indicates a canticle.*

Milton Keynes UK
Ingram Content Group UK Ltd.
UKHW022019160824
447080UK00006B/117